John W Urban

Battlefield and Prison Pen

Through the War, and Thrice a Prisoner in Rebel Dungeons

John W Urban

Battlefield and Prison Pen

Through the War, and Thrice a Prisoner in Rebel Dungeons

ISBN/EAN: 9783744761451

Printed in Europe, USA, Canada, Australia, Japan

Cover: Foto ©ninafisch / pixelio.de

More available books at **www.hansebooks.com**

BATTLE FIELD

AND

PRISON PEN,

OR

Through the War, and Thrice a Prisoner

IN

REBEL DUNGEONS.

A graphic recital of personal experiences throughout the whole period of the late War for the Union—during which the author was actively engaged in 25 Battles and Skirmishes, was three times taken prisoner of war, and incarcerated in the notorious rebel dungeons, Libby, Pemberton, Andersonville, Savannah, and others. An inside view of those dens of death, atrocities practiced, etc., etc.; in fact, a recital of possibly as varied and thrilling experiences as were known during all the wild vicissitudes of that terrible four years of internecine strife.

BY JOHN W. URBAN,

Company "D," First Regiment Pennsylvania Reserve Infantry.

PROFUSELY ILLUSTRATED.

HUBBARD BROTHERS, PUBLISHERS,
PHILADELPHIA, PA.

Entered according to Act of Congress, in the year 1882, by
HUBBARD BROTHERS,
In the office of the Librarian of Congress, in Washington, D. C.

TO
MOTHERS,
WIVES AND SISTERS,
DAUGHTERS AND SWEETHEARTS,
OF THE UNION SOLDIERS, WHO BY HEROIC
SELF-SACRIFICE AND BY LOYAL DEVOTION TO
THEIR COUNTRY, EQUAL TO THE WOMEN OF SPARTA,
GAVE THEIR
SONS, HUSBANDS, BROTHERS, FATHERS, AND LOVERS TO
THE UNION CAUSE, AND WHO BY THEIR STEADFAST
DEVOTION TO THE FLAG, DID SO MUCH TO
PRESERVE THE GOVERNMENT, THIS
VOLUME IS GRATEFULLY AND
VERY RESPECTFULLY
DEDICATED
BY
THE AUTHOR.

PUBLISHERS' PREFACE.

OUR great war is rapidly becoming a thing of the remote past. A generation of young people has already come up into activity, who have little personal knowledge of those terrible scenes. Those who shared in the war, whether as soldiers or as active citizens, are taking their places among 'the older people. It will require only a few more years to place the active participants of that war among the superannuated veterans, and among the dead. The historians of the numberless incidents and the special features of that contest are rapidly passing away. The *present* is therefore the time to gather this class of facts. To-morrow may be too late.

But for this work the present possesses peculiar advantages. It is sufficiently removed from the heat of contest to allow candid views. Men who bore part in the horrors of those days, who felt the leaden hail and the piercing steel, can be just to-day. The time has been when this trait could hardly be expected in them. The *present* is therefore the time to gather up this war record. Yesterday was too early.

At this auspicious time, a volume such as

"Battle Field and Prison Pen" can be written at its best. It is neither premature nor tardy. Its author is still in his prime, though the ardor of his youth has passed away. His experience as a soldier and a prisoner was very extensive. He saw and participated in a phase of army life somewhat exceptional. It is well that he has written. His old comrads, and his old foes, will alike follow his narrative with absorbing interest. Those who remember the events he discusses will review them with satisfaction. Those to whom these events are new will certainly be charmed.

AUTHOR'S PREFACE.

NO event has ever occurred in the history of the world, greater in magnitude, or which has drawn to it more intense interest, than the great Civil War in the United States, or what is more generally known as the Southern Rebellion. This terrible conflict, so fiercely contested, and which swept to bloody graves more than half a million of able-bodied citizens of the country, will ever be a subject of attention to the historian, and to the reader.

Much has been written of this struggle, but the author would surely be presumptuous to imagine that he could fully cover the ground of the four years' mighty struggle that, like a tempest of death, swept over the land. Much also was written at the close of the war, which in the hurry and anxiety to get the literature of the war into the market, was erroneous.

The writer of the present day has an easy task, compared with his predecessors. Much that was then obscure has now become clear and vivid. No chapter in the history of the Civil War is so imperfectly understood as the one relating to the military prisons of the South. This part of the history of our country can only be given by those who endured its horrors, and tasted of its bitterness. Survivors of these terrible dens will tell the story of their sufferings to friends, until the last of them have passed away; but much will remain with the unwritten history of the war.

The object of the author is to give a fair, truthful account of the course of treatment adopted by the rebel authorities toward the poor unfortunate Union soldiers who fell into their hands, and to avoid all artificial coloring or statements that are not in strict conformity with the truth, in such a statement as he would be willing to answer for at the great day of final account. It must, however, be remembered that the stern reality of our prison-life, the horrible scenes there enacted, are more strange, exciting, and wonderful than the most brilliant romance, or stories of fiction; and, reader, if things should appear that may seem incredible to you, remember that in reality comparatively little is known of the terrible suffering of the inmates of these Southern hell-holes; and with all you may glean from those who endured their horrors, and relate their sufferings, yet will it be far short of the whole truth—for no human tongue or pen can describe the agony, wretchedness, and misery the poor soldiers endured who fell into the hands of the rebels.

In Andersonville alone, 13,269 Union prisoners, who were in the prime of life—strong, robust and healthy—perished. And in all the Southern prisons, as near as could be ascertained, about 65,000 men fell victims to rebel brutality. Who can doubt but that it was a fairly concocted, premeditated plan of their captors to destroy them, and *that*, too, in a most horrible manner? The plea of inability to prevent the terrible mortality can avail them nothing. That thousands of their captives died in a land of lumber piles and forests, alone effectually destroys that defense. With such shelter, food, water, and medical attendance, as they could have furnished, and which the laws of humanity would have required, the mortality would not have been one-tenth of the number which perished. But, allowing even twenty per cent., which of itself would have been a fearful mortality, and the fact remains that at least 52,000 helpless men fell victims to inhuman treatment. It would, however, not be just to charge the people of the South with the great crime. The most and worst of these dens of death, the rebel authorities kept away from civilization as much as possible, and comparatively few of the people knew any thing of the barbarities practiced in them, and would have been powerless to prevent it. Especially was this so in Andersonville, the spot where the climax of barbarity was reached. Located in a sparsely-settled country, where but few persons would find out the horrible nature of the slaughter-house, it was well adapted for the purpose it was intended for. To Jefferson Davis, his cabinet advisers, and to the demons whom they sent to these prisons to carry out their devilish plans, and who appear to have been well adapted for that kind of work, belongs the infamy of perpetrating one of the most horrible crimes known in the history of the world, and one that will forever remain a blot and stigma on that page of our country's history. But very little of the terrible barbarity which characterized the prisons in the South, extended to the combatants in the field. While it must be admitted that in a few cases the war was signalized by some acts that were a reproach and disgrace to the participants, the general conduct of the armies in the field was such as reflected honor on the people of the land

J. W. U.

CONTENTS.

CHAPTER I. THE OVERT ACT OF TREASON, AND ITS EFFECT NORTH AND SOUTH, ... 13
The Overt Act of Treason—The Bombardment—Fire in the Fort—Surrender of Fort Sumpter—Beauregard's Congratulation—The North Aroused—Volunteering—Prominent Adherents—A Solid North—Rebel Sympathizers.

CHAPTER II. ADVANCE OF THE GRAND ARMY FROM WASHINGTON AND ITS DEFEAT AT BULL RUN, . . 34
The First Muster—The Storm of Secession—Prevalent Errors—Gen. Scott's Opinion—Advance on Richmond—A Host of Civilians—Disastrous Delay—Battle at Bull Run—Victory at hand—The Critical Moment—The Panic—Defeat—Forces Engaged—The Capital's Peril—Cause of Disaster—Opinions on the Fight—Good Out of Evil.

CHAPTER III. DEPARTURE OF MCCLELLAN'S ARMY FOR THE PENINSULA, ... 69
Organizing the Army—The Army Moving—Strength of Manassas—Off for the Peninsula—Fighting on the Peninsula—On the Chickahominy—Battle of Seven Pines—Interrupted by Floods—Precautions.

CHAPTER IV. ADVANCE OF MCDOWELL FROM WASHINGTON, . 89
Occupation of Fredericksburg—Jackson's Strategy—Defenses of Richmond—Reinforcing McClellan—Welcomed by Negroes—At Mechanicsville.

CHAPTER V. THE SEVEN DAY'S FIGHT ON THE PENINSULA, . 103
Pushing the Fighting—Change of Base—Rebel Preparations—Fight at Beaver Dam—A Creditable Retreat—Cold Harbor—The Battle Raging—Hand to Hand—Repulsing a Charge—Panic—A Rebel Account—A Rebel Report—Retreating—A Horrid March—Terrible Scenes—Leaving the Wounded—Pursuit Checked—Closing up the Fight—Malvern Hill—Harrison's Landing.

CHAPTER VI. MY FIRST CAPTURE, ... 146
Night Movements—Capture of a Spy—Desperate Fighting—Death of Col. Simmons—Fighting Renewed—The Last Shot—Desperate Fighting—Brave Men—Among the Wounded—Taken Prisoner—Rebel Soldiers—Battle of Malvern Hill—Rebels in Retreat—Surgeons at work—Off for Richmond—Libby Prison—Belle Island.

CHAPTER VII. BATTLE OF THE WILDERNESS—OUR CAPTURE AND RE-CAPTURE, ... 180
Gen. Grant in Command—The Shenandoah Campaign—Forward

Again—Counter Movements—In the Wilderness—Skirmishing—Withdrawing the Skirmishers—The Verge of Battle—Still Fighting—The Enemy Repulsed—The Battle Ended—A Close Race—Again in Battle Line—Fleeing for Liberty—A Prisoner Again—Marching to Richmond—Re-captured—Rebel Stores Burned—Contrabands—Brotherly Help—Sheridan's Raid—Sheridan's Gallantry—Leading in Person—Among the Boys Again.

CHAPTER VIII. ADVANCE OF GRANT'S FORCES, . . . 228
Cold Harbor—Working and Fighting—Captured Again—Victory for the Reserves—A Plan of Escape—Shot on the Last Day—Searching Prisoners—Libby and Pemberton—En Route to Andersonville—Planning to Escape—Arrival at Andersonville.

CHAPTER IX. ANDERSONVILLE, , ... 251
Hard to Believe—The Prison Pen Described—Terrible Inhumanity—No Shelter—Miserable Rations—Soaked with Rain—Hopes of Exchange.

CHAPTER X. HANGING OF THE THIEVES, ... 266
Mosby's Marauders—Mr. Kellogg's Book—Pocket-picking—The Hanging—Severity Demanded.

CHAPTER XI. ENLARGEMENT OF OUR PRISON, . . . 276
A New Pen—Religious Work—Prayer Meetings—The Regulators—Rations Served—Molasses Instead of Meat—Commotion Among the Rebs—Mean Workmen—Wretched Water—Indignant at Barbarities—Digging for Water—Tunneling Out—Traitors Among the Prisoners—A Traitor Punished—The Dead Prisoners—Shamming Death—Terrible Mortality—Longing for Death—Idiocy and Mania—News from Without—The Old Flag and the New—Misapprehensions at the South—Loyal Prisoners—Rebel and Federal Prisons—Who was Responsible.

CHAPTER XII. 326
Andersonville in August—Suffering from Scurvy—Trading Buttons—"Yankee Tricks"—Stoneman's Raid—Efforts at Suicide—A Crazy Man Shot—Loneliness in the Prison—Dying of Despair—Cruel Deceptions—The Terrible Storm—Providential Spring—Words of Cheer—Horrors of the Dead-House—Heat and Hunger—The Prison Hospital—Longing for Home—Transfer of Prisoners—Out at last—The "Bull-pen" at Savannah—One Meal a Day—Cold, Disease, and Death—Womanly Nobility--Hunted by Bloodhounds.

CHAPTER XIII. MILLEN PRISON, ... 374
Millen Prison-pen—Poor Shelter—Deaths from Exposure—Dying Comrades—The Candy Business—Clean Candy—Rebel Confusion—Sherman Coming—Robbing the Dead—A Comrade's Death—A Sham Parole—Insult Added to Injury—Charleston Bombarded.

CHAPTER XIV. FLORENCE PRISON, ... 401
Economizing Salt—Unpardonable Cruelty—Selecting for Parole—Off Again—Bound for Charleston—Under the Old Flag—Homeward Bound—St. John's College Hospital—Home Again.

CHAPTER XV. ST. JOHN'S COLLEGE HOSPITAL, . . 421

CHAPTER I.

THE OVERT ACT OF TREASON, AND ITS EFFECT NORTH AND SOUTH.

THE twelfth of April, 1861, will ever be memorable in the history of our country. It was on this day that the first cannon-shot was fired by the traitors in the South on the National flag.

At half past four o'clock in the morning, the flash of a gun from the Stevens' Rebel battery, in Charleston Harbor, followed by the shriek of a flaming shell, which exploded directly over the starry flag on Fort Sumter, announced to the world that the South had rejected all peace overtures of the North, and that they desired that the sword should be the arbiter to settle the issues in question.

It was now evident that the era of compromise and diplomacy was ended, and that terrible war, with all its attending horrors and deluge of blood, only could wash away alike the treason and the curse, which since the formation of the government had been a constant, festering sore on the body politic, and a stigma and reproach on the boasted liberty of our Republic. The first gun was soon followed by others, and in a few moments battery after battery responded, until the entire line of rebel fortifications in the harbor, amounting to more than one hundred heavy guns, was raining a torrent of shot and shell on the fort held by a handful of brave men, who were left by their government to defend and hold the most important harbor in the rebellious States, against a force exceeding their own more than one hundred times; and so ill provided with provisions were they that starvation would have compelled them to surrender to the enemy or to evacuate their position in a few days, even had the rebels not fired a shot. This the rebels fully understood, for Gen. Beauregard sent a message to Major Anderson, a few days before the commencement of the bombardment, requesting him to state at what time he would evacuate the fort if not attacked; and the federal commander replied, "that he would do so at noon on the 15th, three days later, if he did not in the meantime receive supplies or different instructions from the government."

The rebels, however, were too anxious to display their great military skill and prowess to desire so peaceable an ejectment of the hated "Yankees" from Southern soil; and so for fear that by giving them a few hours' time they might evacuate, and thus deprive them of the privilege of distinguishing themselves, they notified Major Anderson that in one hour they would open on the fort. That the bombardment of Fort Sumter, under these circumstances, was entirely uncalled for, and was only a superb act of Southern bravado, is too plainly evident to deceive any one. Had not the rebels for five long months worked most industriously to collect a sufficient force of the most chivalrous soldiers in the South at Charleston, for the purpose of capturing the hated "Yankees" who dared desecrate Southern soil? And now that they had a force of seven or eight thousand men, and had as many cannon in position as Napoleon had at Jena or Waterloo, Meade at Gettysburg, Grant at Vicksburg, and four times as many as the last had at the capture of Fort Donelson; and as the best engineering skill in the South, or, as they boasted, in the world, had been brought into requisition to construct the forts and batteries that were to demolish their enemies, was it reasonable to suppose that when all these stupendous preparations had been perfected, and they were fully prepared to commence the assault with at least a reasonable hope of success, and thirsting for the gore of their enemies, that their hopes of immortalizing their names should be dashed to the ground by the peaceable withdrawal of Major Anderson and his seventy half-starved soldiers? Such a thing could not be thought of. The South must have at least one chance to prove to the world that one Southerner was equal to three Yankees; so, the bombardment commenced.

Major Anderson, the Federal commander was an experienced soldier, and understood perfectly well that his position could not be successfully defended against the tremendous force arrayed against it, unless he should receive aid from a powerful Union fleet. He, however, deemed it necessary so make such a defense as would at least vindicate his flag, and show the enemies of his country that all their efforts to dishonor the nation would not be met with supineness and a willingness to submit to their base dictations. This brave commander, who appears to have, from the first commencement of the difficulty, understood the situation better than his government, had proven his sagacity and forethought by removing his small force from Fort Moultrie, a position even less defensible than Fort Sumter. Here, had he been properly supported, he would at least have made a respectable resistance to the assaults of the rebels.

On account of the small number of his men, and the desire to give them all the rest possible before commencing the unequal contest, Major Anderson kept his men below, where they were safe from the furious shower of iron hail which was making sad havoc with the stone, brick, and mortar above them, until they had breakfasted; when, at seven o'clock, after dividing his command into three squads, he ordered the fort to respond to the enemy's fire. The first gun that thundered back Federal defiance to Southern treason, was fired by Captain Doubleday, since Major-General of United States Volunteers. The small garrison kept up a vigorous fire on their numerous foes during the day; but, as the darkness of night closed over the scene, they ceased firing. Not so, however, the seven thousand men who were determined to overcome the seventy who were shut up in Fort Sumter; and although aware that Anderson would have to surrender in a day or two, they kept up a tremendous bombardment during the entire night.

Major Anderson had ordered the posterns of the fort to be closed, and kept his men inside of the bomb-proofs; and although the beleaguered fort was shrouded in darkness and gloom, when not illuminated by the flashing meteors that fell from the guns of its multitudinous foes, the rebels evidently labored under the impression that some of the heroic defenders of it were still alive, and it would be the safest plan to keep up the grand fusilade until the last of the terrible enemy had been destroyed. Who can tell the disgust these chivalrous sons of the South must have felt when they at last succeeded in getting possession of the fort, to find that, after the furious assault that had cost them about half a million of dollars and several days' hard work, not a Yankee was killed, and not one even seriously injured?

When we read, however (as Schmucker, in his

History of the Civil War, expressed it), "that the wharves and what is called the battery were filled with a delighted and astonished multitude, who gazed with mingled wonder and exultation at the countless shells as they described their symmetrical parabolas through the midnight heavens, and then descended upon the silent fortress," we may come to the conclusion that this demonstration was kept up to still further fire the Southern heart, and excite her sons to greater deeds of valor and daring.

At dawn on the following day, the brave little garrison again opened fire, but were soon compelled to cease firing, on account of a greater danger threatening them than the fire from the enemy's guns. The wooden barracks had caught fire several times during the first day's bombardment, but had been extinguished without calling off the garrison from working the guns; but now the barracks were again on fire, and it soon became evident that the flames could not be controlled without the garrison devoting all their time to it.

An eye-witness thus graphically describes the scene:

"For the fourth time, the barracks were set on fire early on Saturday morning, and attempts were made to extinguish the flames; but it was soon discovered that red-hot shot were being thrown into the fort with fearful rapidity, and it became evident that it would be impossible to put out the conflagration. The whole garrison was then set to work—or as many as could be spared—to remove the powder from the magazines, which was desperate work, rolling barrels of powder through the fire.

"Ninety odd barrels had been rolled out through the flames, when the heat became so intense as to make it impossible to get out any more. The doors were then closed and locked, and the fire spread and became general. The wind so directed the smoke as to fill the fort so full that the men could not see each other; and, with the hot, stifling air, it was as much as a man could do to breathe. Soon they were obliged to cover their faces with wet cloths, in order to get along at all, so dense was the smoke and so scorching the heat.

"But few cartridges were left, and the guns were fired slowly; nor could more cartridges be made, on account of the sparks falling in every part of the works. A gun was fired every now and then, only to let the fleet and the people in the town knew that the fort had not been silenced. The cannoneers could not see to aim, much less where they hit.

"After the barracks were well on fire, the batteries directed upon Fort Sumter increased their cannonading to a rapidity greater than had been attained before. About this time, the shells and ammunition in the upper service-magazine exploded, scattering the tower and upper portion of the building in every direction. The crash of the beams, the roar of the flames, and the shower of fragments of the fort, with the blackness of the smoke, made the scene indescribably terrific and grand. This situation continued for several hours. Meanwhile, the main gates were burned down, and the chassis of the barbette guns were burned away on the gorge, and the upper portions of the towers had been demolished by shells.

"There was not a portion of the fort where a breath of pure air could be had for hours, except through a wet cloth. The fire spread to the men's quarters on the right hand and on the left, and endangered the powder which had been taken out of the magazines. The men went through the fire and covered the barrels with wet cloths; but the danger of the fort's blowing up became so imminent that they were obliged to heave the powder out of the embrasures. While the powder was being thrown overboard, all the guns of Moultrie, of the iron floating battery, of the enfilade battery, and of the Dahlgren battery, worked with increasing vigor.

"All but four barrels were thus disposed of, and those remaining were wrapped in many thicknesses of wet woolen blankets. But three cartridges were left, and these were in the guns. About this time, the flag-staff of Fort Sumter was shot down, some fifty feet from the truck; this being the ninth time that it had been struck by a shot. The men cried out, 'The flag is down! it has been shot away.' In an instant Lieut. Hall rushed forward, and seized the fallen flag. But the halliards were so inextricably tangled that it could not be righted; it was therefore nailed to the staff, and planted upon the ramparts, while batteries in every direction were playing upon them."

Major Anderson, knowing that further resistance would be worse than useless, now surrendered the fort, and his weary, half-smothered men devoted all their energies to extinguishing the flames that were threatening every moment to communicate with the remaining powder, and blow them all into eternity. This was accomplished by evening, and the brave little garrison lay down to rest, feeling at least the consciousness of having done their duty, and that the surrender of this important post to the armed foes of the Government was no fault of theirs.

It must be said to Gen. Beauregard's credit, that the terms given to the Federal commander were very fair and honorable. Major Anderson and his men were allowed to evacuate the fort instead of being held as prisoners of war, and to retain their arms and personal property, salute their flag with fifty guns, and march out with the honors of war. A United States steamship took them on board on Monday, April 15th, and brought them to New

York City, from whence Major Anderson sent the government the following dispatch:

> STEAMSHIP BALTIC, OFF SANDY HOOK,
> April 18th, 1861.
>
> THE HON. S. CAMERON,
> *Secretary of War, Washington, D. C.*
>
> SIR: Having defended Fort Sumter for thirty-eight hours, until the quarters were entirely burned, the main gates destroyed, the gorge-wall seriously injured, the magazine surrounded by flames, and its door closed from the effects of the heat, four barrels and three cartridges of powder only being available, and no provisions but pork remaining, I accepted terms of evacuation offered by Gen. Beauregard (being the same offered by him on the 11th instant, prior to the commencement of hostilities), and marched out of the fort on Sunday afternoon, the 14th instant, with colors flying and drums beating, bringing away company and private property, and saluting my flag with fifty guns.
>
> ROBERT ANDERSON,
> *Maj. First Artillery.*

The news of the bloodless rebel victory in Charleston Harbor was received by the rebels all over the South with the greatest joy and exultation. Seven thousand Southern soldiers had conquered seventy of their enemies, and this great heroic deed set all the South wild with delight. Had the contest been a battle of the magnitude of a Waterloo, or Gettysburg, the Southern rebels could not have been more ardent in their demonstrations of joy. The establishment of the Southern Confederacy was to many of them now an assured fact, and already in the distorted visions they saw the chivalrous sons of the South marching to Bunker Hill, to dictate terms of peace to the subdued and demoralized "mud-sills" of the North.

Gen. Beauregard issued an address to his victorious legions that for silly gasconading, and idle Buncombe, is worthy to be put side by side with Falstaff's best effort. In this remarkable proclamation the general thanks the officers who composed his staff (who, by the way, were more numerous than his foes) for their gallantry, and expresses his admiration for the bravery of the regulars, the volunteers, and even the militia, who composed the army and who had immortalized themselves by their heroism in overcoming the terrible enemy, and giving the death-blow to Federal interference with Southern rights. He declared that "they had all exhibited the highest characteristics of tried soldiers."

It has often been asserted by the rebel sympathizers in the North, that the people of the South did not, in the early part of the war, entertain the idea of an invasion of the North, but would have adhered strictly to a defensive policy to resist an invasion of the States that had seceded from the Union. That that supposition was an erroneous one, subsequent events have fully proven. The capture of Fort Sumter, and the defeat of the Union forces at Bull Run, had aroused the military ardor of the South to the highest pitch, and they not only expected to capture the capital of the nation, but the far-off Yankees up in Massachusetts were to hear, on their own soil, the tramp of the victorious Southern legions, and to hear the fiery Bob Toombs call the long roll of his slaves from the steps of Faneuil Hall, in Boston. The capture of Washington and invasion of the North were fondly-cherished schemes of the leaders of the secession movement very early in the conflict; and the Southern press almost unanimously urged such a step, and declared that the people of the South demanded such an enterprise. The *Mobile Advertiser*, in an article urging such a measure, said:

"We are prepared to fight, and the enemy is not. Now is the time for action, while he is yet unprepared. Let the fife sound, "Gray Jackets over the Border," and let a hundred thousand men, with such arms as they can snatch, get over the border as quickly as they can. Let a division enter every Northern border State, destroy railroad connections to prevent concentration of the enemy, and the desperate straits of these States, the body of Lincoln's country, will compel him to a peace—or compel his successor, should Virginia not suffer him to *escape from his doomed Capital!* Kentucky and Tennessee are offering to send legions south to our aid. Their route is north. They place themselves at the orders of our government, and we have not yet heard that our government has ordered them south."

There can be no doubt but that the South expected an easy victory over the North, and that whatever fighting there might be, they expected but little of it would be fought on Southern soil.

When the news flashed over the country that the rebels had at last fired on the old flag, the excitement in the North became probably as intense as it was in the South; but while in the South it was a feeling of rejoicing and exultation, in the North it was one of the most intense indignation against the dastardly act of the traitors who had now fairly thrown down the gage of battle against the Government. Dastardly, however, as was this act of the rebels, it was yet the very best thing that could have happened the Government. Slow as the loyal North was to believe that the South really meant war, and to accept the true situation of affairs, it needed something of the kind to arouse them to a sense of self-respect, and the necessity of arming and preparing to meet the contest forced upon them. It most effectually accomplished that purpose.

The echo of the first gun had hardly more than died away, when from the pine forests of Maine to the broad prairies of the West, was heard the beat of the drum calling the loyal sons of the nation to arms to save the imperiled Republic. While it must be admitted that in almost every neighborhood in the North a few could be found who still wavered in their allegiance to the Government, and who shed crocodile tears at the prospect of blood being shed by the Government in its endeavors to maintain its existence, yet it is a fact that the vast majority of the people in the free States, and at least a considerable portion in the border States, were loyal, and looked with abhorrence and indignation on this bold attempt to dishonor the flag of the nation. For a time party lines were almost swept away, and the cry, "Rally for the Union," could be heard in every street, hamlet, and highway in the North; and the starty flag was flung to the breeze until it waved from almost every loyal home.

The enthusiasm became indescribable, and the old and the young, men, women, and children, vied with each other in displaying their devotion to the Union. No age in the history of the world has ever witnessed an uprising of the people in defense of an imperiled government as great and grand as the uprising of the people of the North on this occasion. Mechanics and farmers dropped their tools, merchants and clerks left their stores, lawyers, physicians, and even ministers, their professions, and offered their services to the Government, and in the ranks could be found some of the best citizens in the country.

Horace Greeley, in his "American Conflict," relates, "that a regiment from Rhode Island contained a private soldier who was worth a million of dollars, and who destroyed the passage ticket he had purchased for a trip to Europe on a tour of observation and pleasure, to shoulder his musket in defense of his country and her laws."

The first call for troops was so promptly responded to, that in a short time a large number had offered their services who could not at the time be accepted. Thousands of the names entered on the muster-rolls of the Union regiments belonged to boys of sixteen or seventeen years of age, who in their eagerness to serve their country, represented themselves as being eighteen years of age, that being the age required by the government for admittance into the army.

The North, which but a few days before appeared to be a people of compromisers, who could not be aroused to a sense of the danger threatening them flew to arms with an alacrity and enthusiasm that was in strange contrast with their former indifference. Military companies were soon formed all over the North, politics were almost forgotten, and the only thought that appeared to be actuating the minds of the people was how to put down treason and bring the traitors back to their allegiance, or destroy, root and branch, them, and all the institutions which had brought on the rebellion.

A large number of pro-slavery Democrats and Conservatives in the free States, who had earnestly maintained that the North should accede to the demands of the slave power, and for a long time most emphatically opposed any measures that might have a tendency to inflame the South, now came out squarely for war measures to put down the traitors, and warmly supported the government in its efforts to enforce the laws. The action of these men had a most salutary effect, and greatly strengthened Lincoln's administration. Among the most prominent of these men might be mentioned the names of Edwin M. Stanton, subsequently Lincoln's great Secretary of War.

Gen. John A. Dix, whose famous dispatch, "If any person attempts to haul down the American flag, shoot him on the spot," sent, at a later day, an electric thrill through the heart of every loyal person in the country.

Stephen A. Douglas, whose noble support of the administration of his successful competitor for the Presidency did so much to unite the Northern people in support of the Union, and whose bold declaration, at about the beginning of the war, "If the Southern States attempt to secede from this Union without further cause, I am in favor of their having just so many slaves and just so much slave territory as they can hold at the point of the bayonet, and no more!" was the expressed sentiment of thousands of men in the North, who now felt that—

"Once to every man and nation comes the moment to decide,
In the strife of truth and falsehood, for the good or evil side."

"Keep step with the music of Union,
The music our ancestors sung,
When States, like a jubilant chorus,
To beautiful sisterhood sprung."

Gen. B. F. Butler, who, although he had supported Breckenridge for President in preference to Douglas, Bell, or Lincoln, as soon as he saw that the South meant disunion, arrayed himself on the side of the administration, and early proved his loyalty by his works. His services in opening communication with Washington—communication with it and the North having been cut off by the rebels in Baltimore—and his seizure of Annapolis, Md., and marching of troops from that place to the Federal Capital, thus preventing it from falling into the hands of the rebel conspirators, alone entitled his name to rank high in the splendid galaxy of names made illustrious and heroic by our great civil war.

Gen. U. S. Grant, of whom Henry Coppée, his biographer, said: "A decided Democrat before the war, he had in his limited sphere been in favor of conceding to the South all its rights, perhaps more; but when the struggle actually began, his patriotism and military ardor were aroused together."

Directly after the attack on Fort Sumter, he raised a company of soldiers in his own neighborhood, and offered his services to his country; and by his great skill and valor he worked his way up until he is acknowledged as being one of the greatest soldiers of the age.

Gen. George B. McClellan, whose really great services to the country in the early history of the war were not fully appreciated, from the fact that he was in command at a time when the people of the North expected the armies in the field, and its leaders, to accomplish impossibilities, and before the extent and power of the rebellion was understood by the nation; also, from the fact that the movements of the army were, to a great extent, dictated and controlled by men at Washington and New York who understood Blackstone and journalism better than military science. His subsequent acceptance of a nomination for the Presidency of the nation, from a party that was again manifesting considerable hostility against the war as being conducted by the Lincoln administration for the preservation of the Union, and the subsequent abuse and vilifying he, in common with all other men, of whatever party, who have been candidates for high positions in the nation, received, had much to do to prevent him from receiving the credit really due him..

During the excitement that followed the fall of Fort Sumter, a large majority of the Democrats in the North arrayed themselves on the side of the war party, and for a time there appeared to be almost a solid North in support of the administration. The following article, that appeared two days after the fall of Fort Sumter in *The New York Tribune*, fully expressed the situation at the time:

"Fort Sumter is lost, but freedom is saved. There is no more thought of bribing or coaxing the traitors who have dared to aim their cannonballs at the flag of the Union, and those who gave their lives to defend it. It seems but yesterday that at least two-thirds of the journals of this city were the virtual allies of the Secessionists, their apologists, their champions. The roar of the great circle of batteries pouring their iron hail upon devoted Sumter has struck them all dumb. It is as if one had made a brilliant and effective speech, setting forth the innocence of murder, and, having just bidden adieu to the cheers and the gas-lights, were to be confronted by the gory form and staring eyes of a victim of assassination, the first fruit of his oratorical success.

"For months before the late Presidential election, a majority of our journals predicted forcible resistance to the government as the natural and necessary result of a Republican triumph; for months since, they have been cherishing and encouraging the Slaveholders' Rebellion, as if it were a very natural and proper proceeding. Their object was purely partisan—they wished to bully the Republican administration into shameful recreancy to Republican principle, and then call upon the people to expel from power a party so profligate and so cowardly. They did not succeed in this; they *have* succeeded in enticing their Southern *proteges* and sometimes allies into flagrant treason. * * *

"Most of our journals lately parading the pranks of the Secessionists with scarcely disguised exultation, have been suddenly sobered by the culmination of the slaveholding conspiracy. They would evidently like to justify and encourage the traitors further, but they dare not; so the 'Amen' sticks in their throat. The aspect of the people appals them. Democrat as well as Republican, Conservative and Radical, instinctively feel that the guns fired at Fort Sumter were aimed at the heart of the American Republic. Not even in the lowest groggery of our city would it be safe to propose cheers for Beauregard and Gov. Pickens. The tories of the Revolution were relatively ten times as numerous here as are the open sympathizers with the Palmetto Rebels. It is hard to lose Sumter; it is a consolation to know that in losing it we have gained a united people. Henceforth, the loyal States are a unit in uncompromising hostility to treason, wherever plotted, however justified. Fort Sumter is temporarily lost, but the country is saved. Live the Republic!"

It must not be supposed, however, that although

the mass of the people in the North were so enthusiastic in support of the Government, that all treasonable sentiments and sympathy for the rebels had been blotted out in the North. As stated before, almost every locality contained a few traitors, who could hardly conceal their exultation when the Union forces were defeated, and whose cheeks paled at every announcement of a defeat of the rebel army. These were, however, the exceptions, and, whatever mischief they might have wished to do was easily prevented by their more patriotic neighbors, and by the innate cowardice of the rebel sympathizers, who, instead of going to the South and helping their braver co-partners in treason, stayed at home, and, like a bird of ill-omen, kept up a constant croaking about the terribleness of the times. They never tired of lamenting about the dreadful war, but their lamentations were loud in proportion to the whipping received by the South.

The fall of Fort Sumter, although at first received as a disaster, was really a blessing in disguise to the nation; for its loyal sons, now fully aroused to the extent of the danger threatening it, soon prepared themselves to meet treason on the bloody field of battle, and decide once and forever whether this Union was a mere compact between the States, that could be dissolved at will by any of them, or a nation, that could centralize its power, and crush out treason within its borders.

CHAPTER II.

ADVANCE OF THE GRAND ARMY FROM WASHINGTON AND ITS DEFEAT AT BULL RUN.

ON the fifteenth day of April, two days after the fall of Fort Sumter, President Lincoln issued a proclamation calling for 75,000 men to suppress rebellion in the South and execute the laws. This call to arms was so promptly responded to, that in a short time the number who had offered their services far exceeded the call. Unfortunately, they were not accepted, and that this was a short-sighted policy soon became fully evident, and proves conclusively that the Federal administration had entirely miscalculated the magnitude of the rebellion, and the abilities, as well as the desperate character, of the rebel leaders. The North had probably underrated the South as much as the South had the North, and the general supposition among the Northern people was that a small force of troops would soon thrash the seceded States back into the Union. Doubtless there was great disappointment on both sides, and it needed actual war to understand the extent and character of the conflict before them.

A considerable portion of the troops called into service was collected in and about Washington, and was known as the "Grand Army." To this body of men the loyal citizens of the country looked especially as the instrument that was to crush the main power of the rebel army, capture the Capital of the Confederacy, and put an end to the rebellion.

The "Grand Army," as it was absurdly called, consisted of about 40,000 men, all told, including the garrison which would be considered necessary to protect the Capital of the Nation should an advance be made on the enemy. This army, as well as the Union forces, was under the command of Lieut. Gen. Scott, who, being too old for active field service, was to direct the movements from the headquarters at the Capital. To Major General Irwin McDowell, a graduate of West Point, who had distinguished himself in the Mexican War, and who was in every way worthy and competent to command the expedition, was assigned the command of the Union forces which were to make the triumphant march to the rebel Capital.

The army, although almost entirely composed of brave and patriotic men who would have made the most excellent soldiers had the proper time been given to drill and qualify them for active service in the field, was in part little better than an armed mob, for peaceable citizens are not converted into good soldiers, by a few weeks' drill.

About thirty-five miles from Washington is a tract of country known as Manassas Plains.

This place is most admirably adapted by nature for a defensive position against an enemy advancing from the north. In front of it is a small, narrow stream, fordable at intervals of a few miles, known as Bull Run. On the south of the stream, and almost inclosing the immediate valley, are a number of hills or bluffs, which afford most excellent positions for posting batteries, which cover or command all of the roads leading in that direction. The most of these roads were so covered by woods or brush, that batteries occupying them could be so perfectly masked, that the attacking party could not discover them until fired upon. This position, made so strong by nature, was selected by the rebel leaders as the place on which to concentrate the main body of their army, which was to resist Federal invasion; and by a complete system of fortifications, they made the place about as strong as military art could make it. To this formidable position the rebel Government had gathered about 30,000 frantic and maddened men, who had been made fanatical by the political demagogues of the South, who had aroused and excited their worst passions by making them believe that they were to fight an enemy who would destroy their homes, murder or dishonor their families, and carry on a war of rapine, devastation, and plunder, contrary to all the rules of civilized warfare.

The ignorant masses of the South had been

taught to believe that the Northern soldiers were coming South thirsting for their blood, and that with them it was a war in defense of their lives, their honor, and all that was dear to them. A people so inflamed and prejudiced against their opponents are no contemptible foe; and the feeling so prevalent in the North that they would not fight, was a most fearful delusion. Who can doubt that these men, had they had a proper understanding of the true state of affairs, or a true conception of the real state of feeling in the North, would have disbanded and gone to their homes, thus preventing a war that swept to bloody and untimely graves more than one-half a million of the people, which filled almost every home in the land with sorrow. But such are some of the fruits which the teachings of the political demagogue bring forth.

How fortunate it would have been for the South had its people hearkened to the warning voice of one of its great leaders (Alexander H. Stephens), when with prophetic vision, and before he wavered in his allegiance, he proclaimed the terrible results which would follow an attempt of the South to secede from the Union. But the teachings of the rebel leaders had so thoroughly prepared the way for rebellion, that he "was as one crying in the wilderness," and his moaning cry for peace and union was soon drowned out in the raging storm of secession sentiment which swept like a hurricane through the South, and carried its people to financial ruin and untimely graves.

Directly after the firing on Fort Sumter, and when the citizen soldiers of the North were flocking to the Nation's Capital, to save it from falling into the hands of the rebel troops, who were rapidly assembling in Northern Virginia, the press in the Northern States commenced to clamor loudly that an advance should be made by the Union troops on the enemy's lines. The most absurd ideas existed in the North in regard to the extent of the rebellion, the fierce determination of the rebel leaders, and the means required to carry on the war.

To judge from the absurd and ridiculous assertions of the Northern press, and the remarks constantly heard from the people, when discussing the war, its probable extent, and the best means of putting it down, it might have been supposed that all that was necessary to suppress the rebellion was to send a few men to the rebel camps, and by a process similar to the reading of the "riot act," bring peace and quiet to the country; or, that at the worst a few Federal regiments would thrash and bring into submission all the troops the South could bring into the field.

The general impression was that the Southern leaders were only blustering, that the Southern soldiers would not, at least in this war, fight, and that all the preparations the rebels were making to carry on the contest were scoffed at and declared to amount to nothing. The rebel fortifications at Manassas were declared to be mounted with wooden or "Quaker guns," whose harmless muzzles were keeping Scott's army from moving, and that the soldiers gathered at that place were so weakened with drunkenness and debauchery and possessed so little physical endurance, that they would not be able to cope with the more vigorous soldiers of the North.

That these ideas were almost fatal delusions has been well established. It is known that the movement from Washington by the Union forces against the rebel lines at Manassas was commenced against the judgment of the best military men in Washington; but the clamor became so great, and the military editors declaimed so loudly about the inactivity of the army, and the want of energy of its leaders in not advancing and annihilating the rebels, that, against the judgment of those who would be held responsible for any disaster which might follow, the order was given to advance.

If it was not a success in the sense it was expected to be, it had, however, the effect of awakening the Nation from its dream of easy conquest to a sense of the magnitude of the contest before it; and that instead of suppressing the Rebellion in sixty or ninety days, it was engaged in a contest that would be a fierce struggle for its National existence. That the movement was commenced through the influence brought to bear on the Administration by men who had more patriotism than sagacity, and that it was opposed by General Scott, there can be no doubt. A few days after the disaster, the *New York Times* contained the following statement, made to the editor of that paper by Gen. Scott, which proves conclusively that the old veteran was opposed to that advance.

He is there reported to have said, that if the matter had been left to him he would have commenced by a perfect blockade of every Southern port on the Atlantic and the Gulf. Then he would have collected a large force at the Capital for defensive purposes, and another one on the Mississippi for defensive operations. The summer months, during which it is madness to take troops south of St. Louis, should have been devoted to tactical instruction, and, with the first frosts of Autumn, he would have taken a column of 80,000 well disciplined troops down the Mississippi and taken every important point on that river, New Orleans included. "*It could have been done,*" he said, "*with greater ease, less loss of life and with far more important results than would attend the marching of an army to Richmond.* At eight points the river would probably have been defended and eight battles would have been necessary; but in every one of them, success would

LIEUTENANT-GENERAL WINFIELD SCOTT.

LIEUTENANT-GENERAL PHILIP H. SHERIDAN

have been made certain for us. The Mississippi and Atlantic once ours, the Southern States would have been compelled, by the natural and inevitable pressure of events, to seek, by a return to the Union, escape from the ruin that would speedily overwhelm them out of it. This," said he, " was *my* plan. But I am only a subordinate. It is my business to give advice when it is asked, and to obey orders when they are given. *I shall do it.* There are men in the Cabinet who know much more about war than I do, and who have far greater influence than I have in determining the plan of the campaign. There never was a more just and upright man than the President— never one who desired more sincerely to promote the interest of the country. But there are men among his advisers who consult their own resentments far more than the dictates of wisdom and experience, and *these men will probably decide the plan of the campaign.* I shall do, or attempt, whatever I am ordered to do. *But they must not hold me responsible.* If I am ordered to go to Richmond, I shall endeavor to do it. But I know perfectly well that they have no conception of the difficulties we shall encounter. I know the country—how admirably it is adapted for defense, and how resolutely and obstinately it will be defended. I would like nothing better than to take Richmond, now that it has become disgraced by becoming the Capital of the Rebel Confederacy. I feel a resentment for it, and should like nothing better than to scatter the Congress to the winds. But I have lived long enough to know that human resentment is a very bad foundation for public policy; and these gentlemen will live long enough to learn it also. I shall do what I am ordered, I shall fight when and where I am commanded, *But, if I am compelled to fight before I am ready, they shall not hold me responsible.* These gentlemen must take the responsibility of their acts, as I am willing to take that of mine. But they must not throw *their* responsibility on my shoulders."

The advance from Washington on the rebel position at Manassas, commenced on the 16th of July. The column was divided into five small divisions, and was directed to move in the following order: The first division, commanded by Gen. Tyler, in the direction of Viana. The second, commanded by Gen. Hunter, on the road direct to Centreville. The third, by Gen. Heintzelman, on the line of the Orange and Alexandria Railroad. The fifth division, commanded by Gen. Miles, marched in the rear of the first, and the fourth division, commanded by Gen. Runyon, stayed in camp in front of Washington until the main body of the army reached Centreville, when it was advanced to within about seven miles of Fairfax. Gen. McDowell accompanied the column under Gen. Tyler, whose division advanced through Viana and Fairfax to Germantown on the first day's march, where it camped for the night. A considerable rebel column, under the command of Gen. Bonham, had been in possession of Fairfax Court House, but retreated to Centreville on the approach of the Union troops. Early on the following morning, Tyler resumed the advance, and by 9 A. M., had occupied Centreville, the rebels again withdrawing at his approach. About three miles from this place is Blackburn's Ford, one of the numerous fording places on Bull Run, and it was at that place that the rebels made the first effort to stop the advancement of the Federal troops. A reconnoissance made by the Union troops in that direction discovered the enemy in force, and apparently determined to stop the farther movement of the Federals. McDowell ordered Gen. Richardson's brigade, of Tyler's division, to advance to dislodge the enemy. The brigade advanced gallantly to the assault, but were drawn into an ambuscade, and being handled severely, were compelled to fall back in confusion.

The enemy, who, in command of Gen. Longstreet, occupied this position in strong force, being protected by strong entrenchments, easily beat back the Union troops. It was certainly a mistake to advance so small a body of troops to the assault of a strong position, without a better understanding of the nature of the ground and strength of the enemy's position than appears to have been had in this case. As a reconnoissance in force it was, however, a success, so far that it revealed the fact that the advance on the rebel capital could not be continued without fighting a pitched battle. The attack, however, was unfortunate, as it gave the enemy the prestige of success in the very beginning of the fighting. It made them more confident, and had a correspondingly depressing effect on the Union troops. The loss of the Federals in this affray was somewhat over one hundred in killed and wounded. The loss of the enemy is not known, but as they fought almost entirely under cover, it was hardly half as large. The second and third divisions of the Union army arrived at Centreville directly after the fight, and encamped in the rear of Tyler's division. Miles' division, the fifth, was close in the rear, and Runyon's, the fourth, about half-way between Arlington Heights and Fairfax Court House. Everything appeared in readiness to commence the first great conflict of the war. Gen. McDowell had intended moving on the enemy's position early on the following morning, July 20th, when it was discovered that a deficiency of ammunition existed, which necessitated a delay of twenty-four hours. Finally, at half-past two o'clock on Sunday morning, July 21st, the order was given to advance, and soon the mixed host of soldiers, teamsters, and civilians moved forward in the direction of the enemy's lines. That the authorities permitted a large number of the last-named class to accompany the army to the immediate vicinity of the field of battle, was a most deplorable error, and can only be accounted for on the supposition that the impression was pretty general that the destruction of the entire rebel army was considered a sure thing, and that all that was necessary was to march forward and capture it. Had everything gone well, their presence would probably not have been a misfortune; but at the first indications of a disaster occurring to the army, they were sure to flee to the rear like a flock of frightened sheep. So, at least, it proved in this case. When the first few regiments gave way, the host of civilians, who had approached as near as prudence would allow, to witness the destruction of the rebels, fled to get out of the way; and in almost an incredibly short time, the road to Centreville was filled with these people, who evidently had now witnessed all the battle scenes they desired to see; and, among the torrent of humanity that fled in such hot haste from the battle-field to Washington on that disastrous day, Congressmen, Government officials, politicians, and other civilians, took the most prominent part; and as they had kept in the rear of the army in the forward movement, they now as determinedly kept in the van, and the most demoralized, fleet-footed blue-coat was no match with them in the race to get into the fortifications at Washington.

Gen. Tyler's division, accompanied by Gen.

McDowell in person, pressed directly on to the stone bridge that crossed Bull Run, and at about six o'clock opened fire on the enemy, who were intrenched in strong force on the opposite side of the stream. The divisions of Hunter and Heintzelman crossed Cub Run, and making a circuit of three or four miles, crossed Bull Run at Sudley, about three miles above the stone bridge. This movement placed the two divisions on the flank of the rebel army, and was in accordance with Gen. McDowell's plan of battle, which was to merely menace the enemy's right and centre in the beginning of the engagement, while the main attack would be made by Hunter and Heintzelman on the left.

The object of this strong concentration of troops on the right of the Union lines was to turn the left of the enemy's position in such a manner as to drive it back on its centre at the stone bridge, where Tyler's division was in line ready to cross the bridge and complete the defeat of the enemy. Miles' division was kept at Centreville as a reserve, and for the purpose of guarding against an attack from the direction of Blackburn's Ford. That the plan of battle was a most admirable one, and failed of success only by a combination of circumstances which are often the overruling fatalities of war, and that Gen. McDowell can in no way be held accountable for the disaster that followed, there can be no doubt. Unfortunately for the success of the movement on the enemy's left, the most of the troops were newly organized into brigades and divisions, and the inexperience of some of the officers caused a delay of several hours in the morning, before the two flanking divisions were properly on the way, and it was fully eleven o'clock before the column was in position on the enemy's left. When the distance from Centreville to the battle-field is remembered, it can easily be comprehended that had the Union force consisted of old and tried soldiers, and all the divisions, brigades, and regiments been led by experienced officers, the column might have been in line ready to commence the assault by at least seven o'clock.

This delay was most unfortunate, for had the movement been made before daylight, as was McDowell's intention, the position desired would have been obtained without the rebels understanding the intention of the Union commander; but the nature of the ground is such that Beauregard, from his position on the south side of the stream, could see plainly all the movements of the troops on the north side, and consequently was prepared for the assault.

As already stated, Gen. Tyler's division, directly after arriving at the stone bridge, opened a brisk fire with artillery on the enemy's position. The rebels paid very little attention to this attack, not even replying with artillery to the fire of the

Union guns. Gen. Beauregard, who was fully aware that this was only a demonstration to cover the real assault on his position, was moving the main body of his troops to the left wing of his army, to meet the shock that he knew would soon fall like a thunderbolt on that part of his line.

The fire of Tyler's batteries eliciting no reply from the rebels, he ordered several regiments to advance and reconnoiter the enemy's position. These troops soon encountered the rebels, and became severely engaged; but owing to the great strength of the enemy's position, they were compelled to retire with heavy loss. The rebels had a number of batteries so concealed as to be invisible to the Union troops, until they were opened on with a torrent of shot and shell that compelled them to retire from the unequal contest. As the Union troops fell back, Gen. McDowell ordered Carlisle's battery of heavy guns to move to the front, and open fire on the rebel batteries. This was accomplished in the most gallant style, and the terrific and accurate fire of these guns soon silenced several of the enemy's batteries.

In the meantime the divisions of Hunter and Heintzelman had succeeded in getting into line. Hunter's division was on the right, and after the advance brigade, commanded by Gen. Burnside, crossed Bull Run at Sudley Springs, and was marching down the south side of the stream, he was opened upon with a heavy fire of artillery and infantry. He, however, pressed on, driving the rebels for some distance when, encountering a vastly greater number of the enemy, his further advance was for a short time checked. The remainder of Hunter's division was soon brought into action, and after the most desperate fighting, the enemy was compelled to give way, contesting, however, every foot of ground with the fiercest determination. As the Union column advanced they were met with the most furious volleys from infantry and artillery; but most gallantly they pressed on. In spite of the great advantage of the enemy in position and numbers, their extreme left wing was being turned and driven from the field; and the victorious shouts of Hunter's men, as they pursued the retreating foe, were re-echoed by Heintzelman's men, whose division had crossed the stream about half the way between Sudley's Springs and the stone bridge, and was also fiercely engaged with the enemy. The larger part of Tyler's division had also crossed the stone bridge and engaged the enemy, and the battle now became general along the entire line. It was at this time that the gallant Irish regiment, the Sixty-ninth New York volunteers, made the famous charge so characteristic of the heroic bravery of the Irish soldier. The battle now raged with most intense fury. The rapid volleys of musketry, the thundering of cannon, the shouts of the victorious Federals as they forced the rebels from the field, the frantic yells of the maddened rebels as they were compelled to yield one position after another, made an indescribable scene. The rebels fought with the utmost desperation, and as the Union troops pressed forward, they were confronted with battery after battery, and line after line of troops, who poured a continued volley of shot into their ranks. Occasionally a furious charge from the enemy would compel the Federals to fall back, only to again press forward to dislodge their assailants. The tide of battle was now decidedly in favor of the Union army, and in spite of the desperate fighting of the rebels, the general nature of the contest was everywhere favorable to the Union forces. The Federal right wing had completely rolled up the rebels' left, which was slowly but surely being forced back on the centre of their line, or in the direction of the stone bridge, where Tyler's division was prepared to receive it, and complete the rebel defeat. A part of his division had not yet crossed the bridge, it being held in reserve to strike the enemy at the critical moment. Gen. Jos. E. Johnston, the ablest commander in the Southern army, was on the field with most of the troops who had slipped Patterson at Winchester, and was personally directing the movement of the Confederate forces. He and Gen. Beauregard were making the most frantic efforts to stop the further retreat of their commands, but according to their own acknowledgments in vain; and at 1 P. M., in spite of all the advantages the rebels possessed in fighting from fortified positions, which were constructed in such a manner that every repulse would enable them to fall back into intrenchments, and concentrate a terrific fire on their assailants from masked batteries, the Union troops were everywhere successful. The toils were now slowly but surely infolding the rebel army with a circle of death, that would have insured the destruction of its entire force, had not an event now occurred which turned the tide of battle, and reversed the order of things to such an extent that, what promised to be a most decided victory, was turned to a disgraceful defeat. To prove that the rebels were completely whipped at this period of the battle, it is only necessary to refer to their own published accounts. The correspondent of the *Louisville Courier* said, in describing the battle:

"The fortunes of the day were evidently against us. Some of our best officers had been slain, and the flower of our army lay strewn on the field, ghastly in death or gaping with wounds. At noon the cannonading is described as terrific. It was an incessant roar for more than two hours, the havoc and devastation at this time being fearful. *McDowell, with the aid of Patterson's division of* 20,000 *men, had nearly outflanked us, and they were just in the act of possessing themselves of the railway to Richmond. Then all would have been lost. But, most opportunely—I may say, providentially—at this juncture, Gen. Johnston, with the remnant of his division—an army, as we fondly call it, for we have been friends and brothers in camp and field for three months—reappeared, and made one other desperate struggle to obtain the vantage ground.* Elzey's brigade of Marylanders and Virginians led the charge; and right manfully did they execute the work."

The correspondent of the Richmond *Dispatch* wrote as follows:

"Between 2 and 3 o'clock large numbers of men were leaving the field, some of them wounded, others exhausted by the long struggle, who gave us gloomy reports; but as the firing on both sides continued steadily, we felt sure that our brave Southerners had not been conquered by the overwhelming hordes of the North. It is, however, due to truth to say that the result at this hour hung trembling in the balance. We had lost numbers of our most distinguished officers. Gens. Barton and Bee had been stricken down; Lieut. Col. Johnson, of the Hampton Legion, had been wounded. But there was at hand the fearless general whose reputation as a commander was staked on this battle. Gen. Beauregard promptly offered to lead the Hampton Legion into action, which he executed in a style unsurpassed and unsurpassable. Gen. Beauregard rode up and down our lines, between the enemy and his own men, regardless of the heavy fire, cheering and encouraging our troops. About this time a shell struck his horse, taking his head off, and killing the horses of his aids, Messrs. Ferguson and Hayward. * * *

"Gen. Johnston also threw himself into the thickest of the fight, seizing the colors of a Georgia regiment, and rallying them to the charge. His staff signalized themselves by their intrepidity, Col. Thomas being killed and Major Mason wounded.

"Your correspondent heard Gen. Johnston say to Gen. Cocke, just at the critical moment, 'Oh, for four regiments!' His wish was answered, for in the distance our reinforcements appeared. The tide of battle was turned in our favor by the arrival of Gen. Kirby Smith from Winchester, with 4,000 men of Gen. Johnston's division. * *

"They were at first supposed to be the enemy, their arrival at that point of the field being entirely unexpected. The enemy fell back, and a panic seized them. Cheer after cheer from our men went up, and we knew the battle had been won!"

Gen. Beauregard, in his official report, says:

"Now, however, with the surging mass of over 14,000 Federal infantry pressing on their front, and under the incessant fire of at least twenty pieces of artillery with the fresh brigades of Sherman and Keyes approaching—the latter already in musket-range—our lines gave back, but under orders from Gen. Bee.

"The enemy, maintaining their fire, pressed their swelling masses onward as our shattered battalions retired: the slaughter for the moment was deplorable, and has filled many a Southern home with life-long sorrow."

When Johnston, with the most of his command, left Winchester to re-enforce Beauregard, Gen. Kirby Smith's brigade was left to watch Gen. Patterson; but the rebel commander, finding he had absolutely nothing to fear from that officer, ordered it also to Bull Run, and it was the unfortunate arrival of these troops that turned the tide of battle in favor of the rebel arms. The rebel brigade was being moved on the railroad, and as it approached Gainesville—a small village on the Manassas Gap Railroad—Smith heard the roar of battle. He immediately stopped the train, and unloading his men, marched them across the fields to the field of battle at the very moment when his services would be of the most benefit to the rebel cause. A brigade of rebel troops commanded by Gen. Early, which had just arrived from Richmond, and had not yet been engaged, formed on the right of Smith, and the two brigades advanced to the assault in the most gallant style. The frantic yells and cries of the advancing rebel host, which could be seen emerging from the woods, and which appeared to make their number almost innumerable, struck dismay into several Union regiments in the immediate front of the advancing enemy, who commenced to give way, and in a few moments broke completely and fled from the field. The regiment on the extreme left of the Union lines, which was still fighting desperately to hold in check the advancing host of the enemy, discovering that a part of the line had given way, and that the rebel column was winding itself around their left, thus threatening to cut off their retreat, and not being able to see or hear of a single regiment being sent to their relief, now commenced to fall back, at first contesting fiercely with the enemy; but at last becoming panic-stricken, they broke and fled in dismay from the field. The panic now spread with fearful rapidity from one part of the line to the other, and then ensued that stampede that will always be a blot on the history of the Union army; regiment after regiment now broke and fled in the utmost confusion. To add to the terror and confusion of the scene, a body of rebel cavalry charged on a number of unarmed teamsters, who had been left most injudiciously to advance with their teams to a position where they would be in the way, and could not be withdrawn in case of a retreat.

In an almost incredibly short time, regiments of infantry, squadrons of cavalry, batteries of artillery, teams without teamsters, ambulances—in short, almost all that was in the front, came rushing across the field and down the road toward Centreville. At this place the presence of Miles' division, which kept an unbroken front, and calmly awaited the approach of the victorious rebels, had the effect of reassuring some of the fugitives, and to some extent restoring order but a large number of the troops which had broken continued their flight in the direction of Washington, and did not stop until they found themselves safe inside of its fortifications. The host of civilians that had fled at the first alarm were well on their way to Washington by the time the panic-stricken soldiers reached Centreville, which no doubt accounted for the pedestrian victory which they had won over the blue-coats in getting to that place. The rebels appear to have been astonished at the flight of their foes, who had fought so desperately all day, and made very little effort to pursue or take any advantage of their unexpected victory. Their cavalry did advance in the direction of Centreville, but getting a view of the fifth division, which was eagerly awaiting their attack, and a volley from Blenker's rifle brigade, they fell back in haste to their old position along Bull Run. They evidently considered their victory as being won merely by a lucky accident, and that it would be best to let well enough alone. This defeat and retreat of the Union army, although disastrous and important in its results, was most outrageously exaggerated by the press, and all kind of theories, but the right one, were advanced by the military editors of the North to account for the disaster.

The army was declared to be destroyed, and the number of killed and wounded was sometimes stated greater than the number engaged. Washington was declared to be perfectly at the mercy of the enemy, and its capture a foregone conclusion. These stories were, however, the results of the exaggerated reports brought to the Capital by the fleet-footed, panic-stricken racers, who fled to Washington and represented all killed but themselves.

The arrival of Runyon's division, and later that of Miles, Richardson's brigade, as well as smaller organizations whose ranks were unbroken, and who marched back to their old camp in perfect order, gave a more reassuring view of the situation; and by the time the official account of the battle was given, the fact was ascertained that, serious as the disaster was, it was not nearly so bad as at first represented. The Union loss was officially reported as being four hundred and eighty-one killed, one thousand and eleven wounded, and one thousand two hundred and sixteen missing. The missing included the number who had escaped the slaughter and then deserted the service. Gen. Hunter was severely, and Gen. Heintzelman slightly, wounded, and among the Union killed was Col. James Cameron, of the 79th New York Volunteers, and brother of Hon. Simon Cameron, Secretary of War. The rebel loss was hardly less, although reported to be so by Gen. Beauregard. A rebel officer, De-Kay, who was in the battle, in a letter to the *Louisville Courier*, said:

"Our loss is fully two thousand in killed and wounded. Among the killed are Gen. Bee of South Carolina; Gen. Bartow, of Georgia; Col. Moore and all of the Alabama field officers; Col. Fisher and all of the North Carolina field officers; Adjutant Brush, and a host of leading men."

Other reports also show that the rebel loss, in officers especially, was very great; and as nearly as can be ascertained, the loss in the two armies was about equal. The entire number of troops that marched with McDowell from Washington to Centreville was about 30,000 men of all arms. Runyon's division was not in his command, and did not advance farther than to Fairfax Court House. Miles' division, the smallest in his command, did not take any part in the engagement. Richardson's brigade, of Tyler's division, was in position about two miles from Centreville, on Blackburn's Ford road, and did not take any part in the fighting on the twenty-first; so the actual number of men that were engaged did not exceed 20,000 men.

The rebel force has been variously estimated; but from the most reliable information that can be gathered, it numbered about 36,000 men. All —or, at least, very nearly all—took part in the engagement. The Southern historian, Pollard, in describing the battle, says: "Our effective force of all arms on the field on the eventful morning was less than 30,000 men." How many less he does not say, but it is not to be supposed that he meant more than a few hundred; and as that was before the brigades of Kirby Smith and Early came on the ground, it can be easily seen that the rebel force could not have been less than 36,000 men. Julius Bing, an intelligent English citizen, who was on the ground as a spectator, was captured by the rebels and sent to Gen. Beauregard's headquarters, and who appears to have had good opportunities to find out the strength of the Southern army, says their force was 40,000 men, and describes it as follows:

"Beauregard's force at Bull Run was 27,000, which was increased by the arrival of Johnston, on the day before the battle, by 8,000, and by 5,000 more during the engagement."

That the rebels, who had all the advantages in position and numbers, should win the victory is not strange, and can reflect no dishonor on the Union troops. A retreat under the circumstances was perfectly justifiable; but it was made in too precipitate a manner, and continued too long, for the credit of the men who had acted so heroically just before the panic seized them. The impression—at one time so general in the North, and still maintained by some writers—that the rebels could have marched their army into Washington and captured it, had they pursued our demoralized army, is not sustained by facts. According to their own admissions, they had been severely punished, and were in no condition to make a very vigorous movement in pursuit; and had one been attempted, the Federals could have confronted them at Fairfax Court House with the two full divisions of Miles and Runyon, Richardson's brigade, and at least a considerable portion of the better class of soldiers in the broken organizations, making a force fully as strong as the part of the army that made the attempt, and came so near whipping the rebels in their strongly intrenched position. At this place the Union troops would have been entirely on the defensive, and on ground of their own choosing, so the chances of success would certainly have been better than it was on the field at Manassas. The mass of panic-stricken fugitives were from the two divisions of Hunter and Heintzelman, which had also borne the brunt of the battle; but it must not be supposed that these two divisions were entirely routed, or in such a condition that no troops from them could have been made use of in a second action. Some of the better organizations, including the regulars, although compelled to fall back when the panic took place, were still, however, in a condition to make a desperate resistance, had the occasion presented itself. Runyon's division had reached Fairfax Court House, and here, joined by Miles' division and Richardson's brigade, it could have formed a nucleus for the broken organizations to rally around, so that, had the rebels pursued and attacked them in this position, it would have almost certainly resulted in a defeat to the rebel arms. But had the enemy pursued, and the Federal commander declined to give battle, and retreated with his force to Washington, the idea of the Capital falling into the hands of the pursuers is not only improbable, but extremely absurd; for, by the time the rebel army would have reached the Potomac river, the Government would have withdrawn Patterson's 22,000 men from Harper's Ferry, about half that many from Baltimore, and with the full division of troops en route then from the State of Pennsylvania to Washington, the Federal force would have amounted to more than 80,000 men; and it is not very reasonable to suppose that this large body of men could have been forced from its strong fortifications by 35,000 rebel troops, who already had been severely punished by 20,000 of their foes, and that, when fighting on ground of their own choosing.

The idea is perfectly ridiculous, and the fact of its ever being believed in the North can only be accounted for on the theory that the Northern people expected such astounding results from the movement, and had so fully made up their minds, that it would result in the destruction of the entire rebel army, that when they found that, instead of their expectations being realized, it was really a defeat, they became so astonished, disappointed, and so full of indignation, that they ran directly in the other extreme, and the rebel army, which was to fall so easy a prey to the prowess of the North, was now magnified into an army of invincibles, that could storm the forts and intrenchments of Washington, even when manned by a force of Federals exceeding their own number two or three times. The army of new, green soldiers, who had really performed prodigious feats of valor on the plains of Manassas, and were only defeated by a combination of adverse circumstances that might well have beaten an equal number of the best veteran soldiers, were now belittled in a manner which was as disgraceful as it was ungenerous and uncalled for.

Gen. McDowell, who had handled his troops with great skill and gallantry, and who, had the promise given to him when he left Washington that he would not have any of Johnston's men to fight, been fulfilled, would have destroyed Beauregard's forces, came in for a full share of the blame. He was declared incompetent, and not a few, who had more patriotism than knowledge or good sense, declared that he was a traitor to his country. Had Johnson been prevented from coming in the field, McDowell would certainly have been successful, and then the public that now denounce him would have declared that he was the greatest soldier of the age! Such are the fortunes of war.

Much has been said, and many theories advanced, as to the cause of the disaster, and in the excitement and alarm which followed the battle, much was written that was sheer nonsense. The fact of Miles' division being kept at Centreville during the engagement, has been severely criticised, on the ground that it was too far in the rear to be of any service as a reserve, should a defeat threaten the army. That would be a strong argument, had the division been kept there for no other purpose than a reserve. But it must be remembered that it was kept at Centreville more especially for the purpose of guarding against an attack by the way of Blackburn's Ford, than as a reinforcement for the storming column in front. Had such not been the case it would have been moved close to Tyler's division, at the stone bridge. It does not require a very careful examination, however, of the battle-field to discover that such a step would have been highly dangerous. It does not appear probable, either, that Gen McDowell believed that the services of this division would be required to storm the rebel position; but if he had any doubt in regard to that matter, he certainly knew that to move Miles from his position would endanger his rear, and in case of a rebel advance across Bull Run at Blackburn's Ford, cut off his retreat and communications to Washington.

The rebel line of fortifications extended from a short distance below Blackburn's Ford, along the south side of Bull Run, to within about one mile of Sudley Springs. The distance from Centreville to the stone bridge is seven miles, south; and Sudley Springs three miles farther distant, and northwest from the bridge. Blackburn's Ford is southeast of Centreville, and distant about three miles. As already stated, the advance of Richardson's brigade on Blackburn's Ford road was only intended as a feint, and to strengthen Miles' division, should the rebels make an attempt to advance in force on Centreville. The advance of Tyler to the stone bridge, although a more serious demonstration, was to divert the attention of the rebels from the main assault to be made by the two divisions of Hunter and Heintzelman, on the left of the enemy's position at Sudley Springs, The nature of the ground is such that, while the rebel leaders could watch the movements of the Union troops, they could move their own from one end of the line to the other without being discovered; so it can easily be seen how important a position the troops at Centreville occupied during the battle. The advance of Hunter's and Heintzelman's divisions to Sudley's Springs, ten miles to the right, and Tyler's to the stone bridge, without leaving Centreville guarded against an advance from the enemy's right—but three miles distant—would certainly have been a very dangerous experiment, as the rebels could have marched, unobserved, a considerable number of men on their right, and in an hour's march gained the rear of the Union army. The consequences would have been the capture of the trains containing the ammunition and supplies for the Union army, and a stampede would have followed without the advantage of an open line of retreat. That the rebels would have taken advantage of the advance of Miles' division is fully borne out by the fact that they did advance troops on the road to Centreville, to feel the strength of the Union lines at that place, and were driven back by Davis' brigade and the artillery belonging to Miles' division. Gen. Beauregard, in his official report, says:

"I sent orders to Gen. Ewell, holding my extreme right at the Union Mills' Ford, next south of Blackburn, to advance and attack; and they did advance a mile toward Centreville, on the Union Mills' road, but retreated again under a sharp fire of artillery."

That Gen. McDowell made a skillful and judicious disposition of his command, and only failed to win a decisive victory from circumstances which he could not control, and for which others are responsible, there can be no reasonable doubt. The mistake was in not sending Runyon's division to Centreville, instead of leaving it back so far in the rear, where it could be of no earthly good for anything or to any one. This would have enabled McDowell to move Miles' division in supporting distance of his assaulting column; but as McDowell did not control Runyon's command, that mistake cannot be imputed to him.

A number of adverse events occurred which helped to bring about the disaster; but the first great mistake was in hurrying the army from Washington before it was properly organized, drilled, and fitted for the campaign, and before it was strong enough for the accomplishment of the great work before it. It was also a serious blunder in not having a sufficient amount of ammunition with the army when it reached Centreville. This neglect caused a delay of twenty-four hours, which prevented the battle from being fought before the troops of Kirby Smith, and Early came on the field. The host of citizens and non-combatants on the ground; the length of time taken by Hunter and Heintzelman to get their commands into position; the superior numbers of the enemy, and the strongly-fortified positions they occupied; the inexperience of a number of Union officers, and a want of proper knowledge of the strength of the enemy's position—were all serious disadvantages to the success of the Union arms. With all these disadvantages, however, Gen. McDowell would have beaten Gen. Beauregard from the field, had not the rebel troops that slipped Gen. Patterson arrived on the ground at the critical moment, and turned the tide of battle in favor of the enemy.

The battle of Manassas, although a defeat to the Union army, was not, in the full acceptance of the word, a great national disaster, as all at first believed it to be, for the light of subsequent events has fully revealed the fact that the defeat of the Union forces in that battle was productive of more good than evil to the country. The success of the Union forces would have been succeeded by a still further disregard of the extent of the rebellion, and of the means required to crush it out. The grand hunt for rebels by the "grand army" in the direction of Richmond would have become more popular than ever, the number of spectators and bummers would have greatly increased, and the small army pressed forward by a still lower estimate of the prowess of the enemy, would have been met by a rapidly-concentrating Confederate army at Richmond, and compelled to fight when two or three times as strong as at Manassas, and a defeat would have followed to which Bull Run would have been no comparison.

And had it been possible to make the victory so decisive as to crush out the rebellion, the great curse which was the cause of it would have remained, and the Union would have been restored with the same disturbing element to keep up a constant discord, and before many years again to plunge the country into war. The defeat was also beneficial from the fact that the people, now sobered, stopped boasting, and went to work to prepare for the mighty conflict before them; and in a short time a well armed, drilled and equipped force of several hundred thousand men was in the field ready to confront the foe.

CHAPTER III.

DEPARTURE OF M'CLELLAN'S ARMY FOR THE PENINSULA.

AFTER the battle of Manasses, the Federal Government made a requisition on the loyal States for a large number of troops. This call was promptly responded to, and as the Capital was believed to be in the most imminent danger, a very large portion of these new troops were gathered in and about that place. The fortifications also were greatly strengthened, and every preparation made to make it impregnable. It was known that the rebel army at Manassas was being strongly reinforced from all parts of the South, and it was daily expected that an advance from that direction would be made on the Capital, or for the purpose of attempting an invasion of the North. It was, therefore, felt to be highly necessary to place the Capital in such a fortified position that a small garrison could hold it against an attack, and leave the main part of the army free to operate against the enemy.

The south side of the Potomac, in front of Washington, was strongly fortified before the battle of Manassas, but the city was ill protected on the north side, and immediate steps were taken to fortify it against an attack from any direction. A considerable number of troops were also kept along the river above the Capital, to guard against an attempt of the enemy to cross over.

Gen. George B. McClellan, whose brilliant services in West Virginia had brought his name into great prominence, was called to Washington to take command of the Union forces. Gen. Scott, although not removed from office until later, was virtually set aside by the foundation of a new military district. This department included the troops in Washington and North-eastern Virginia, and to its command McClellan was appointed. The troops were immediately organized into brigades and divisions, and the most energetic measures taken to drill and discipline the troops, and to form an army equal to the great task of crushing the armed hosts of treason, who had gathered in front of the Capital of the Nation.

The formation of the army into corps was not, however, effected until March, 1862, just before the army left on the Peninsula campaign. On the 15th of October, McClellan reported the number of troops of all arms in and about Washington, including all along the Potomac south of Harper's Ferry and at Baltimore, at 152,025 men. This estimate did not include Gen. Banks' troops at Harper's Ferry. During the following winter the time was occupied in drilling and fitting the army for the spring campaign, and by that time the best drilled and disciplined army undoubtedly ever marshaled on the American continent was ready to take the field. The ninety-day hallucination had now been effectually dispelled, and the men who composed the army had enlisted for two or three years, and expected that hard blows would be necessary to put down the Rebellion. All were volunteers, not a conscript then, as yet, being in the army; and the morale of the army was certainly better than at any time during the war. The lines of this magnificent array of men extended from Alexandria to Pierrpont, Virginia, and presented a solid phalanx to any attempt that might be made by the rebels against the Federal Capital. The army in front of Washington was now known as "The Army of the Potomac."

On the eighth of March, this force was divided into four army corps. These were commanded by Gens. McDowell, Sumner, Heintzelman, and Keyes. On the 11th of March President Lincoln issued an order confining McClellan's command to these four corps, the troops along the Potomac above and below Washington and in Baltimore, being taken from it. On the following day, McClellan was ordered by the President to advance on the enemy's position at Centreville and Manassass. The President had, as early as the middle of January, prepared an order for the army to move on to Richmond by way of Manassas; but

Gen. McClellan made some objection to that route, and argued that it would be better to attack Richmond by first concentrating the principal portion of the army at Annapolis, Md., and then ship them down the Chesapeake Bay and up the Rappahannock river to the town of Urbanna, then march them across the country to Richmond, and capture it before the enemy could concentrate a strong force to defend it. The city of Washington had been made as strong by fortifying during the winter as engineering science could make it, and McClellan believed that a small force could successfully defend it against any attempt that could be made by the enemy in the absence of the greater portion of the army. A council of war, composed of twelve of the most prominent officers in the army, was held, and to them was submitted the two plans of operation, as proposed by the President and Gen. McClellan. These officers almost unanimously favored the route as proposed by McClellan, and the President at first yielded to their judgment; but as the rebels had blockaded the lower part of the Potomac, and he believed that the plan would not interfere with the rebel batteries, he became alarmed for the safety of the Capital, and would not consent to the withdrawal of so large a portion of the army from its defense until the rebel line was driven from the river. He issued an order "that no more than two army corps of said army of the

Potomac should be moved *en route* for a new base of operations until the navigation of the Potomac from Washington to the Chesapeake Bay shall be freed from the enemy's batteries, and other obstructions, or until the President shall hereafter give express permission."

This order effectually broke up the plan as proposed by McClellan, and the order was given to move on Richmond by way of Manassas Junction. Gen. McClellan issued a spirited proclamation to his command, in which he stated that they had been thoroughly organized and drilled, and that the time for action had arrived. He urged them to discharge "all the duties that may devolve on them with bravery and fidelity." About this time, however, it was discovered that the enemy were evacuating their position along the lower Potomac, and withdrawing from the front of the Union army.

It was believed that the intention of the rebels was to concentrate all their forces on the old battle-field of Bull Run, and the army advanced in that direction to give battle. As the advance of the Federal troops reached Centreville, the rebels fled, leaving a large amount of stores burning, and the fact was soon after discovered that the entire rebel army was evacuating its strong position along the line of Bull Run, and the miles of fortifications they had erected with so much skill and labor fell into the hands of the Union troops without striking a blow. Much has been written in regard to the strength of this position, and of the number of Rebel troops who occupied it during the winter, when the Army of the Potomac was in camp in front of Washington, and it has often been contended that it was not large enough to justify the inactivity of the Union forces during that time. A prominent writer, in writing about the hesitancy of the army to move at this time, said: "The loyal masses—awed by the obloquy heaped on them, falsely accused of having caused the disaster at Bull Run, by their ignorant impatience and precipitancy—stood in silent expectation." As the writer of the above, before Fort Sumter was fired on advocated "letting the wayward sisters depart in peace," but shortly after that event became so belligerent that he kept up a constant clamor about the inactivity of the army, and as he was responsible for a full share in creating the popular feeling which forced McDowell's undisciplined troops on the intrenched rebel position at Manassas, the reader can easily see with what silent expectation he looked on the scene. The same writer, in a published history of the war, in writing about the strength of the rebel army at Manassas, after stating that McClellan estimated the rebel force in Eastern Virginia at about 150,000 men, says: "Judging by information received from 'contrabands' and deserters who came into our lines during the fall and winter, the strength of the enemy could not have been more than 60,000 men." When the average intelligence of the Southern contraband and deserter is taken into consideration, it can easily be understood how nearly correct their statements were likely to be. That the commander of the United States army, with all the advantages of having an able corps of detectives, spies and scouts at his command, would be likely to form a better estimate of the force of the enemy than the editor who received his information from the first-named class, is certainly more than probable.

The possession of the rebel position at Manassas did reveal the fact that more than one hundred thousand men had occupied it during the winter; and so strong had the position been made, that had an advance been attempted as early as was demanded by the impatient North, a great national disaster would no doubt have been the result.

Standing at Centreville, and looking east and west, as far as the eye could reach could be seen forts, mounted not only with field artillery, but with large-sized guns of the best pattern, and commanding every foot of ground for miles. South of this line, in the direction of Manassas Junction, a continuous wave of intrenchments met the view. From this position 50,000 men might well have repulsed twice that number of assailants, had the attack been made in front. McClellan's army, which was, however, considerably larger than the enemy's force when the final advance was made, would have endeavored to outflank their position west of Centreville, resorting to the same plan that McDowell had pursued; and the superiority of his command would, in all probability, have given him the victory.

The rebels, for the purpose of concentrating their forces close to the Confederate Capital, evacuated their strong position, and, as the Union troops advanced, they fell back in the direction of the Rappahannock river, which they crossed, and then marched to the fortifications of the rebel Capital. The advance guard of the Union army pursued the rebels as far as the Rappahannock, when the pursuit was discontinued, and the entire army returned to the vicinity of Washington. It had now been decided to advance on Richmond by way of Yorktown and up the Peninsula. The army was rapidly marched to Alexandria, to which place transports had been ordered to carry the troops to Fortress Monroe. Gen. McClellan expected to take with him for the reduction of Richmond the four corps constituting the Army of the Potomac, and had left Alexandria with the advance of the army, when the President, who had been informed by some of his military advisers that McClellan was moving too many troops from Washington, ordered that McDowell's corps—the strongest and most efficient should remain.

The embarkation had commenced on the 17th day of March, and by the close of the following day, the three army corps which constituted McClellan's command, numbering about 110,000 men, had sailed for Fortress Monroe. Gen. McClellan had hoped to make a rapid movement on Yorktown before the enemy could concentrate their forces at that place; but an unforeseen event occurred in the beginning of the campaign which caused a considerable delay. It appears that in planning the campaign the course of the short but deep stream known as the Warwick river was not perfectly understood, and it was not known that it ran directly across the Union army's line of march. It was found to be strongly fortified, and consequently, it considerably impeded the advance.

The rebels, in the meantime, had been strongly reinforced at Yorktown, and by the time the Union forces arrived before its works, they found a force of between sixty and seventy thousand, and the place so strongly fortified as to be almost a Gibraltar in strength. The defences were found to be too strong to carry by assault, so preparations were immediately made to lay siege to the place. The rebel Gen. Magruder had been in command of this position with about 20,000 men; but the rebel Government, finding the Federal army was marching on that place, advanced both Johnston and Lee to his assistance. McClellan approached the place by erecting counter-works, and the siege was progressing with great vigor, when suddenly, on the 3d of May, the enemy evacuated the place and retreated in the direction of Richmond. On the night of the evacuation the enemy kept up a heavy bombardment until midnight, when, dismounting as many of the guns as they could take with them, they began to retreat and daylight revealed the fact that the immense forts and long line of intrenchments were deserted. The fruits of the victory were, however, considerable, seventy-one large cannon and a large amount of supplies falling into the hands of the Union troops. The abondonment of this strong position was one of the strangest events in the history of the war. The enemy had concentrated the bulk of their army in Eastern Virginia at this place, for the purpose of making the most earnest resistance to the further advance of the Union troops in the direction of their Capital. The place was made so strong that it would have been impossible to carry it by direct assault, and it would have required a considerable time to reduce it by siege.

Immediately after the retreat, McClellan ordered a vigorous pursuit, and the rear of the rebel army was overtaken by the Union advance under Gen. Stoneman, about two miles from Williamsburg, and a spirited engagement ensued in which the rebels were defeated and driven on their main

ROAD BETWEEN YORKTOWN AND WILLIAMSBURG.

column, which had taken position at that place. A sanguinary battle ensued, and the rebels were again defeated, being driven from the field with heavy loss. The enemy left over 700 dead on the field. The fighting on the Union side was done by the divisions of Hooker and Keyes. The brigade commanded by Gen. Hancock especially distinguished itself by a most brilliant flank movement on the left flank of the enemy's position, which decided the victory in favor of the Union arms. The enemy retreated in the direction of Richmond, and the Union troops continued the pursuit until the banks of the Chickahominy river were reached. Two days later, the enemy again suffered a defeat at West Point, on the York river. The division of troops commanded by Gen. Franklin had landed at that place to reinforce McClellan's army, and were directly after attacked by a strong force of rebels, who were defeated and driven back with severe loss. After this action, Franklin's troops formed a junction with McClellan's army, and the combined force continued the pursuit of the enemy in the direction of Richmond.

The two divisions of Keyes' corps, commanded by Gens. Casey and Couch, constituting the van of the Federal army, crossed the Chickahominy river about eight miles from Richmond, and camped at a place known as the Seven Pines. The column crossed on one bridge, and as they were considerably in advance of the remainder of the army, they occupied an isolated position, which proved most unfortunate. A heavy rain greatly increased the dangerous position of these troops, as the stream in their rear became so swollen that it would have been impossible to recross it at any place but on the frail bridge upon which they had crossed over, and which was now in momentary danger of being swept away.

The enemy, discovering the dangerous position of these troops, immediately conceived the idea of destroying them before reinforcements could reach them, On Friday, May 30th, the enemy made a strong reconnoissance for the purpose of finding out the location of the Union camp; and on the following day, after firing three shots as a signal for their assaulting columns to advance, an immense rebel force rushed on the Union lines. To add to the misfortunes of the situation, Casey's division, which held the most advanced position of the Union line, was composed of the newest troops in the army, and at the time a very large number of the men were disabled by sickness. These troops, however, at first made a firm resistance, and for about one hour held the enemy at bay, but finally broke, and in spite of the most determined efforts of Gen. Casey, who, with all the skill, daring, and gallantry of the most accomplished commander, was endeavoring to steady his line, the entire division was driven in confusion from the field. Couch's division had also, by this time, become severely engaged, and although fighting with the most desperate determination, it was borne down by superior numbers and was compelled to fall back. The situation was now most critical. The enraged enemy, fighting in sight of their Capital, swept over the field with frantic yells of rage and exultation. The entire Federal line was slowly but surely being driven back to the banks of the Chickahominy, which presented an impassable barrier. At this most critical moment, Gen. Sumner, at the head of Sedgwick,s division of his corps, who had been ordered to advance to the assistance of the hard-pressed Union troops, arrived on the banks of the stream. The river was still rising rapidly, and the bridge was floating, and could only be kept in place a short time.

Fortunately Gens. Sumner and Sedgwick were two of the greatest of soldiers, and as they took in the situation at a glance, they knew that the division must cross this bridge or certain destruction fall on the troops on the other side, and they were not the sort of commanders to hesitate and make the plea that the same misfortune would probably overtake them should they advance to the assistance of their comrades. As the head of the division reached the bridge, the men hesitated, when Gen. Sumner shouted, "Forward, men! your weight will keep it in place!" The men, encouraged by the presence of their great leader, sprang on it with a will, and in an almost incredibly short time the entire division was in line of battle on the other side of the stream. General Sumner made a most judicious disposition of his command, and the troops of Casey and Couch, reassured by the presence of reinforcements, again formed line of battle and presented a solid front to the enemy. Fortunately a large number of rebels had stopped to search for plunder in the camps the divisions of Casey and Couch had been driven from, and this gave Gen. Sumner a better chance to form his line. Never was time more industriously employed, and the Union line was soon in a position to mete out deadly vengeance on the enemy for their first success.

In the formation of the new line, Gen. Sumner ordered the 31st Pennsylvania, the 1st Minnesota, and a New York regiment to lie down flat on the ground in such a position that they would be concealed from the enemy, and then ordered the Anderson Zouaves to form line in the rear of these regiments. This disposition was hardly more than made when the rebels rushed forward in immense numbers, expecting no doubt to finish the destruction of the Union forces. The bright, showy uniforms of the Zouaves soon attracted their attention, and they charged on the Union line with the greatest impetuosity. The hidden line reserved its fire until the enemy was almost on top of them, when they poured into their ranks a shower of lead which swept their lines like a maelstrom of death.

Perhaps no volley fired from the same number of troops has ever resulted in such terrible destruction to an enemy as that from those three regiments. The carnage was dreadful, the ground being literally heaped up with the dead. The enemy, dismayed by this dreadful repulse, broke in confusion, and the Union lines advancing, drove them from the field. This ended the battle of Seven Pines, or perhaps what might be more properly called the first day's fighting of the battle of Fair Oaks. The enemy, although severely repulsed at the end of the conflict, had the advantage, all things taken into consideration. They had captured and held Casey's camp, with all of its camp equipage and several batteries of artillery; and no doubt the Union troops waited with great anxiety during the following night for the dawn of day, when the conflict was expected to open again. Important changes had, however, taken place during the night. Large reinforcements had arrived, and the following morning, Sunday, June 1st, found the Federals in strong battle line ready to confront the foe. Early in the morning the battle was renewed by the advance of the enemy, who no doubt felt confident of completing the destruction of the Union troops. Gen. Hooker was ordered to make a counter-charge, and the battle soon opened furiously.

The action soon spread along the entire line, and a battle of the fiercest description raged until 10 o'clock, when the rebels gave way and were driven from the field. By 11 o'clock the battle was over, the Union troops having regained the position they had lost the day before. The Union loss, as officially reported by Gen. McClellan, was 5,739 in killed, wounded, and missing. The loss of the enemy, as officially reported by Gen. Joe E. Johnston, was 6,697. After the battle of Fair Oaks, the loyal people of the North who expected that the fall of the rebel Capital would follow this victory, were considerably disappointed that no immediate advance was made by the Union troops. It was contended that, had such an advance been made before the rebels received reinforcements, as they shortly did, it would have resulted in the capture of Richmond. But such an advance at the time would have been a physical impossibility. The greater part of McClellan's forces had not yet crossed the Chickahominy, and those which had, had been so severely handled as not to be in a condition to make a very vigorous pursuit of the enemy. The few bridges along the stream had been swept entirely away during the battle, and the high water overflowed the bottom to such an extent as to make it almost impossible to move an army over it.

The rebels had fought with a desperation un-

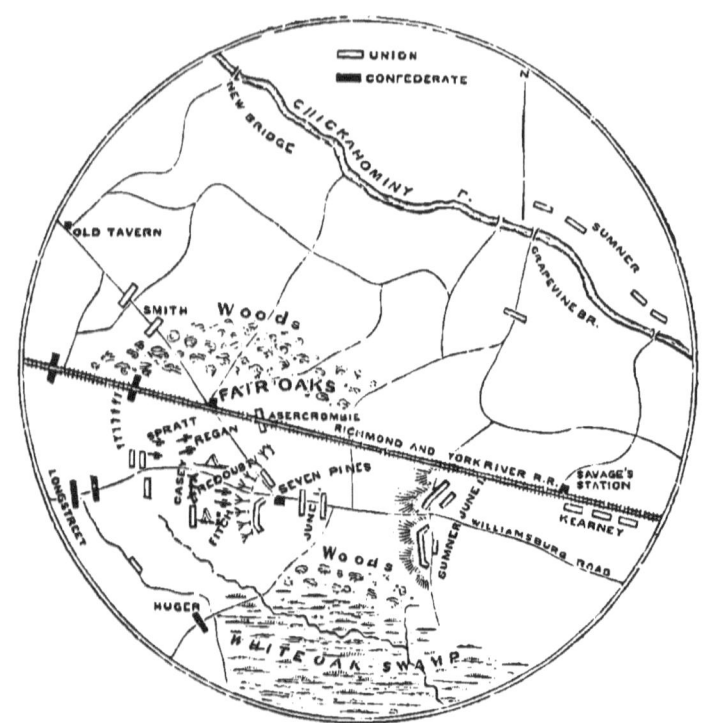

BATTLE OF SEVEN PINES AND FAIR OAKS.

BATTLE-FIELD OF THE SEVEN PINES.

surpassed in modern times, and to attack them in the strong forts around Richmond, with the troops on the south side of the river, would have been sheer madness, and could only have resulted in a fearful repulse to the Union arms.

The clamor in regard to this matter arose from the fact that the people did not understand the situation, and were, therefore, unreasonably unjust. Gen. McClellan, in a dispatch to the Secretary of War, said:

"On the 31st, when the battle of Fair Oaks began, we had two of our bridges nearly completed; but the rising waters flooded the log-way approaches, and made them almost impassable, so that it was only by the greatest efforts that Gen. Sumner crossed his corps and participated in that hard-fought engagement. The bridges became totally useless after this corps had passed, and others, on a more permanent plan, were commenced.

"On my way to headquarters, after the battle of Fair Oaks, I attempted to cross the bridge where Gen. Sumner had taken over his corps on the day previous. At the time Gen. Sumner crossed, this was the only available bridge above Bottom's bridge. I found the approach from the right bank, for some four hundred yards, submerged to the depth of several feet, and on reaching the place where the bridge had been, I found a great part of it carried away, so that I could not get my horse over, and was obliged to send him to Bottom's bridge, six miles below, as the only practicable crossing.

"The approaches to New and Mechanicsville bridges were also overflowed, and both of them were enfiladed by the enemy's batteries, established on commanding heights on the opposite side. These batteries were supported by strong forces of the enemy, having numerous rifle-pits in their front, which would have made it necessary, even had the approaches been in the best possible condition, to have fought a sanguinary battle, with but little prospect of success, before a passage could have been secured.

"The only avaliable means, therefore, of uniting our forces at Fair Oaks for an advance on Richmond soon after the battle, was to march the troops from Mechanicsville, and other points on the left bank of the Chickahominy, down to Bottom's bridge, and thence over the Williamsburg road to the position near Fair Oaks, a distance of about twenty-three miles. In the condition of the roads at that time, this march could not have been made, with artillery, in less than two days, by which time the enemy could have been secure within the intrenchments around Richmond. In short, the idea of uniting the two wings of the army in time to make a vigorous pursuit of the enemy, with the prospect of overtaking him before he reached Richmond—only five miles distant from the field of battle—is simply absurd, and was, I presume, never for a moment seriously entertained by any one connected with the Army of the Potomac. An advance, involving the separation of the two wings by the impassable Chickahominy, would have exposed each to defeat in detail. Therefore, I held the position already gained, and completed our crossings as rapidly as possible.

"In the meantime, the troops at Fair Oaks were directed to strengthen their position by a strong line of intrenchments, which protected them while the bridges were being built, gave security to the trains, liberated a larger fighting force, and offered a safer retreat in the event of disaster."

Three days after the battle, Gen. McClellan, in a dispatch to the authorities in Washington, said:

"Terrible rain-storms during the night and morning—not yet cleared off. Chickahominy flooded, bridges in bad condition. Are still hard at work on them. I have taken every possible step to insure the security of the corps on the right bank, but I cannot reinforce them here until my bridges are all safe, as my force is too small to insure my right and rear, should the enemy attack in that direction, as they may probably attempt. I have to be very cautious now. Our loss in the late battle will probably amount to seven thousand. I have not yet full returns. On account of the effect it might have on our own men and the enemy, I request that you will regard this information as confidential for a few days. I am satisfied that the loss of the enemy was very considerably greater: they were terribly punished. I mention the facts now, merely to show you that the Army of the Potomac has had serious work, and that no child's play is before it. You must make your calculations on the supposition that I have been correct from the beginning, in asserting that a serious opposition was to be made here.

"Please inform me, at once, what reinforcements—if any—I can count upon having at Fortress Monroe or White House Landing within the next three days, and when each regiment may be expected to arrive. It is of the utmost importance that I should know this immediately.

"If I can have five new regiments for Fort Monroe and its dependencies, I can draw three more old regiments from there safely. I can well dispose of four more raw regiments on my communications. I can well dispose of from fifteen to twenty well-drilled regiments among the old brigades, in bringing them up to their original effective strength. Recruits are especially necessary for the regular and volunteer batteries of artillery, as well as for the regular and volunteer regiments of infantry. After the losses in our last battle, I trust I will no longer be regarded as an alarmist."

CHAPEL IN THE CAMP.

CHAPTER IV.

ADVANCE OF McDOWELL FROM WASHINGTON.

WE will now leave the army under McClellan on the banks of the Chickahominy, and return to that portion of it which had been left under McDowell in front of Washington.

When Gen. McClellan made arrangements to ship his command from Alexandria to the Peninsula, the first army corps, under Gen. McDowell, was to be shipped first, and land at West Point on the York river; but a delay having occurred by the transports not arriving in time, and then only in such numbers at a time as to compel the army to be shipped in smaller detachments, the first corps was kept back until the balance of the army had been shipped. McClellan desired the first corps to be moved in a body, and it was with the expectation of getting enough of transports together for that purpose that it was kept back until the last. As already stated, at about the time it was ready to start, some of the military advisers at Washington, who were about as numerous as "the leaves at Vallambrosia," and some of them about as useful, succeeded in persuading the President that the removal of so many troops would leave Washington unprotected, and he issued the order already stated, that McDowell's corps should not be moved to the front.

That the taking of the strongest and most efficient corps from his command, after he himself had sailed with a part of his army, interfered very seriously with McClellan's plans, there can be no doubt; and it had more to do with causing the failure of the campaign on the Peninsula than anything else. Aside from the question of who was right or wrong, of one thing there can be no doubt—that the support given to the commander of the Union army by the government was in strange contrast to that given to the Union commanders during the last year of the war.

Gen. McDowell's large corps was kept in front of Washington, perfectly inactive, for one month, when it was finally ordered to march along the line of the Alexandria and Orange Railroad to Manassas.

After camping a few days at that place, McDowell moved a part of his command along the railroad in the direction of Culpepper Court House, and had proceeded as far as Catlett Station, when he received an order from the Government to the effect that, as his corps was intended to cover Washington, he was to act entirely on the defensive. After camping a short time at this place. Gen. McDowell, who was impatient in having his command so long inactive. and who felt keenly the absurdity of having his large force in a position where it could be of no service, requested permission to advance and capture the city of Fredericksburg. About this time, Franklin's division of his corps was sent back to Alexandria, and shipped to West Point, in response to McClellan's requests for reinforcements. Permission being granted, McDowell with the remaining two divisions of his army, advanced on Fredericksburg. The enemy occupied Falmouth—a small town on this side of the river, and nearly opposite the city—in small force. After a sharp conflict with the van of the Union troops, the rebels fled across the river and burned the bridge.

About this time, McDowell received an order from Washington that he was not to cross the river, or make any effort to reconstruct the bridge; so the small number of rebels were left in undisturbed possession of the city for a short time. The Union troops encamped near Falmouth for several weeks, when McDowell, finding that the enemy was removing supplies to Richmond, and arresting loyal citizens and conscripting them into the rebel service, begged of the authorities at Washington for permission to cross the river and occupy the city. The request was at last granted, but with the understanding that he was not to advance any troops beyond the city. The river was then crossed by the Union troops, and the city fell without any opposition into the hands of McDowell's command.

Gen. McDowell now became very anxious to march his command down the Richmond pike to form a junction with McClellan's army, and several times requested permission of the authorities at Washington to do so. This was also McClellan's request, but the authorities would not at this time consent to it, and McDowell was ordered to recross the river to Falmouth, where his command was encamped and inactive for about one month longer. Finally, however, it was decided to send a strong force of troops to McClellan's assistance, and Gen. Shields' division of Banks' army in the Shenandoah was ordered to march to Fredericksburg and report to Gen. McDowell, who was to march with the combined force and form on the right wing of the army in front of Richmond. Gen. McDowell immediately ordered his cavalry to advance and reconnoiter the road in the direction of Richmond as a preliminary movement before the grand advance. These troops proceeded to within about eight miles of Hanover Court House, driving the enemy before them, when a messenger from McDowell reached them with an order immediately to return to Fredericksburg.

This was in compliance with an order McDowell received from the War Department, and was issued on account of the rebel Gen. Jackson moving up the valley and threatening the command of Gens. Banks and Fremont. McDowell was ordered to march his command, with the exception of McCall's division, to intercept Jackson. A wild-goose chase was the result, in which nothing was accomplished, and the troops finally returned to Fredericksburg. Gen. Jackson, by a rapid, bewildering series of movements, drove General Banks out of the valley, and so alarmed the authorities at Washington that they kept the commands of McDowell, Banks and Fremont frisking about without accomplishing anything definite, when the wily rebel commander finally skipped off to Richmond in time to take a most prominent part in the great Seven Days' battle which ensued soon after. The object of the enemy in making this raid was to prevent McDowell's army from marching to the relief of McClellan's troops. It appears strange that the combined force of Banks and Fremont, together with the troops around Washington, could not have held the line of the Potomac against Jackson's 30,000 men, and let McDowell march to the Peninsula; but such a chronic fear existed at Washington that the Capital might by some chance fall into the hands of the enemy, that the first report of a rebel army moving up the valley set half of the Union armies in motion. Gen. McClellan, in accordance with the movement made by McDowell's cavalry, sent Gen. Fitz John Porter with the fifth corps to Hanover Court House to engage the enemy. The result was the battle of Hanover Court House, in which the Union troops were victorious.

The way was now open for a junction between McClellan's and McDowell's forces, and had such a junction been effected the rebel captain would in all probability have fallen into the hands of the Union troops. After the battle of Fair Oaks, Gen. McClellan, believing his force too weak to capture Richmond by assault, selected his camp and commenced to erect lines of intrenchments and fortifications for a regular approach to within commanding distance of the city, and to protect his men from an assault by the enemy. Almost one month was employed in this work, and by that time the army occupied a strongly fortified position, extending from the swamps below White Oak to the right of Mechanicsville, a distance of about fifteen miles. A part of this immense line was in sight of the rebel Capital, at which place the main strength of the rebel power was concentrated. The people of the North and South looked on with almost bated breath for the result which would follow. The rebels had employed the time as industriously as the Union troops in fortifying and strengthening their position, and preparing for the mighty conflict before them.

A large part of Gen. Beauregard's forces had been transferred to Richmond, and with the thirty thousand Jackson brought with him from the valley, the entire force in the defences of Richmond was not less than 135,000 men. To this was added the division of Gen. Magruder during the fighting, which numbered about 15,000 men. Gen. McClellan's force when he first landed on the Peninsula was rather less than 115,000 men; to this was added the division of Gen. Franklin, numbering about 12,000, the greater part of McCall's division, numbering about 10,000 men, and about 11,000 from other sources, making a total of about 148,000 men,

Directly after landing on the Peninsula, sickness commenced to spread with fearful rapidity through the Union army, and in a short time the number of men in hospitals was fearfully great. The losses in the different actions had also been quite heavy, and it is not probable that McClellan had a man more than 100,000 men when the Seven Days' battle commenced. This force could not even all be depended on in an engagement with the enemy, as it required the services of a full division to guard our base of supplies, and keep up communication with it at White House Landing.

McClellan, finding that he could not hope for a junction with McDowell's corps, again requested that reinforcements be sent to him, and it was decided to send him McCall's division of that corps. On the 7th of June, Secretary of War Stanton advised McClellan of the departure of reinforcements, and desired to know "whether he would, on their arrival, be in a situation to advance?" to which McClellan replied:

"I have the honor to state that the Chickahominy river has risen so as to flood the entire bottoms to the depth of three or four feet. I am pushing forward the bridges in spite of this, and the men are working night and day, up to their waists in water, to complete them.

"The whole face of the country is a perfect bog, entirely impassable for artillery, or even cavalry, except directly in the narrow roads, which renders any general movement, either of this or the rebel army, entirely out of the question until we have more favorable weather.

"I am glad to learn that you are pushing forward reinforcements so vigorously.

"I shall be in perfect readiness to move forward and take Richmond the moment McCall reaches here, and the ground will admit the passage of artillery. I have advanced my pickets about a mile to-day, driving off the rebel pickets, and securing a very advantageous position."

To give a proper description of the events which followed, it will be necessary to again return to McDowell's command at Fredericksburg. The division of that command which had marched to the assistance of Banks' troops had not as yet returned to occupy the position at Fredericksburg; but the necessity now appeared so great that some reinforcements should be sent to the Peninsula, that McCall's division was ordered to move without waiting for the other division to arrive and take its place.

On Sunday morning, June 4th, the division marched to Gray's Landing—ten miles below Fredericksburg—at which place a fleet of transports was in waiting to take us down the river. The march was made in the darkness of night, for the purpose of deceiving the enemy in regard to the movement.

At daylight on the following morning the embarkation commenced, and by 10 o'clock the first brigade was on board. At about 2 P. M., the steamers with the first and second brigades on board steamed into line, and commenced to move down the river. The third brigade was delayed for the want of transportation, and did not get off until two days later.

We had been greatly disappointed in being severed from the Army of the Potomac, and prevented from going with it from Alexandria to the Peninsula, and the men were wild with delight at the prospect of joining it again. Cheer after cheer reverberated through the forest along the shore as the steamers steamed down the stream; and to judge by the joy and mirth of the men, it might have been supposed that they were going on a grand pleasure excursion instead of to a great battle, and it must not be supposed that these men expected anything else than hard work and severe fighting when they arrived in front of Richmond. They all believed that a grand effort would be made to storm the rebel Capital, and the result would be terrible battles, with great loss of life—but the men were eager for the fray, and rejoiced at the prospect of meeting the enemy. The playing of bands, the rolling of drums, and the wild cheering of the troops, made a most inspiriting scene, and one not soon to be forgotten by those who witnessed it.

Three weeks later, more than one-fourth of these men were lying dead or bleeding along the banks of the Chickahominy river, or in the swamps of the Peninsula. Such are the fortunes of war.

On Monday evening we anchored at Fort Conroy, where we stopped until the following morning, when we again continued our voyage, and by 4 o'clock had reached the Chesapeake Bay. The weather was most delightful, and we all enjoyed the trip probably better than anything else we had experienced in our soldier life. On the way down the river we passed a number of very fine plantations, and large numbers of blacks, with a few whites, gathered along the shore to witness the sight. The blacks were wild with joy and excitement, and it was highly amusing to the boys to see their demonstrations of delight. Some of them waded into the water and shouted for "Massa Lincoln" to take them on board; others gathered in groups, and jumped, shouted, and clapped their hands, until they sank down on the ground exhausted. The few whites looked on in sullen silence. We were probably the first Union troops these people had ever seen, and to them, no doubt, we seemed a mighty legion, and to the blacks an army of deliverers who had come to set them free.

These poor, ignorant people instinctively knew that the marching of Union troops, or "Massa Lincoln's men"—as they called us—South, would in some way, lead to their good; and no doubt in the privacy of many an humble cabin was discussed that night the joyful news, and many earnest, sincere prayers ascended to Almighty God in thankful praise that the day of deliverance was nigh, and that the promised "Moses" had at last appeared to lead them to freedom; and who can say how much the prayers of these poor, oppressed people had to do with the deluge of blood which swept its crimson waves from shore to shore of our country?

On Wednesday, June 11th, the fleet steamed up the Pamunky river to White House Landing, at which place we disembarked as rapidly as possible, and marched a few miles up the York River and Richmond railroad, where we encamped for the night.

On the following morning the march was resumed, and we marched to Tonstall Station, and on the next day to Dispatch Station, where we were to encamp and wait for the third brigade before continuing our march. Directly after going into camp Gen. McCall received a dispatch stating that the enemy had attacked the guards and laborers at Tonstall Station in our rear, and that the immense amount of army supplies at White House Landing was in danger of being destroyed. Our brigade was immediately ordered to fall into line and march back to the station. It was already night, and the men felt tired after the day's march; but the news that the enemy was in our rear, and that there was some prospect of meeting them, caused the men to form line with alacrity and in the best of spirits. After marching about eight or nine miles, and a good part of the way on double-quick, we arrived at the station. The enemy fled at our approach, leaving a number of cars and the station in flames. The bodies of several unarmed laborers whom the rebels had murdered were lying near the railroad track. After extinguishing the flames, the march was renewed in the direction of the Landing. We had not marched very far, however, when we received word that the third brigade had landed at that place, and thus prevented the enemy from doing any mischief there. The rebels had appeared in sight of the Landing, but discovering the presence of a considerable number of troops, they fled. It was fortunate that the division arrived so opportunely in the rear of the army, thus saving the Union supplies from falling into the hands of the rebels.

The force which had thus threatened the rear of the Union army consisted of Gen. Stuart's cavalry, and as it was, of course, useless to think of pursuing them with infantry, we marched back to camp.

On the 17th of June, the division, with the exception of the regiment of cavalry, the sixth infantry, and part of the Bucktail regiment, was again united at Dispatch Station, and ready for action. The cavalry and four companies of the Bucktails had been left with Fremont in the valley, and the sixth regiment was to guard Tonstall Station. The effective force now in the division was about 10,000 men.

On the morning of the 18th of June, the march was commenced for the position the Reserves were to occupy in the army. On the day before the march commenced, we received orders to fall into line, as Gen. McClellan was coming to review the division. The boys were very anxious to see that popular commander again; but as he did not put in an appearance, they suffered a disappointment. After marching two days, sometimes in sight of the rebel pickets, and sometimes under fire, we reached the extreme right of the Union position at Mechanicsville, at which place we went into camp.

The position thus assigned to the Pennsylvania Reserves was a most important one, and immediate steps were taken to make it as strong as possible. The first brigade was placed in position across the Walnut Grove Church road, its line extending from Beaver Dam creek on the left to a large swamp on the right. The second brigade formed on the left of the first, its line extending along the Beaver Dam creek. The third brigade was in position on Gaines' farm, a short distance in the rear of the two other brigades.

By the 25th of June everything was in readiness to commence the grand assault upon the rebel Capital. The bridges had all been completed, and the troops, placed in the most advantageous position, eagerly awaited the order to advance.

CHAPTER V.

Position of the Two Armies—McClellan Orders an Advance—Receives Information of the Enemy Receiving Strong Reinforcements—Danger to the Union Rear—A Change of Base Decided on—Moving of the Stores from the Pamunky to the James River—Beauregard's and Jackson's Commands join Lee's—Critical Situation of the Union Army—Successful Withdrawal of the Union Supplies—Advance of the Rebels on the Union Right Wing—Battle of Mechanicsville—Gallant Fighting of the Pennsylvania Reserves—The Rebels Defeated with Terrible Loss—Withdrawal of the Union Troops to Gaines' Mill—Battle of Gaines' Mill—Terrible Fighting by Both Armies—Results—Battle of Golding's Farm, on the Union Left—Gallant Fighting of Hancock's Brigade—Defeat of the Enemy—Retreat of the Union Right Wing across the Chickahominy—Attack of the Rebels on Sumner's and Heintzelman's Corps at Allen's Farm—Repulse of the Enemy—Union Troops Withdrawn to Savage Station—Rebel Attack on the Union Position—Great Slaughter and Repulse of the Rebel Army—The Withdrawal of the Union Army through White Oak Swamp—Battle of New Market Cross Roads—Results—Great Battle of Malvern Hill—Complete Defeat of the Rebel Army—Results of the Campaign.

TWO armies—the largest ever marshaled on the Western continent—now stood confronting each other in such close proximity that the advance pickets of the contending forces could converse together, and all felt that a mighty struggle was close at hand. As a preliminary movement to the great one that was to follow, Gen. McClellan ordered Gen. Heintzelman's corps, and Richardson's division of Sumner's, to advance and feel the enemy in their front. The object of this movement was to place the corps of Heintzelman and Sumner in a more favorable position for the opening of the great assault that was to commence on the morrow.

McClellan had received information that Gen. Jackson, with 30,000 men, was approaching along the line of the Virginia Central Railroad, to reinforce Lee's forces, and he now determined to strike before they could form a junction. In the evening, after leaving the field where the advance had been made, and arriving at his headquarters, McClellan received additional information that Jackson was much closer than at first reported, and that he was moving with his entire force directly on the rear of the Union position, which greatly endangered his base of supplies. It now became plainly evident that the advance on the rebel Capital must be given up until the danger that threatened our rear was removed. Gen. McClellan immediately issued an order that the immense amount of supplies be removed from White House Landing and shipped to Harrison's Landing, on the James river. He had for some time before favored a movement of this kind, as he considered the James river a safer base of supplies, from the fact that it would be under the protection of the Federal gunboats, and would not require so many men to guard it. Unfortunately, it did not at first meet the views of the Government, and it was delayed until it was absolutely necessary to remove them, or let them fall into the hands of the enemy. The immense amount of supplies was tumbled on transports, and sent down the Pamunky as fast as possible, and a considerable number of troops sent to hold the enemy in check until the supplies could be got out of the way.

McClellan had, however, not given up the plan of fighting on the Chickahominy, but merely delayed it until the change of base was effected. He intended to renew the fighting, if possible, on the battle-field of the Fair Oaks, and compel the rebel commander to fight a great battle on the south side of the river. He had a number of good, strong bridges over the stream, which would have enabled him to concentrate his force in a short time on either side of the stream; and if the enemy would refuse to fight on the south side, so far from their Capital, he could, at least, advance his line nearer to the city, with the great advantage of having his base of supplies nearer and in a much safer position.

Early in the evening, after the advance of Heintzelman, Gen. McClellan telegraphed to Washington :

"The affair is over, and we have gained our point fully, and with but little loss, notwithstanding the strong opposition. Our men have done all that could be desired. The enemy has been driven from the camps in front of this place, and is now quiet." * * * * * *

A few days later Gen. McClellan received information that both Beauregard and Jackson had united their commands with Lee, and that they would, in all probability, assume the offensive on the morrow, and by flanking his right, compel him to fight on the north side of the Chickahominy. That this information was correct, subsequent events fully proved. At about 6 o'clock in the evening, McClellan telegraphed to the President as follows:

"I am inclined to think that Jackson will attack my right and rear. The rebel force is stated at 200,000, including Jackson and Beauregard. I shall have to contend against vastly superior odds, if these reports be true. But this army will do all in the power of men to hold their position and repulse any attack.

"I regret my great inferiority in numbers, but feel that I am in no way responsible for it, as I have not failed to represent repeatedly the necessity of reinforcements, that this was the decisive point, and that all the available means of the Government should be concentrated here. I will do all that a General can do with the splendid army I have the honor to command, and, if it is destroyed by overwhelming numbers, can at least die with it and share its fate. But if the result of the action, which will probably occur to-morrow, or within a short time, is a disaster, the responsibility cannot be thrown on my shoulders; it must rest where it belongs."

McClellan now believed the situation to be most critical, and he took the most energetic measures to get the immense amount of supplies, wagons, and army material, out of the way of the enemy. The cars were kept constantly running from the rear of the army to White House Landing, loaded with army supplies, where it was tumbled on boats and moved down the river. Immense trains of loaded wagons were kept moving along the rear of the army to the left, and all supplies on the way to the front were ordered back and up the James river to Harrison's Landing.

It is certainly creditable to Gen. McClellan that, although the fighting commenced on the following day, and raged with great fury for seven days, so little of the army supplies fell into the hands of the enemy, and the change of base to the James river was so successfully effected. The change of base at so late a day was, however, unfortunate, from the fact that it to some extent impaired the morale of the army. The fact that something unusual was going on could not be kept from the men, and the reports of the enemy being so strongly reinforced spread through the army, and the fear of a disastrous retreat, instead of a successful forward movement, soon became felt.

This was greatly increased after the second day's battle, when the right wing of the Union army retreated across the Chickahominy, and the excitement and confusion proved conclusively that the army was retreating from its fortified position in front of Richmond. That the occupation of White House Landing for a base of supplies was a mistake, there can be no doubt. Who was responsible for it will ever be a matter of dispute, but McClellan was certainly in favor of removing it before it was done.

It has been contended by some that it was the commencing of this change of base which brought on the rebel attack on the 26th, but that is not borne out by the facts in the case. The order for commencing the movement was not made until in the evening of the 25th, and that the rebel commanders had, in council of war, decided to assume the offensive before that order was issued, is proven by the statement of a rebel officer who was present at said council. This officer said:

"On the 25th of June another great council of war was held. In it were assembled nearly all that was eminent in the Confederate army. There stood like a rock General Lee, gazing cheerfully over the countenances of his comrades, for each of whom he had a part already assigned. Thoughtfully his eyes wandered from one to the other, as though he wished to stamp the features of each upon his memory, with the feeling that he perhaps should never behold many of them again. Close beside him towered the knightly form of Gen. Baldwin; at his left leaned passively Stonewall Jackson, the idol of his troops, impatiently swinging his saber to and fro, as though the quiet room was too narrow for him, and he were longing to be once more at the head of his columns. A little aside stood the two Hills, arm-in-arm, while in front of them old Gen. Wise was energetically speaking. Further to the right stood Generals Huger, Longstreet, Branch, Anderson, Whiting, Ripley and Magruder, in a group. When all these generals had assembled, General Lee laid his plans before them, and in a few stirring words pointed out to each his allotted task. The scheme had already been elaborated. It was compact, concentrated action, and the result could not fail to be brilliant.

"When the conference terminated, all shook hands and hastened away to their respective army corps, to enter upon immediate activity."

Early on Thursday, June 26th, the day that McClellan had intended to move on the enemy's works, indications of an advance of the rebels on our extreme right commenced to show themselves. Gen. Jackson's command had left Ashland at 3 o'clock in the morning, and after driving the Union pickets back in the direction of Atley's Station, advanced and engaged the Union cavalry under Gen. Stoneman at Hanover Court House.

This movement uncovered the front of Gen. Branch's rebel division on the left of Lee's lines, and it crossed the river at the Brook turnpike bridge and attacked the eighth Illinois cavalry, which was in position between that bridge and the Meadow bridge. The cavalry, after a short resistance, fell back to Meadow bridge, where six companies of the Bucktails and four companies of the First Pennsylvania Reserves were stationed. A sharp conflict ensued; the Union troops were compelled to fall back, and a number of men belonging to one of the Bucktail companies were cut off by the enemy and taken prisoners.

In the meantime Gen. Reynolds, with the first brigade, had advanced beyond Mechanicsville and formed line of battle; but it soon became evident that the rebels were in such force that it would be useless to try to oppose them with so small a force, and the brigade was withdrawn to its line of intrenchments this side of Beaver Dam creek. The second brigade was formed in line of battle on the left of the first, and the third brigade in the rear of the first and second, as a reserve. The disposition of these troops had hardly been more than effected when two full divisions of rebel troops, commanded by Gen. Lee in person, advanced to the assault, and the battle opened with great fury along the front of the first brigade. As the enemy's troops came within range of McCall's artillery, the batteries of Cooper and De Hart opened on them with the most terrific effect; but the enemy, encouraged by the presence of Lee, pressed forward to the assault with the most desperate courage. The enemy, who were suffering dreadfully from the fire of the Union batteries, were evidently determined to come to close quarters as soon as possible, and with frantic cries of rage they threw themselves on the Union lines.

In front of the first brigade a part of the ground was low and swampy, making it almost impossible for troops to cross. Into this a part of the rebel column charged, and a scene of the most indescribable confusion, horror and tumult ensued. Hundreds of the men and horses sank into the mire, and were shot down by the deadly rifles of the first brigade. Again and again the enemy advanced to the assault, only to be driven back with the most terrible slaughter. Gen. Lee, finding he could not storm the position held by the first and second brigades of the Pennsylvania Reserves, sent a strong column down the Ellison Mill road, for the purpose of turning the left of the position held by McCall's troops. That general, however, was equal to the sly rebel leader, and he had already dispatched both infantry and artillery to that point, and the enemy met the same repulse they had received on our right. The battle raged at different points along Mc-

Call's lines until after dark, when the fighting ceased. At about sunset Griffin's brigade of Morrell's division and Edwards' battery came on the ground and became engaged; but almost all the fighting was done by McCall's division. The rebels had two full divisions engaged, one of which, commanded by A. P. Hill, was officially reported as having 14,000 men when the battle commenced. The loss sustained by the Union troops was less than 300; the rebel loss exceeded 2,000.

Although the Reserves had inflicted a terrible defeat on the enemy, and were abundantly able to hold their position against almost any force that might attack them in front, their position nevertheless was one of great peril. The rebel division commanded by Gen. Branch was advancing to turn their right, and Jackson's corps was moving on the left of Branch's division, for the purpose of getting into the rear of the Union army. It became highly necessary to withdraw McCall's division from the dangerous position it occupied to one in closer proximity to the main army. Gen. McClellan in his report says:

"The position on Beaver Dam Creek, although so successfully defended, had its right flank too much in the air, and was too far from the main army, to make it available to retain it longer. I therefore determined to send the heavy guns at Hogan's and Gaines' houses over the Chickahominy during the night, with as many wagons of the fifth corps as possible, and to withdraw the corps itself to a position stretching around the bridges, where its flanks would be reasonably secure, and it would be within supporting distance of the main army. General Porter carried out my orders to that effect.

"Meade's and Griffin's brigades were the first to leave the ground; Seymour's brigade covered the rear with the horse batteries of Captains Robinson and Tidball; but the withdrawal was so skillful and gradual, and the repulse of the preceding day so complete, that, although the enemy followed the retreat closely, and some skirmishing occurred, they did not appear in front of the new line in force till about noon of the 27th, when we were prepared to receive them."

The withdrawal of the troops commenced at daylight, but as the rebels opened fire directly after, and it was necessary to keep up a show of resistance for the purpose of deceiving the enemy, it was not fully accomplished until 9 A. M., when the last of the brave division which had fought and defeated three times their number was in retreat in the direction of Gaines' Mill. Gen. McCall, justly proud of his command, said:

"In fine, our killed had been buried and our wounded had been sent off by 7 o'clock A. M. on the 27th, and not a man nor a gun nor a musket had been left on the field. The regiment filed past as steadily as if marching from the parade ground; and it must have been some time before the enemy were aware that we were gone, as no attempt was made to follow immediately."

The loss of the enemy was heavy beyond precedent in this war in proportion to the numbers engaged. I learned from official authority while a prisoner in Richmond that Lee's loss in killed and wounded did not fall short of two thousand men. In the official reports published it was admitted that the First North Carolina regiment lost nearly one-half its effective force, and the Forty-fourth Georgia nearly two-thirds.

In this, the first great battle in which the Pennsylvania Reserves had taken part, they won laurels that well might make any commander feel proud of them. Gen. Porter had been ordered to withdraw the whole of his corps to a position a short distance beyond Gaines' Mill, and the retreat continued in that direction. The Reserves covered the line of retreat, which was made in the most orderly manner, the last of the column destroying the bridge at the mill after crossing. The enemy, finding that our troops were retreating, and being strongly reinforced, rushed forward in pursuit, and as we were leisurely retiring, we were soon overtaken by them. The destruction of the bridge did not detain them very long, as they soon had a temporary causeway, on which they crossed their artillery, and the stream was so

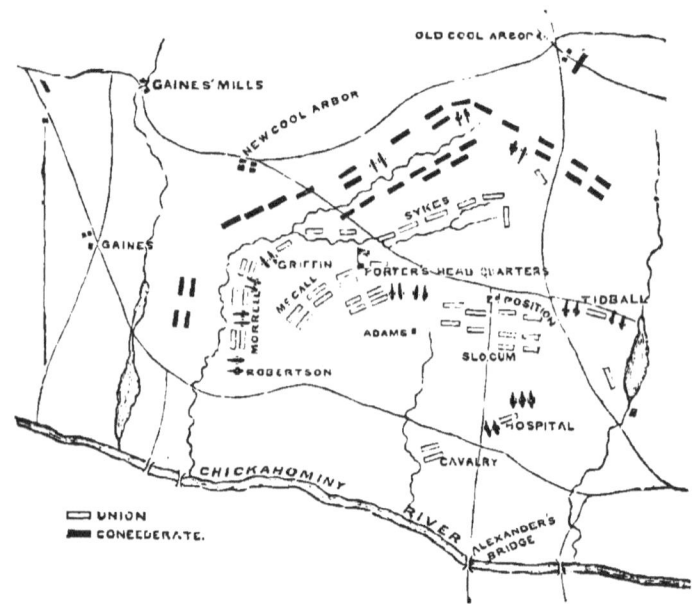

BATTLE OF GAINES'S FARM.

RUINS OF GAINES'S MILL.

insignificant that it did not long retard the advance of the infantry. The entire mass was soon across the stream and in pursuit of the Federal army.

Gen. McClellan, finding that it would be necessary to fight another battle on the north side of the Chickahominy river to hold the enemy in check long enough to get his trains over the river, ordered Gen. Porter to take a position about two miles this side of Gaines' Mill, and resist the further advance of the enemy until that was accomplished. Gen. Porter formed his corps in line of battle in the following order: The divisions of Morrell and Sykes were advantageously posted in position, with the left of Morrell's line extending almost to the Chickahominy, and the right of Sykes to the rear of Cold Harbor. McCall's division was held in reserve, being in position about one mile in the rear of the first line. By 11 o'clock everything was in readiness to receive the enemy, every man and every gun being in position.

The scene, as witnessed by the author from the position held by his regiment, was one of the grandest and most inspiring imaginable. The space of ground presented to the eye, and on which was soon to be fought one of the most desperate and destructive battles known in modern warfare, was about two miles in length and nearly as wide. It was made up of beautiful green meadows, large fields of waving grain, several swamps and ravines, which at some places interposed between the two armies, and a strip of wood skirting along the rebel line opposite to the Union position. The long array of glittering steel, the waving of the numerous starry banners, which gracefully and majestically flung their folds to the breeze from every regiment, the dashing of officers from one part of the line to the other giving orders, and the knowledge that the rebels in immense numbers were close upon us, all convinced us that the loyal sons of the Nation would soon again have to meet armed treason on the bloody field of battle.

The retreat from Mechanicsville, and the reports of the immense number of reinforcements which the rebels had received, had the effect of filling the hearts of the Union soldiers with apprehension for the result of the conflict they knew would soon take place, but undismayed they awaited the approach of the enemy. The period of suspense did not last long. At a few minutes before 1 o'clock the enemy emerged from the woods along the entire front in countless numbers, and with wild yells advanced on the Union lines. The battle had opened almost instantaneously along our entire front, and the great superiority in numbers of the enemy soon compelled Gen. Porter to use his reserve division, and in a short time almost his entire command was engaged.

At 2 o'clock he sent a request to McClellan for reinforcements, and also for axes to fell trees, but unfortunately the message did not reach McClellan till late in the day, when a part of Slocum's division was sent to his support. The battle raged all the afternoon with the utmost intensity, and, although a panic seized several regiments which at one time threatened the most serious consequences, the mass of the Union troops fought with a desperation unsurpassed in the history of the war. For four long hours 27,000 men held 60,000, led by the ablest chieftains in the Southern army, at bay. At about 4 o'clock there was a short lull in the battle, when it again burst forth with even greater fury than before. The enemy had again been strongly reinforced, and, with the most frantic yells of rage, they in overwhelming numbers charged on the Union lines.

The Union troops, with shouts of defiance, and the most destructive volleys of infantry and artillery, met their assailants, and the battle raged with all the fury which characterizes an engagement in which brave men fight for victory or death. The fighting was now of the most terrible description, and would often be at such close quarters that the savage thrust of the bayonet, and the crash of the butt of the musket, as it struck through the head of some poor unfortunate, added to the horror and tumult of the occasion. In the rear of a portion of the Union position was a low, marshy swamp, and into this the rebels tried with the utmost desperation to drive the Union troops; but our men, knowing the nature of the ground, and that it would be certain destruction if the enemy succeeded, fought with all the desperation of despair to prevent it.

It was fortunate that at about this time the reinforcements arrived from the south side of the river, and reached the front; for, even the most heroic fighting could not much longer have held the overwhelming hosts of the enemy at bay. During the battle, the regiments belonging to the division of the Pennsylvania Reserves were sent to combat where their services would be the most needed, and were frequently in the severest parts of the battle. One of the fiercest conflicts that occurred during the battle was fought by Col. Duryea's regiment of Zouaves and a large force of rebels. The Zouaves held a position on an open sandy piece of ground, and the enemy occupied the wood in front of them. A rebel column, six or eight men deep, cautiously advanced to the edge of this wood, when, rushing forward, they charged with frantic yells on the Union regiment. The Zouaves poured into their ranks a deadly fire, and then, with a wild shout, charged bayonets. The rebels for some time bravely stood their ground, and then ensued a conflict as terrible as human beings could make it. When the fighting was the severest, our regiment was ordered forward to reinforce the gallant Zouaves; and, as we advanced for that purpose, we could distinctly see the desperate nature of the fighting. Neither side appeared to think of loading their muskets, but depended entirely on the bayonet. We advanced as fast as possible to the assistance of the Zouaves, but by the time we reached the ground, the gallant fellows had beaten the rebels back into the woods and out of sight. They had, however, paid dearly for their victory, as about 300 of this heroic band lay dead or terribly wounded on the field. The regiment was completely disorganized, and left the field in squads. Its brave commander stayed for some time with our regiment, evidently regretting that he did not have a fresh regiment to seek revenge for the noble fellows lying dead in front of him. When the two Colonels met, Col. Roberts remarked, "Well, Colonel, they have used you up pretty badly;" to which Duryea replied, "Well, yes; but, by the Eternal,"—pointing with his sword to the heaps of rebel dead—"I think we have paid them back in their own coin."

For a few minutes after we arrived on the field, there was a lull in the fighting, and Col. Roberts ordered the regiment to advance over the ground so hotly contested a few moments before. As we advanced, I had a good opportunity of seeing the terrible character of the conflict. The ground was so thickly covered with the dead and wounded that it was with the utmost difficulty we could advance without treading on them. To accomplish this the regiment were compelled to break ranks and get over the ground as best they could, regardless of system or discipline. The red uniforms of the Zouaves, showing more conspicuously than the gray of the enemy, gave us at first the impression that the Union loss was the severer; but a closer inspection of the field revealed the fact that the loss of the enemy was even greater.

The nature of the wounds inflicted proved the close proximity in which the combatants contested for the mastery. Some of the dead had their heads broken in by blows from butts of rifles, and others lay dead with bayonets thrust through them, the weapon having been left sticking in their bodies. Some of the wounded begged piteously to be helped to the rear; and altogether, it was the most sickening sight I had ever witnessed. We had hardly more than advanced over the ground when Col. Roberts received orders to about-face his regiment, and march a few steps to the rear of the position held by the Zouaves. At this place the ground formed a small elevation several feet high, and behind this Col. Roberts formed his line. He had hardly more than done so when a chorus of yells, which was enough to make us believe that all the demons from the lower regions had broken loose, announced that the enemy was advancing to the assault. Col. Roberts ordered the regiment to lie down, and not fire a shot until the rebels reached the open ground. Some of the men could hardly be restrained from firing as they came yelling through the woods; but the officers kept telling them to keep cool and wait for the word of command.

After a few moments of painful suspense, the enemy like a swarm of bees burst from the wood into the open ground. The single word "Fire!" from our gallant Colonel, and the rifles of the first regiment sent a shower of lead into the rebel mass which swept their line like a scythe of death. The rebel line broke and fled in the utmost confusion, and in a few moments after the men, with loaded rifles and without the loss of a man, were prepared to give them the same reception. We did not have to wait long, however, to get the chance; for they, having reformed their lines, again advanced to the attack. They were again driven back with great slaughter, and we were commencing to congratulate ourselves on having a soft thing of it, when the yells of the enemy again announced their advance. They had now a fresh and a stronger column, and were evidently determined to force us from our position at any cost. We again reserved our fire until they were out of the woods, and then gave them the contents of our rifles. The rebel line wavered for a moment, but soon recovered, and then, giving us a volley, rushed forward to come to close quarters. A fierce conflict ensued, which raged for almost an hour, when they again fled from the field, leaving us in victorious possession. It was most fortunate, however, for us that they did, for our ammunition was running short, and after a few more volleys at the retreating rebels some of the men were entirely out; and the regiment which was advancing to relieve us made so poor a record after they became engaged, that, had we been compelled to fall back, they would, no doubt, have fled from the field before they did.

Our regiment and the 8th Pennsylvania Reserves, which had been engaged on our right, and was also out of ammunition, were now ordered to march to the rear for the purpose of getting a new supply and a short rest. The two regiments marched to the rear, stacked arms, and threw themselves on the ground. We had hardly more than done so, when a wild commotion in our front caused us to jump to our feet, when we discovered that a serious break had taken place in the line we had just vacated. The New York regiment which had relieved us broke and fled as soon as the rebels charged on them, and the enemy, pouring through the gap thus created, flanked several regiments, which were also compelled to fall back. To add to the confusion, a body of cavalry under the command of Gen. McCook, who, according to

HAND TO HAND FIGHTING AT MECHANICSVILLE.

the report of Gen. Porter, had been commanded to remain behind the hill, and not under any circumstances to appear above the crest, but to operate against the enemy on the bottom land on the left, should an opportunity present itself, charged on the rebel line. "This charge in the face of a withering fire of infantry, and in the midst of cannonading, resulted, of course, in their being thrown into confusion; and the bewildered horses, regardless of the efforts of the riders, wheeled about, and, dashing through the batteries, convinced the gunners that they were charged by the enemy."

Several of the batteries fell into the hands of the enemy, and a scene of the most indescribable confusion ensued. Horses plunged madly about, and sometimes ran into the ranks of the soldiers. Batteries fled to the rear, and from the point where the break occurred in the infantry line came a stream of flying fugitives, some of them throwing away guns and everything that could impede their flight. Everything now indicated a terrible disaster to our arms. Looking at the mass of running fugitives who came rushing toward us, I remarked to a comrade, "Now look out for a Bull Run stampede;" but happily such was not to take place. Col. Roberts had formed his regiment in line, and to keep them steady commenced to drill, throwing his command into columns by companies, and then into regimental line, with as much coolness as if he had had us on a parade ground in camp, when an officer dashing up, exclaimed, "Colonel, fire into those men who are falling back!" The Colonel replied, "We are out of ammunition." In a moment after Gen. Porter came riding up in haste, and exclaimed, "Col. Roberts, can't you take these two regiments and stop those men?" To which Roberts replied, "I will try; but get me some ammunition to stop the enemy."

Col. Roberts formed the two regiments, and, although the shells from the enemy's batteries fell thick around them, and the shouts of the now victorious enemy, who were in hot pursuit of the broken Union troops, could be heard coming nearer and nearer, they stood as firm as if on dress parade, and presented a solid front of steel to the demoralized fugitives, who tried to pass them and get to the rear. The two regiments succeeded in stopping the most of them, but they were now in a most serious situation, as the rebels would soon be upon them, and they without ammunition to defend themselves.

Fortunately just at this time the cheering in our rear announced the fact that reinforcements were at hand, and never were such more eagerly welcomed. The Irish brigade, commanded by Gen. Meagher, and a brigade commanded by Gen. French, both of Slocum's division, came on the ground on the double-quick, and charging on the enemy with the ferocity of tigers, stopped their farther advance; and finally the entire line, which was now again in good condition, advanced and drove back the enemy. The approach of night put an end to the fighting, and closed one of the severest battles, for the number engaged, in the history of the war.

This battle, fought for the purpose of covering the retreat of the Union army over the Chickahominy, fully accomplished that purpose. The siege guns, wagons and army material on the north side of the river were safely crossed to the south side, and Porter's corps followed in perfect order during the night. The loss sustained by the Union forces was, however, very great, and as the rebels captured several batteries of artillery and held the battle-ground, the prestige of success was held by them. Gen. Fitz John Porter's corps, which did almost all the fighting, numbered about 27,000 men, and lost nearly one-third. Fearful as was the Union loss, the enemy's was even yet greater. The Union troops fighting most of the time on the defensive, inflicted the most terrible slaughter on their enemies.

A distinguished rebel officer thus describes this terrible conflict:

"The attack was opened by the columns of Hill (1st), Anderson and Pickett. These gallant masses rushed forward with thundering hurrahs, upon the musketry of the foe, as though it were joy to them. Whole ranks went down under that terrible hail, but nothing could restrain their courage. The billows of battle raged fiercely onward; the struggle was man to man, eye to eye, bayonet to bayonet. The hostile Meagher's brigade, composed chiefly of Irishmen, offered heroic resistance. After a fierce struggle our people began to give way, and at length all orders of encouragement were vain—they were falling back in the greatest disorder. Infuriate, foaming at the mouth, bareheaded, sabre in hand, at this critical moment Gen. Cobb appeared upon the field at the head of his legion, and with him the Nineteenth North Carolina and the Fourteenth Virginia regiments. At once these troops renewed the attack, but all their devotion and self-sacrifice were in vain. The Irish held their position with a determination and ferocity that called forth the admiration of our own officers. Broken to pieces and disorganized, the fragments of that fine legion came rolling back from the charge. The Nineteenth North Carolina lost eight standard-bearers, and most of their staff officers were either killed or wounded. Again Gens. Hill (1st) and Anderson led their troops to the attack, and some regiments covered themselves with immortal glory. Our troops exhibited a contempt for death that made them the equals of old, experienced veterans; for,' notwithstanding the bloody harvest the destroyer reaped in our ranks that day, no disorder, no timid bearing, revealed that many of the regiments were under fire and smelt gunpowder then for the first time. But the enemy, nevertheless, quietly and coolly held out against every attack we made, one after the other. Notwithstanding the fact that some of their brigades had to stand their ground from four until eight o'clock p. m., they performed feats of incredible valor; and it was only when the news came that Jackson was upon them in the rear, that, about eight, they retired before our advance. Despite the dreadful carnage in the ranks, they marched on with streaming banners and rolling drums, and carried with them all their slightly wounded and all their baggage; and when the cavalry regiments of Davies and Wickham went in pursuit, repelled this assault also with perfect coolness.

"By this time night had come on, and overspread the field of death with darkness, compassionately shutting out from the eyes of the living the horrid spectacle of slaughter, * * I hastened with one of my aids to that quarter of the field where the struggle had raged the most fiercely. The scene of ruin was horrible; whole ranks of the enemy lay prone where they had stood at the beginning of the battle. The number of wounded was fearful, too, and the groans and imploring cries for help that rose on all sides had, in the obscurity of the night, a ghastly effect that froze the blood in one's veins. Although I had been upon so many battle-fields in Italy and Hungary, never had my vision beheld such a spectacle of human destruction."

The troops referred to by this officer as making so desperate a resistance were not, as he thought, the Irish Brigade, that body of troops not coming into action until late in the evening. During the time that this battle was in progress, the enemy made an attack on McClellan's left wing, for the purpose of preventing him from sending reinforcements to the troops fighting on the north side of the river. The rebels, who were under the command of General Toombs, suffered a severe defeat, and were driven from the field with heavy loss. The enemy renewed the engagement at this point on the following morning, but were again defeated by the desperate fighting of Hancock's brigade of the Union army. This action is known as the battle of Golding's farm, and as already stated, had been brought on for the purpose of preventing strong reinforcements being sent to Porter. Some writers contend that it had that effect, but that is not in accordance with the facts in the case. Gen. McClellan had fully made up his mind to withdraw his army to the James river, and the reinforcements he did send to Porter's aid, although late through the miscarriage of the order from that general requesting aid, yet had the effect of checking the farther advance of the enemy, and enabled the army to concentrate on the south side of the river.

The rear of the Union troops, after crossing the Chickahominy, blew up the bridges and encamped on Trent's Farm. The greatest activity, however, prevailed in the Union army, and the most extensive preparations were made to get the siege guns, wagons and army supplies safe off on the line of retreat. The army had succeeded in cencentrating on the south side of the river, but the greater task of getting it through the White Oak Swamp still remained. During the night of the 27th, between five and six thousand loaded wagons, a drove of three thousand head of cattle, and an immense number of ambulances and other war material, were started on the way to the James. There were but two passable roads on the line of retreat to Savage Station, and over them flowed a constant stream of wagons, cattle and men.

The magnificent corps of reserve artillery of the Army of the Potomac, commanded by Gen. Hunt, and numbering over one thousand guns, was still parked on Trent's farm, waiting to get possession of the road, on the morning of the 28th, and it was of the utmost importance that this most valuable auxiliary of the army should be prevented from falling into the hands of the enemy. This splendid park of artillery consisted of thirteen batteries, its guns being of the most improved pattern, and was intended to be used in the bombardment of Richmond. It was a few days later used with terrible effect on the enemy from Malvern Hill, and did much to win us that splendid victory.

There was great danger that these guns, being so heavy that they could only be moved slowly, might fall into the hands of the enemy before they could be moved to another battle-field.

A writer (J. R. Sypher) in describing the movement said:

"Gen. McClellan nervously, and in deep anxiety, called to mind his ablest generals and his trustiest troops. Gen. McCall and his division of Pennsylvania Reserves had been intrusted with the defense of the right wing at Mechanicsville; they had fully justified the confidence reposed in them by the commanding general. At Gaines' Mill, too, they had put to shame the regulars, and paid a terrible price in blood for their valor. There were other divisions which had rested while the Reserves had been fighting and marching, without sleep and without rations. But McClellan would take no risks in a labor so momentous. Gen. McCall was therefore ordered to guard Hunt's artillery, and conduct it in safety from Trent's Farm to the Quaker road south of White Oak Swamp."

The giving of this important trust to Gen. McCall and his men was certainly a very great honor. In the two great battles that had been fought on the north side of the river, the rebels had gained no decided advantage; in fact, had been severely punished; but the rebel leaders, mistaking the withdrawal of the Union forces for a hurried flight to White House Landing or down the Peninsula towards Yorktown, made a quick movement in that direction to cut off McClellan's retreat. They, however, soon discovered their mistake, and commenced to press the Union rear. The army was now in a position where a pitched battle with the enemy was out of the question, and it would require the finest generalship to extricate it from the labyrinth of difficulties which surrounded it. This was accomplished with the most consummate skill. It was fully 9 o'clock in the evening before the road could be cleared for the departure of the artillery train, and then, with the regiments equally distributed along the line, the march commenced. This artillery corps, with the wagons and batteries of our division made a train six or seven miles long, and this valuable property we were to guard over the swamps and bogs of one of the worst of the wretchedly bad roads which crossed the Peninsula. It was raining, and the night was as dark as pitch, and, as the mud at some places was almost knee deep, it was one of the most miserable marches imaginable. A constant watch had to be kept against a surprise from the enemy. But the men, feeling the importance of the trust confided to their keeping, kept cheerfully to the work, and by the following morning reached Savage Station. This place is a railroad station on the Richmond and York River railroad, running from Richmond to White House Landing, and was being used by the Union commander to send supplies from the latter place to his army. Since the change of base to the James river had been decided on, the road had been used to its utmost capacity to send army material and wounded to the landing for shipment. A large number of sick and wounded were still at the station waiting to be moved, and a train loaded with them was just in the act of leaving when the telegraph stopped working. It was, of course, at once believed that the enemy had cut our communications with White House Landing, but the train proceeded cautiously down the road a few miles, when it was discovered that the rebels had possession of Dispatch Station. It was now evident that all the supplies yet with the army and the wounded that could be got away would have to be sent through White Oak Swamp, and the greatest terror and alarm fell on these poor unfortunates, who had anxiously hoped to be sent away on the cars from the terrible scenes surrounding them.

The rapid movement of the troops as they

marched past the station, the hurry and confusion of the countless teams as they left on the road to James river, the endless string of ambulances that were still arriving loaded with sick and wounded, the touching cries of those unfortunates, who had been unloaded and laid under the trees, and who were begging piteously not to be left behind, together with the wild reports about the enemy having cut off our retreat, created a scene of the wildest excitement and confusion. About 3,000 sick and wounded were at the station, and a constant stream still coming in. The most active preparations were being made to get them away, but it soon became evident that a large number would have to fall into the hands of the enemy.

A writer, in describing the scene at the station, writes:

"The poor broken and wounded men, whose hearts had borne them up to endure all hardships, still waited on the cars, hoping against hope, and rejecting the offers of their friends to remove them to beds on the ground. Between two and three thousand sick and wounded were in the houses and tents, and under the trees at Savage Station. Deep gloom and sore distress fell upon all; there were a thousand rumors of things most improbable, but the despondency of the men prepared them to believe the most extravagant stories, and the confusion that surrounded them increased their consternation.

"When, therefore, on Sunday morning, the Reserves halted at the station, the men left the ranks, and amid the army of wounded, sought out their companions, and ministered to their many wants. For such as could walk they made canes and crutches; they bound up the wounds of some, and aided many to follow their regiments in the retreat across the swamp; to others who could not follow them, they gave water, and rations of bread, meat, sugar, and coffee; and each noble patriot placed in the pocket of his wounded companion all the money he had in his possession. The parting of brave men, companions in arms, is rarely witnessed under more distressing circumstances; the strongest heart was melted in sorrow; many a manly cheek was wet with tears as the soldiers bade farewell to each other, expecting never to meet again. Fathers dragged themselves away from the couches of their sons, son forsook father, and brother parted from brother. Both were patriotic and brave—one well, robust, and strong; the other all bleeding, maimed, and dying. They parted like brave men; those who went, to die gloriously in battle, or to survive with the vindicated honor of their country; those who remained, doomed to the most terrible hardships that befall men who, in war, become the prisoners of a vengeful foe. Without physician, nurse, or attendant, many died beneath the trees where their companions had left them; others, carried towards Richmond, either died on the way, and were buried in the swamps, or, taken to the Confederate prisons, died of neglect, filth, and abuse."

Rev. Dr. Marks, who was chaplain of the sixty-third Pennsylvania Volunteers, said:

"When it became manifest that such was to be their fate, the scenes of distress could not be pictured by human language. Some of the wounded men, who were left in their tents, struggled forth through the grounds, exclaiming, they 'would rather die than fall into the hands of the rebels.' I heard one man cry out, 'O, my God! is this the reward I deserve for all the sacrifices I have made, the battles I have fought, and the agony I have endured from my wounds?' Some of the youngest soldiers wept like children, others turned pale, and some fainted. Poor fellows! they thought this was the last drop in the cup of bitterness; but there were yet many to be added."

The rebel commander appears to have been somewhat perplexed by the movements of the Union army on Saturday, but on Sunday he discovered that the line of retreat was in the direction of the James river instead of the Pamunky, as he had at first supposed, and he immediately made the most desperate efforts to cut off the Union forces from the James river.

The left wing of the Union army abandoned their intrenchments on Sunday night, and also fell back in the direction of Savage Station. The rebels immediately closed in pursuit, and Gens. Sumner and Heintzelman, who were in command of the Union forces on the left, were ordered by Gen. McClellan to form their commands in line of battle on Allen's Farm, and check the advance of the enemy. The rebels advanced on the Williamsburg road, and, forming line of battle within a short distance of the Union lines, advanced to the attack. They were met with a terrific discharge of artillery and infantry. They fell back in confusion, but soon again advanced, and the battle raged with great fury until nearly noon, when the rebel line gave way and fled from the field. This action is known as the battle of Peach Orchard or Allen's Farm, and it was a severe repulse to the rebel army. It was deemed best, however, that Sumner and Heintzelman should fall back to a position nearer Savage Station; and after the close of the battle they retired and formed line of battle near that place.

The position held by the Union forces extended over an almost level tract of land, comprising several hundred acres; and on this open ground, like a living wall of fire, stood the rear of the Union army to check the advance and save the Union forces from destruction. It was necessary to give the enemy one more repulse, and hold them in check long enough to enable the part of the army and trains that had left the station, to get through the White Oak Swamp before the rear corps could follow. A defeat of this line would have insured the destruction of a considerable portion of the Union army; for had it been driven on the mass who were struggling to get out of the way, the most terrible consequences would have followed.

That great soldier, Gen. Sumner, had been intrusted with the command of the rear-guard, and never was trust placed in more loyal or abler hands. He had beside his own corps a part of Heintzelman's corps and Franklin's division, and, forming his column, he calmly awaited the assault of the enemy. At about 5 P. M. the battle opened with a furious discharge of artillery from the enemy's batteries, which was responded to by the Union batteries, and for almost an hour the thunder from these guns was incessant. The enemy's infantry had in the meantime advanced through the woods skirting the front of the Union position, and, at a given signal, in almost countless numbers, with the most frantic yells, they rushed on the Union lines. A sheet of fire from the Union lines, and the roar of musketry was added to the thunder of artillery. The battle raged with indescribable fury until eleven o'clock at night, when the rebels, defeated in every assault and at every point, sullenly withdrew from the field. The attempt of the enemy to drive our rear in confusion on the retreating army was a most signal failure; there is no doubt that Gen. Sumner could have held at bay almost any force the enemy might have been able to concentrate in his front; but the trains of artillery, wagons, ambulances, cattle, and supplies, in the van of the army, had by this time all left the station, and were either over or on the way through White Oak Swamp. So, at twelve o'clock, Gen. Sumner received orders from Gen. McClellan to evacuate his position as rapidly as possible, and follow the rest of the army.

It is said that Gen. Sumner, who now had his blood up, retreated with the greatest reluctance, and before doing so requested reinforcements, that he might renew the conflict in the morning; and that he was so disgusted with the order to withdraw from the position he had so nobly defended, that from some expressions which he made, he received the sobriquet of "Bull Sumner." Subsequent events, however, fully proved the wisdom of the order, as the rebels had already started a strong column in the direction of White Oak creek, to cut off the retreat of the rear of the army, and it became highly necessary that all of the army should get across the swamp, and over the creek, before the enemy could intercept them. Gen. Sumner rapidly withdrew his men, and, before two o'clock the last of the troops, with the exception of the wounded, had left the station. As the troops marched away, and the wounded found that they would really have to fall into the hands of the enemy, the scene was absolutely heart-rending; and to add to the terror of these unfortunates, the woods had caught fire and were burning with great rapidity, threatening death to hundreds of them.

The rebels had also again opened fire with artillery, and, in spite of the hospital signs over the buildings that contained some of the wounded, fired into them. The flames lit the heavens as bright as day, the air was full of the most dismal sounds, and the shrieks of the flaming shells, with the piteous cries of the wounded, made a scene of horror no pen can describe, and a sudden demoralization appeared to seize upon all in the rear of the army.

The entire retreat had so far been made with the greatest coolness, the troops retreating from one position to another leisurely, and nobly contesting every foot of ground; but the movement now degenerated into a rapid flight, and the men who had so nobly sustained themselves were now compelled to flee to save themselves from destruction; and a scene the most indescribable ensued. The race was, however, won by the Union troops, and before ten o'clock in the morning the last of them had crossed White Oak creek, and had blown up the bridge in their rear.

The race for position on White Oak creek had been won, but it soon became evident that the army had secured very little time for rest. The pursuing enemy, as soon as they reached the front of the position occupied by the Federal right wing, opened with artillery, and also made several efforts to cross the stream, but were driven back by Gen. Smith's division. This demonstration was, however, only made for the purpose of diverting the Federal troops from the real attack of the rebels, who were marching to intercept the Union army at Charles City cross roads. This movement again compelled McClellan to give battle, as it was necessary to hold the enemy in check until the trains of siege guns, wagons, and other war material, could be safely transferred to Malvern Hill, and then to Harrison's Landing on the James river. The line of battle extended from near Turkey Bend on the James river to White Oak creek, a distance of about four miles.

Sumner's corps held the right of the position, Gen. Porter's the left, and Gen. Heintzelman's the center. Gen. Franklin guarded the passes of White Oak Swamp. McCall's division of Porter's corps was in position on the New Market road, which is the principal one running from the direction of Richmond. This position was the most important one in the Union line of battle, as the main body of the rebel army approached on the New Market road for the purpose of cutting through the Union lines and getting between McClellan's army and the James river. Hancock's brigade of Sumner's corps held the extreme right of the line, and the battle opened by a vigorous fire of artillery on that command. This fire was most destructive, and caused a short panic in several Union regiments, but order was soon restored, and the rebels repulsed. This demonstration, as well as several others on our right, was, however, only intended to cover the movement to be made by the enemy on the New Market road. It was not, however, before three o'clock that the enemy, in strong force, appeared in front of McCall's division; but the battle soon after opened with great fury along his front, and rapidly spreading along the line held by the Union troops, raged with the most desperate fury until night put an end to the conflict.

The enemy fought with a desperation unsurpassed in the history of the war, and at several periods of the battle the total defeat of the Union army appeared to be certain; but the equally desperate fighting of the latter at last drove them back, and when the battle closed the ground was in possession of the Union troops. Several batteries of artillery had, however, fallen into the hands of the enemy, and the Union loss in killed and wounded was very great. During the following night, the army was successfully withdrawn to a strong position at Malvern Hill. The army was now again united, and in one body presented a solid front to the enemy. Harrison's Landing was only six miles below, and to this place all the army material not wanted in the coming conflict had been sent.

The soldiers, almost worn out by the marching and fighting, were now concentrated in a strong position, under the protection of the splendid train of artillery which we had guarded through the White Oak Swamp, and the gun-boats on the James river; but their task was not yet finished, for the approaching day was to witness one more great conflict in the war for the Union. General McClellan posted his men with great skill, and by daylight the formation of the Federal line was completed. It was drawn up in a semicircle, with the artillery in such a position as to command the entire front. At about nine o'clock the enemy appeared in front of the Union position, but the battle did not open until about noon, when it commenced with a most terrific discharge of artillery, and for almost two hours the earth shook beneath the thunder of the combined artillery of the two armies. The enemy were worsted in this conflict, and finding that they could make no impression with artillery on the Union line, advanced a massive column of infantry, commanded by Generals Lee, Jackson, Beauregard and Magruder, to storm the Federal position.

A battle of the most terrible description ensued, and the rebel line was driven back with the most dreadful slaughter; but again and again they renewed the assault, only to be again driven back with the same fearful loss. The battle raged until night, when the rebel army, fearfully beaten, fell back out of range of the Federal guns. The siege guns on Malvern Hill and the gunboats on the James river did most effective service, and did much to win the victory. A storm of shot and shell from these guns was hurled on the retreating rebel column with fearful effect, until it succeeded in getting out of their range; and until nine o'clock the occasional flash of a gun from Malvern Hill, followed by the crash of a flaming shell, gave notice to the rebels that the vigor of the Union guns was not exhausted.

This ended the great Seven Days battle before Richmond, undoubtedly one of the bloodiest series of battles in the annals of modern or ancient times. After the battle of Malvern Hill, the Union troops marched to Harrison's Landing and the change of base was effected; it is true, not without great loss. But the loss of the enemy was yet greater, and they could not fairly boast of a victory. They had captured the larger number of prisoners, from the fact that the Union forces falling back were compelled to allow a large number of wounded to fall into their hands; but as the Union troops fought almost all the time on the defensive, and often from strong positions, the enemy lost a much larger number in killed and wounded. The rebels were, however, loud in their boasts of having gained a great victory; and the fact of their getting possession of the field after the fighting gave their claim some semblance of truth; but a more careful examination of the campaign disclosed the fact that they had suffered much more than the troops they claimed to have defeated. They had gained no important advantage over the Union troops in any of the seven battles, and had been driven from the field with great slaughter in every action but one, and on that occasion they had lost more men than the Union forces. The boast of having driven the Union army to the James river cannot be sustained, as it is unquestionably true that the Union forces would have been withdrawn to the position they occupied after the battle of Malvern Hill had the rebels not pursued a step after the first day's fighting. The rebels had fought with a desperate courage, well worthy of a better cause; but the fighting of the Union troops had been fully as brilliant, and they were handled by their officers with at least as great daring and skill. It is certainly to the credit of the Union commander, that, although greatly outnumbered by the enemy, and attacked at the unfortunate time when the removal of his base of supplies became a positive necessity, so little fell into the hands of the enemy. It was perhaps a mistake in not following his decisive victory at Malvern Hill by a pursuit of the fleeing enemy; but it must also be remembered that his men were well-nigh worn out with incessant marching and fighting, and consequently not in a condition to make a vigorous pursuit; and if they had, they would have been compelled to fight the enemy in the strong fortifications of Richmond, and the result would probably have been as disastrous as the assault on Malvern Hill was to the enemy, when they charged on the Union lines in that strong position.

Harrison's Landing, the place selected by Gen. McClellan for his new base, was admirably adapted for a defensive position, and was soon made so strong that it could easily have been held against any force that the enemy might have brought to bear upon it.

CHAPTER VI.

MY FIRST CAPURE.

IN writing the narrative of my first capture by the enemy, it will be necessary to give a more detailed account of the part taken by my regiment on the sixth day of the Seven Days' fighting before Richmond, than in the previous chapter, in which was given but a general description of the battle.

As already stated, by Sunday morning, June 29th, our division had safely guarded the reserve artillery corps of the army from Trent's farm, on the Chickahominy, to near the James river; and on the following day this most important arm of the service was removed to Malvern Hill, where it took a prominent part in the great conflict fought at that place. Relieved of that important trust, and as we had now reached the James river, we hoped to get some rest; and weary and almost worn out by the long marching and fighting we had passed through, we threw ourselves on the ground for that purpose. We were soon, however compelled to realize that our rest would be a short one, for we had hardly more than nestled down when our brigade was ordered to fall in line, and marched down the New Market road to picket and watch the movements of the enemy in our front.

It had already been discovered that the rebels were advancing on this road in strong force, and that in all probability our division would have to stand the brunt of the attack, and that it was of the utmost importance that a strict watch be maintained along our front, to guard against a surprise. The terrible days of battle, and toilsome marching, had told severely on us all, and a large number of the men still in line were better subjects for the hospital than for the battle-field. But not a murmur or word of complaint could be heard; and when the order was received to fall in and advance in the direction of the enemy, it was obeyed with as much spirit and alacrity as the weary spirit of the men would allow.

Since the capture at Gaines' Mill of our beloved commander, Gen. John F. Reynolds, the brigade was commanded by Col. Simmons, of the Fifth regiment, who immediately advanced his command about one mile, and then placed it in position to guard the New Market road. The night was so intensely dark that it would have been impossible to distinguish an enemy a few steps from us, and in advancing we had been compelled to move with the greatest caution, feeling our way at every step, until we reached a private road running at right angles with the New Market road, into which we filed, expecting every moment to meet the enemy; and it was certainly a considerable relief when we were halted and ordered to lie down.

A picket line was established a few yards in front of the line, and we were then informed that we might lie down and sleep, but with loaded rifle in hand, and ready in a moment's notice to jump into line and receive the enemy. I soon found out that, at least with me, sleep was out of the question, for it was a night of constant alarm. At one time a volley of musketry almost in our rear made us spring to our feet in alarm, as we supposed that the enemy was making an effort to cut us off from the army; but it subsequently was learned that two Union regiments had fired into each other in mistake. At another time, a number of artillery horses, which had broken loose, dashed along the line snorting with terror, giving us the impression that a cavalry charge was being made on us. The almost constant barking of dogs at several farm-houses in our front gave us the impression that the enemy was advancing, keeping us in a state of constant alarm, and preventing us from getting the sleep we so much needed to prepare us for the desperate work on the morrow.

At daylight we were withdrawn from this advanced position, and rejoined the division, which was in position in a large open field completely surrounded with woods of scraggy, low pines and scrub oak. We had prepared a hasty meal, expecting we could then lie down and rest, when a fellow having the appearance of a mulatto, or very dark-complexioned white man, came into camp and gave some information which led to our regiment being ordered out on a reconnoissance, the stranger accompanying us as guide. After marching a short distance through the pines, we struck on a by-road, and had proceeded but a short distance when we discovered that we were in the most imminent danger of being ambuscaded and our retreat cut off. The Colonel immediately gave the order to about-face, and double-quick for the rear.

The stranger, who no doubt had been sent to decoy us into the rebel lines, made an effort to escape, but Col. Roberts ordered the men to secure and bring him along. We had unconsciously been marching right into the enemy's lines, and as they endeavored to close in and cut us off, it became a desperate race with us to get out of the trap. We had about got rid of the pursuing enemy, when a line of Union sharpshooters, who had advanced in our rear, mistook us for the enemy and fired into us. A large ditch that intervened between us and the sharpshooters afforded a good protection; we jumped into it, and after considerable difficulty we managed to let them know who we were, and after they ceased firing we rejoined the brigade.

The fellow who so nearly succeeded in leading the regiment to destruction, trembled with terror, and his fears were not groundless; for as soon as we got to the rear, one of the men shot him dead on the spot. Under any other circumstances, we might have considered it a cowardly act to shoot him after being a prisoner; but under the present circumstances we could not help but feel that the act was justifiable, and that the miscreant richly deserved his fate.

It soon became evident that the enemy were swarming along our entire front, and that a desperate conflict would soon ensue. Gen. McCall formed the division in line of battle, with the second brigade on the right, the third on the left, and our brigade, the first, was held in reserve in the rear of the two other brigades. The position was a fairly good one, but the division was too small to properly occupy it; and before the opening of the battle it was considered best to call the regiments of the Reserve brigade into position in the front line. Immediately after the battle opened, the entire division became fiercely engaged, and for several hours held three times their number at bay, without having a single regiment as a support in their rear. Our regiment and the Ninth Reserves had been placed in position in the rear of Kern's and Cooper's batteries as a support to them, but we were soon after ordered to advance with the Third regiment, and endeavor to feel the enemy and draw them from the wood. We soon found that the enemy occupied the wood in strong force. They appeared shy about advancing, but kept up a scattering fire with our regiment. This was no doubt for the purpose of deceiving us in regard to their strength, and for the purpose of getting us to charge into the wood, where almost sure destruction would have been the result. Finding, however, that we would not be entrapped in that way, they at last advanced and made a violent attack on the Third regiment on our right. At the same time everything indicated the advance of the enemy along the entire line, and we were ordered to fall back to our former position in the rear of Kern's battery.

The rebels had made a desperate effort to cut off the Third regiment, but after considerable difficulty it succeeded in extricating itself, and getting back into the main line of battle. About this time the enemy opened a heavy artillery fire along our entire front, and under cover of this cannonading, their infantry advanced to the assault. A strong column threw itself with terrific fury on the left of our division line, and through the cowardly conduct of a New York German battery they at first gained a slight advantage in that direction. This battery became panic-stricken, and fled to the rear in the utmost confusion, and its base conduct might have resulted in a terrible disaster to our division, and perhaps to the entire army. The frantic horses attached to the caissons dashed right through the infantry lines, and threw them into disorder. The enemy, taking advantage of the confusion, charged with frantic yells on the now broken ranks, and the Twelfth regiment, which was in position on the extreme left of our division line, was cut in two, and the greater part of it driven back to the right and rear of Hooker's division. The enemy pursued them, but being taken in flank by Hooker's men, they were driven back on the Reserves, and then driven from the field.

When the break occurred on the left, Gen. McCall immediately ordered Col. Simmons, with the Fifth and Eighth regiments of his brigade, to move to the left and support that part of the line. Col. Simmons was one of the finest soldiers in the army, and no braver spirit ever led an assaulting column than he. Taking the two regiments, he advanced to the point of greatest danger, and ordering the Ninth and Tenth regiments in position on the left to change front, he formed the four regiments into line, and then his trumpet voice rang out "*Brigade, Forward, Charge!*" and the four regiments with a loud cheer, which rang out above the roar of battle, charged on the enemy.

A conflict of the most terrible description ensued; the rebels with the most frantic yells of rage contested the ground with the brave Reserves with the utmost desperation, but were finally driven from the field with the most dreadful loss. The left wing of the division was saved, and the enemy, after leaving the ground covered with killed and wounded, and three hundred prisoners in the hands of the victors, were driven from the field; but the Union troops had also suffered severely, a large number of brave patriots being left dead on the field, and they had also to mourn the loss of their leader, who fell mortally wounded while leading the charge.

The death of Col. S. G. Simmons was a great loss to the army and the country. With no disparagement to the other able commanders of regiments he was probably the ablest officer in command of a regiment in the division. He was a graduate of West Point, and after participating in the Mexican and Seminole war, was connected with military schools up to within a short time before the commencement of the Civil War, when he was in the far West. At the first commencement of hostilities he came to Harrisburg, and connected himself with the Pennsylvania Reserves, and was immediately appointed Colonel of the Fifth regiment, being one of the most accomplished soldiers in the army. The result was soon felt by his regiment, and under his skillful leadership it soon became one of the best organizations in the army.

When Gen. Reynolds was captured, Simmons was given the command of the brigade, and had he lived he would have added one more to the three great army commanders produced by the division of Pennsylvania Reserves.* The entire division, as well as his gallant regiment, deeply felt his loss, and mourned his sad death.

Directly after the enemy made the desperate charge on the left of our division, they also advanced in strong force on the position held by Kern's and Cooper's batteries. As already stated, these batteries had been supported by the Ninth and our regiment; but as the Ninth had been taken to reinforce the left, our regiment was the sole support of these batteries during a considerable portion of the engagement.

As the rebel lines advanced to the assault, we were ordered to lie down behind the barriers, and let the artillery first deal with them. On came the yelling mass of rebels until within a short distance of the Union guns, when a discharge of double-shotted grape and canister from these plowed through their ranks with fearful effect. The enemy recoiled a few steps, when quickly reforming, they rushed with the most hideous yells on the batteries. Our regiment was now ordered to fire, and then charge bayonets. This was accomplished with the greatest gallantry, the boys charging on the yelling enemy with

*Mead, Reynolds and Ord.

shouts of defiance, and in a short time we drove them from the field and into the wood beyond. They, however, soon reformed and advanced to the attack, and we soon again became fearfully engaged; but the result was the same, the enemy being again driven from the field.

After this assault, we had a few moments rest, and as the enemy had disappeared from our front, we were commencing to hope that the conflict was over, when the sharp whiz of a bullet over our heads, which was soon followed by others, gave indications that our work was not yet over, and that we would have at least one more attack from the enemy. They had now advanced a strong line of sharpshooters to the edge of the wood, and under the protection of the trees, endeavored to pick off the gunners of the batteries. The batteries thundered volley after volley into the woods; but as the rebels were well protected, they probably sustained very little loss, and the fire from their rifles was telling fearfully in the ranks of the batteries. A detail of the regiment now advanced to dislodge the enemy, and a sharp skirmish ensued between them and the rebels. It soon after became evident that the enemy was again preparing to charge, and our men were ordered to fall back into line.

The enemy had been strongly reinforced, and in a few moments after our skirmishers fell back, they rushed in a massive column from the wood, and, yelling like fiends, came swarming across the field and against our line. As the dense mass of humanity, maddened by former repulses, and driven to desperation by the desire to overcome the batteries that had so severely punished them, rushed over the field, the Union batteries, double-shotted with grape and canister, opened on them, and a scene of the most indescribable horror ensued. The batteries fired with almost lightning rapidity, and every discharge plowed horrible gashes through the enemy's ranks, and strewed the ground with the dead. It appeared as if no flesh and blood could withstand these terrible discharges; but the enemy filled up the chasms in their ranks, and pressed forward with a recklessness and desperate courage that was unsurpassed in the history of the war. The artillery men at last commenced to load triple charges of grape, and the overloaded guns recoiled with such force as to endanger the lives of those around them.

Our regiment, inspired by the valor of the brave artillerymen, could hardly wait until the order was given to open on the enemy, and when the order was at last given, they went to work with a will, and crowding on the spaces between the guns, poured a constant stream of bullets on the advancing enemy. For almost two hours the battle raged with the most intense fury, the enemy rushing up to the mouths of the cannon with the fury of demons, and the slaughter was horrible in the extreme; the artillery often fired into them when only forty or fifty steps from the muzzles of the guns, and we kept up a fire so rapid that the guns commenced to heat so badly as to blister our hands; but the rebels displaying a contempt of death that was almost incredible, pushed forward over the dead bodies of their comrades, and it now appeared as if the batteries would have to fall into their hands, but the terrible volleys of death were at last too much, and they fell back. But a terrible crisis was now approaching. Kern's battery was running out of ammunition, and its brave commander, who had in vain been trying to get a new supply, was compelled to withdraw his guns. After firing the last round of his ammunition at the enemy, Captain Kern, with tears in his eyes, ordered his battery to withdraw from the position it had so nobly defended.

The enemy mistaking the movement for a retreat of the Union forces, immediately re-formed their lines, and charged on the now defenseless battery, and it would have fallen into their hands, had not the prompt measures of Col. Roberts prevented it. In the few moments which intervened between the repulse of the enemy and the withdrawing of the battery, the Colonel had reformed his thinned and broken ranks; and when the enemy with cries of exultation rushed forward to take advantage of the break in our line, his voice rang out, "*First Regiment, Forward, Charge*

Bayonets!" and with a loud cheer we rushed on the advancing enemy. We did not fire a shot, but relying on the bayonet we charged with an impetuosity that broke the rebel line, when we poured a deadly volley into their backs, and pursued them over the fields. Unfortunately the momentum of the charge carried us too far, and it soon became evident that we had got ourselves into a bad fix. A column of fresh rebel troops flanked us, and we were soon in the most imminent danger of being surrounded and cut off by them. We had also suffered fearfully in the charge; our gallant captain, George H. Hess, and a large number of officers and men of the regiment had fallen, and we were compelled to fall back in confusion to the edge of the wood in the rear of Cooper's battery.

The enemy in strong force now rushed on the battery, and capturing it, were on the point of turning the guns on our lines, when Col. Roberts ordered us to take cover behind the trees and open on the enemy. We immediately opened a deadly fire on the rebels, who had possession of the guns, and for a short time we would tumble them over as fast as they could lay hands on the battery; but we could not accomplish impossibilities, and the immense hordes of the enemy would soon have dislodged us and secured the battery, had we not at this most critical moment received reinforcements.

The Ninth regiment was hastening from the left for that purpose, and when informed that Cooper's battery was in the hands of the enemy, they demanded to be led against them for the purpose of recapturing it. This battery was a great favorite with the Reserves, and the fact of it now being in the hands of the enemy filled our hearts with rage and a fierce determination to recapture it or die in the attempt. The noble Ninth regiment, joined by our regiment, with a tremendous cheer now charged upon the enemy, and a most terrific conflict ensued. Both sides discharged their pieces, and then with the most frantic yells of rage rushed on each other; never was battle more severely contested, both sides fighting with all the desperation of the most infuriated men. No time could be secured for loading, so all had to rely on the bayonet or such weapons as they might have in their possession. Bayonet thrusts were frequently given, muskets clubbed, and even knives were used in this fearful struggle. The dead bodies of men and horses, and broken caissons were literally piled up around the guns of the battery, and in some cases afforded barricades for the contestants.

On the left, the charge of the four regiments under the gallant Simmons had cleared the field, and on our right Randell's battery of regulars, supported by the Fourth and Seventh Pennsylvania Reserves, were sweeping the enemy like chaff from the field, so the rebels in our front could expect no relief from that quarter; and the desperate fighting of the Ninth and First regiments, who now appeared to be seized with a supernatural frenzy, was at last too much for them, and they broke and fled from the field. With shouts of rage we pursued them over the field, thinning their ranks at every step, until compelled by our officers to halt and return to the rear of the battery. The battery was now re-captured, and the enemy was driven from the field, but at a fearful cost, and we looked with dismay on our thinned ranks, and listened with horror to the pitiful pleadings of our wounded comrades who were lying around us.

As already stated, our brave Captain had fallen mortally wounded in the desperate conflict for the possession of the battery; and as he was lying on the ground requesting to be helped to the rear, we were compelled to fight over his body for some time to drive back the enemy before his request could be complied with.

More than one half of the company that went into this action a few hours before were either killed or suffering from wounds. Among the killed in our company was Sergt. John R. Courtney—and the army did not contain a braver or more loyal spirit than his. But among the noble slain in our company it would be hard to make a distinction, and the army of the illustrious dead that lined the swamps of the Chickahominy from Mechanicsville to Malvern Hill, contained no heroes that gave their lives in defense of their country, more patriotic and brave than George H. Hess, John R. Courtney, Gottlieb Gainer, Samuel Gordon, Amos Haverstick, Henry Pickle, Samuel Robinson, and Robert Scott.

Col. Roberts re-formed his line at the edge of the wood, and made preparation to meet the enemy, should they again advance; but we were not again called into action. The Irish brigade had come to relieve the regiment, and advancing until they met the enemy, after a short conflict drove them still further from the field.

It has been said that Kern's and Cooper's batteries were captured from the Reserves; but that is not true. These batteries remained in possession of the Reserves after the close of the conflict, and were left on the field when the army retreated the night after the battle. Sometime during the night, some of the officers of the batteries requested permission to make an attempt to withdraw the guns, and take them to the rear; but this request was refused by Gen. Heintzelman, on the ground that it would renew the engagement. The batteries had suffered terribly, a large number of men and almost all the horses being killed; and it may be true that it would have been imprudent, under the circumstances, to make an attempt to remove the guns; but it was certainly highly unjust to charge the men who had so nobly defended them with their capture by the enemy.

As we made the last charge on the enemy, a sharp pain in my right arm, followed by a rush of blood over the hand, announced to me the unpleasant fact that I was wounded. I loaded and fired several shots after the fleeing enemy, when the copious bleeding from my arm alarmed me, and I went to the rear. In the excitement of the moment I strayed to the left, instead of going directly to the rear; and as it was some time before I got to an hospital, and the ball had opened a vein in my arm, I felt weak and sick from the loss of blood. My arm, however, was soon dressed, and the flow of blood stopped, when I threw myself on the ground for a rest. I had hardly more than done so, when the color-bearer of our regiment, William Lafferty, who was wounded in both arms, and also slightly in the side, came to me and said, "Urban, let us get out of this. I do not believe that it will be safe for us to stay here." To my question as to what made him think so, he replied, "Well, I wouldn't be surprised if this hospital is in the hands of the enemy before to-morrow morning." I told him I did not think so; as we had now reached the James river, and did not think there would be any farther retreating; and even if the army did retreat down the river, we would no doubt be informed of it, so as to give us a chance to es-

FIELD HOSPITAL.

cape. Lafferty, did not, however, appear to think so, and he left, and it was not long before I wished I had followed his example. I did not get to see him again, and what became of him has always remained a mystery, as no one heard of him afterwards.

The cries and groans of the wounded were so terrible that I could not sleep, so I moved away a short distance from the house, where I could not hear them so plainly, but still I could get no rest.

On Friday before, at the battle of Gaines' Mill, I had given myself a severe wound in my hand with the bayonet while in the act of loading. My gun having become heated from the rapid firing, the ball I was trying to ram down stuck about half way, and it was some time before I could move it. Becoming excited in my efforts to ram it down, I finally, in ramming, bent the ramrod, and the bayonet catching my thumb, tore it open almost the full length, and to the bone. In the last fighting I lost the bandage, and in loading, powder and sweat would get into the cut, and the consequence was that it was getting exceedingly painful, and now prevented me from getting the sleep I so much needed. Late at night, however, I fell asleep, and when I awoke I found that it was daylight. I then moved back to the hospital and took a survey of the place. The house, outbuildings and yard were full of wounded, and among the sufferers were quite a number from my company and regiment. Captain Hess was lying in a room up-stairs, and I went up to see him, but I found him in so sad a condition that I could not speak to him, so I soon left the room. In and about the house I found William Wright, Jacob Finney, and several other members of our company, badly wounded.

I was looking around to find familiar faces, when hearing some one say that the enemy was coming, I walked out into the yard; and, sure enough, but a short distance from the house was a line of rebel skirmishers. Flight or resistance was out of the question, so we could only submit to the inevitable and hope for the best. The enemy immediately took possession of the hospital, and their skirmishers advanced in the direction of Malvern Hill. The house we were at stands but a few steps from the road on which most of the rebel army marched in the advance on the Union position at Malvern Hill, and it was but a few moments after the rebels had possession of this house when a rebel column came marching rapidly past. I secured a good position, and for hours watched the rebels marching along. Most of the regiments appeared to be well equipped and drilled, and under any other circumstances I might have enjoyed the sight; but under the present circumstances, I felt so vexed and chagrined that it was anything but a pleasant sight to me. To look at the long lines of armed men marching along, with secession flags flung to the breeze, and in pursuit of my comrades and the dear old flag, and to realize that I was a helpless prisoner among them, made me feel most wretched, and filled my heart with dark forebodings of the future.

The rebel regiments all carried two flags, and these emblems of treason were a great annoyance to the Union wounded lying on the ground. "Look at their dirty rags!" and similar expressions, could be heard frequently, and some of the boys cared very little who heard them. The finest body of rebel troops that marched along this road was Gen Magruder's division. Some of the rebels who came to the pump inside of the yard for water, informed us that these troops had not yet been engaged; and they did have the appearance of being fresh troops. The regiments had from seven to nine or ten hundred men. I counted seventeen regiments, and the division must have had at least 13,000 men. As the rebel army marched past, some of their men were constantly coming inside of the yard for water, and some of them sometimes stopped and exchanged a few words with us.

After Magruder's troops had passed, and troops which I think belonged to Gen Jackson's corps, were passing, an officer who was surrounded with a numerous staff came riding into the yard, and I soon came to the conclusion that he was some leading officer of the rebel army. Directly after riding into the yard, one officer came dashing up and handed him a paper, which I suppose was some kind of a dispatch, for, after reading it, he galloped rapidly down the road, followed by his escort, in the direction of the front. I was intently watching him, and wondering who he might be, when a rebel soldier who was standing close to me asked if I knew who he was. On my replying in the negative, he informed me that it was "Stonewall Jackson."

I had considered him a very ordinary-looking kind of a man, but the mention of his name caused me to look closer, and I at least imagined that his face betokened a strong, resolute and brave character, and that he had the appearance of being a great soldier; but then had it happened at the present day, and I been informed that it was Guiteau, I might have come to the conclusion that the face indicated a character of quite a different kind. After all, we greatly judge men's faces from what we have heard of them, and the appearance of a person is a poor criterion to judge character from. The general appearance of Jackson on horseback was not of the kind that would impress the beholder with the idea that he was a great military leader, but rather that of a sturdy old farmer, who was riding along with his knees drawn up and shoulders stooped, contemplating the probable value of his crops.

I had also the pleasure during the day of seeing the great Confederate leader, Gen. Lee, and I considered him one of the finest-looking military men I had ever seen. Sitting on horseback he appeared to be of medium height, strong built, with short, slightly gray, full beard, and warlike cast of feature, which made him look every inch a soldier.

The stream of rebel soldiers kept marching along the road in the direction of Malvern Hill all the morning, and as early as nine o'clock indications of a conflict began to show themselves in the direction of that place. Gen. Magruder's division after passing the hospital filed right, and formed in line of battle with his left but a short distance from the hospital, and his right extending towards the James river. They then advanced in the direction of the Union position. This body of men was to lead the assault on the Union lines, and after advancing to within the distance it was to occupy before making the charge, it came to a halt to await the formation of the rebel line of battle. A strong body of troops now advanced to within supporting distance of Magruder's line, and a strong column also marched to the left of his position in the direction of the Union right. A large number of batteries of artillery also passed during the forenoon, and were placed in position along the rebel line. It soon became evident to us that our men had made a stand for the purpose of contesting the farther advance of the enemy, and that in all probability a great battle would be fought in our sight; and we became very anxious as to what would be the result. Up to about noon the moving of the rebel columns and the occasional firing indicated that the enemy was feeling the Union position, and we waited with the most painful suspense for the opening of the conflict.

Directly after noon the enemy opened on the Union lines with a terrific discharge of artillery. This was soon responded to by the Union guns on Malvern Hill, and for several hours the earth shook from the effects of the terrible cannonading. We could plainly see that the advantage in this contest was with our men, and that the rebels were getting the worst of it; their artillery apparently making no impression on the Union lines, and some of their batteries being driven from position. It was well on to three o'clock when the loud cheering of the enemy indicated that they were advancing to the assault, and soon the crash of musketry announced the fact that the opposing forces had come into close contact.

A severe contest ensued, and the rebels were driven back with fearful loss. They, however, soon re-formed, and again advanced to the attack, and the battle again raged with the most intense fury, and lasted for about one hour, when the rebels were again compelled to fall back.

After this repulse there was a short lull in the fighting, but we soon discovered that the enemy had not yet given up the hope of carrying the Union position, and that they were making the most earnest preparations to renew the conflict. Between five and six o'clock the rebel army suddenly opened a terrific fire on the Union lines, and then with loud cheers their infantry advanced to the assault, and soon the battle opened with greater fury than ever. We could see brigade after brigade, and division after division charging through the woods and over the open ground in front of the Union lines, only to be driven back with the same dreadful loss.

The guns of the Union fleet on the James river had also opened fire on the enemy's lines, and with the artillery along the Union position, kept up a constant shower of shell, which played havoc with the enemy. The scene was now one of the most terrible grandeur. The flash of the large guns from the ships, the shrieks of the two and three hundred pound shells, as they rushed through the air, and burst in the rebel lines with a report as if the globe had exploded, carrying death and dismay into the enemy's ranks unparalled in the history of the war, the continuous flash and roar of the long train of artillery on Malvern Hill, the vivid flashes and incessant rattle of musketry, the shouts of the enraged combatants, all gave proof of a terrible battle.

The enemy fought with the recklessness of despair, but they could not accomplish impossibilities, and one assault after the other met the same result. No troops on the face of the earth could have carried the Union position, and it seemed like sheer madness for the rebel leaders to thus sacrifice their men. The battle raged till almost sundown, when the rebel columns, no doubt now fully aware of the utter hopelessness of the contest, broke and fled in the wildest confusion from the field. Never had men more resolutely advanced to an assault, and never were they more justifiable in falling back, than the column of rebel troops that charged on Malvern Hill.

I was in the yard watching the progress of the battle, earnestly hoping and praying that our troops would be successful, but fearing every moment that some part of our line would give way, and disaster follow our army, but while thus engaged, I was surprised and delighted to see a stream of flying men issuing from the wood in the rear of Magruder's position. It soon became evident that his entire division was completely broken, and was leaving the field in the utmost confusion. In a few moments after, the field in the rear of the woods was crowded with a mass of fleeing fugitives, and the shells from the Union guns cutting them down at every step. The panic soon spread along the entire rebel line, and it fell back in terrible disorder.

The greatest excitement existed among us at the hospital, and some of the men could hardly be kept from cheering when witnessing the flight of the enemy. Some of the shells from the Union gunboats commenced to fall in rather close proximity to the hospital, but we were too much elated at the defeat of the enemy to care much for that. In the excitement of the hour we commenced to entertain a strong hope that we would be re-captured by our men. Had the Union troops advanced after the defeat of the enemy, we certainly would have been, as the rebels had enough to look after themselves without molesting us. The defeat of the rebels was most thorough and complete; they had not only failed in accomplishing the purpose they had in view when they made the assault, but had been driven from the field with the most frightful slaughter, and it was with the utmost difficulty that they could get any of their men to rally as far back as the hospital. I saw Gen Magruder riding back and forth, swearing and raving like a madman, trying to re-form his lines, but all in vain. I do not believe that he succeeded in re-forming a regiment of his division that night. Close in the rear of the house I saw the colors of an Alabama regiment with less than a dozen men around them, and an officer making the most frantic appeals to the balance of the regiment to halt and form in line; but the most of them made in hot haste for the fortifications of Richmond, and I am confident that not twenty men of the regiment re-formed with the colors that night.

The Union guns kept up a slow, continuous fire on the enemy in the early part of the evening, but by ten o'clock the last shot was fired, and the great Seven Days' struggle had come to a close. During the night large numbers of rebel wounded were brought in and laid on the ground around us, and a constant stream of them were being loaded in ambulances and wagons and sent in the direction of Richmond. The cries and groans of the poor wretches rang in our ears all night, and I commenced to think that in the confusion and hurry of getting the wounded out of the way the enemy might not keep a strict watch over us, and consequently there might be some chance to escape to our lines, so I determined to make the effort. I left the yard, and cautiously passing through the long rows of wounded, took a survey of the situation. I found, however, that a line of rebel guards extended around the hospital, and that escape was impossible. In the morning a line of rebel skirmishers advanced a short distance in the direction of Malvern Hill, and we found with sorrow that the Union forces had fallen back, and we were sure of having a taste of prison life in the South.

A number of Union surgeons were captured with us, and they with the rebel surgeons were kept busy amputating limbs, and in other ways attending to the wounded. I here witnessed the most extraordinary display of nerve and courage I have ever witnessed in my life. A captain in a Union regiment had his leg so badly shattered that he was informed that amputation was necessary. He was propped up, and without giving him anæsthetics of any kind, the doctors took off his leg, the unfortunate man watching the operation with as little display of fear or nervousness as if the doctors were performing the simplest service for him.

On the morning after the close of the fighting, the most terrible reports commenced to come in about the condition of a large number of Union wounded who were yet lying on the field, who had fallen in the battle on Monday, at Charles City cross roads. It had rained very heavily since the battle, and it was said that the low grounds being overflown with water, some of the men had drowned, and others were in the most wretched condition, and would have to perish if speedy relief was not sent to them. The Union surgeons secured the consent of the rebel authorities at the hospital to fit out an expedition and try to save them, and a number of wagons were furnished for that purpose. A number of prisoners, some of them wounded, but in such a manner as not to interfere with their duties, were selected to go with the train and load the wounded. I was selected to take charge of the squad, and furnished with paper and pencil, and instructions to return a written report of the condition of the field. We were accompanied by a few guards, and to farther protect us from the rebel soldiers who might be rambling over the field, we had white strips of muslin tied around our caps. Thus fitted out, we proceeded on our mission of mercy, and it was not long before we reached the battle field.

The dead had not been buried, and the sight that met our eyes was horrible to behold. They lay thick on the ground, and in some places were heaped on top of each other, and presented a sight so sickening that we could hardly proceed. All had the appearance of being plundered by rebel stragglers, their pockets being turned inside out. Lying among the dead were a number of wounded, and the hope of helping them gave us nerve and strength to do what, under other circumstances, would have been an impossibility. I had been instructed to remove only such as would probably have a chance of recovery, and not disturb those who were past hope; but I soon found it hard to discriminate between them. They begged with tears in their eyes to be taken, and I soon loaded as many as we could take. We lifted quite a number out of the water and mud, and made them as comfortable as we could, and then started with our load for the hospital. On the way, several died, and I was told by one of the

DEATH IN THE TRENCHES.

doctors that I should not have loaded men who were so hopelessly wounded. We had expected to be sent out again; but, in the meantime, it had been decided to bring no more wounded to our hospital, and we did not get to go.

As we were shortly afterward sent to Richmond, I never found out what means, if any, were taken to help the poor fellows; but I have no doubt that hundreds of them perished that might have been saved, had the proper means been taken. On the morning of the Fourth of July, all of the wounded not nursing at the hospital, and who could walk, were ordered to fall into line, and, after bidding our comrades a sad farewell, we left for Richmond. We had proceeded but a short distance, when I made a narrow escape from being shot by one of the guards. I was walking along carelessly, thinking of our miserable condition, when I unthinkingly stepped a few steps to the side of the column. A guard, who at least pretended to think that I was going to make an attempt to escape, raised his rifle to his shoulder and aimed it for my head, and I suppose would have shot me down like a dog, had not one of my comrades caught me by the arm and jerked me back into the ranks. The brute of a guard cursed me, and said that if I attempted that again he would blow the head off my shoulders. The idea of making an attempt to escape had never entered my mind.

It had been confidently asserted by the Northern press that Richmond would be in possession of our troops by the Fourth of July, and the rebels appeared to be fully aware of this, and we had to hear it oftener than was pleasant. "Well, you Yanks did get to Richmond by the Fourth, did you?" greeted our ears along the way, and by the time we had reached the city, it appeared as if the entire population had prepared themselves to join the grand chorus. Our appearance seemed to give them intense delight; but some of our boys would keep telling them that they would some day see the "Yanks" enter the city, when the laugh would be on the other side of the mouth. As we marched through the city, we felt somewhat anxious as to what kind of a place we were to be shut up in; but we were not kept long in suspense, for we soon marched up to a long, dingy-looking brick building, something over a hundred feet long, and nearly as wide. The sign at the one end, "Libby & Son," convinced us that we had arrived at the infamous prison of that name. It certainly presented a dreary and uninviting appearance, and we sincerely hoped that our stay in it would not be long. After being searched for arms and valuables, we marched into the building, and our first experience of life in Southern prisons had commenced.

After finding myself locked from the outer world, I looked around to examine what kind of a place we had been shut in. I found it to be a room about forty feet wide, and nearly one hundred feet long. At one end of this room was a wooden water trough, and a spigot to draw water from, which gave us at least the privilege of washing. The room was without furniture of any kind, and the floor was filthy in the extreme. The few low windows at the front but poorly lit up the room, giving it a dreary and desolate appearance. I was informed that five more rooms of the same size, and several basement rooms, composed what was known as Libby Prison—a name that will be synonomous with all that is horrible and cruel; and as the Tower of London and the Black Hole of Calcutta appear in English history, and the military prison of Paris in French history, so will Libby prison appear in American history, and it will ever remain a blot on the boasted civilization of the age, and a stigma on the American people.

In this dreary and desolate room, crowded to overflowing with prisoners, almost all sick or wounded, I stayed twenty-three days; but as I was subsequently a much longer time a captive in the hands of the enemy, and at a time when prison-life was even less endurable, I will not give a detailed description of my imprisonment at this time. I deem it but just to say, however, that the treatment we received at this time, although bad, was yet much better than the prisoners received during the last two years of the war. The food was of a better quality and also more of it, and more attention was paid to the sick and wounded at this time than later. Several United States surgeons, who had also been captured, were allowed to come and see us daily, which was considerable of a comfort and benefit.

A few days before my parole we had been informed that we would be sent to Belle Island, in the James river, and as it was represented as being quite a pleasant place as compared to Libby, we all felt anxious to go and stay there as long as we should be compelled to be prisoners of war. About this time, however, the wound in my arm was getting somewhat troublesome. The arm from the wound to the hand had become full of dark spots, and threatened to get very sore. My lacerated thumb was also in a highly inflamed and painful condition, and I was terribly alarmed one morning to find that my jaws were aching fearfully and appeard to be getting stiff, and that I could not without the greatest difficulty swallow food. One of the men in the room had died a few days before of lock-jaw, and the fear of taking that terrible disease filled my heart with gloom, and I could hardly wait until the arrival of the doctors. As soon as I could get to them, I informed them of it. They examined my arm and thumb carefully, and then put me under treatment, as I supposed for lock-jaw.

It was on this day that the removal of prisoners

to Belle Island commenced, and, as stated before, we all felt anxious to go; but it appears that a number of the worst wounded were to be paroled and sent to our lines, and that I was one of the number selected for that purpose. But as I did not know this, I felt very indignant when the most of my comrades marched out and I was compelled to stay. To add to my misery, I found that I could not swallow any of the food which I received during the day, and I was settling down in utter despair, when it was announced to us that we were to get ready to be sent to the Union lines. My sorrow was immediately turned to joy, and although I felt fearful about the disease that appeared to be fastening itself on me, I felt rejoiced that I could at least have the satisfaction of dying away from the terrible scenes surrounding me, and under the folds of the dear old flag.

We were immediately sent down the James river to Mill Creek Union Hospital, near Fortress Monroe, and there surrounded with all the care and kindness we could wish for. In about one month I regained good health, and was sent to Camp Parole, at Annapolis, Maryland. After being at that place for about six weeks, I was exchanged and sent to my regiment.

CHAPTER VII.

BATTLE OF THE WILDERNESS—OUR CAPTURE AND RE-CAPTURE.

ON the first of March, 1864, Congress passed an act authorizing the President to appoint an officer of the grade of Lieutenant-General, who was to assume command of all the land forces of the Government. On the tenth of the same month, President Lincoln appointed General U. S. Grant to that important position. Grant was in Nashville, Tenn., at the time he was notified of his appointment, and immediately hastened to Washington to take command. In a general order, he announced his intention of making his headquarters with the Army of the Potomac, and accompanying it in person in the campaign against Richmond. The army was in winter quarters at Culpepper, Va., and was under the gallant Major General Geo. C. Meade, whose fitness to command that splendid organization had been fully tested at Gettysburg.

Meade had, during the winter, thoroughly reorganized his command, and when it entered on the spring campaign, it was probably (with the exception of McClellan's army when it marched for the Peninsula) the best equipped and drilled army ever marshaled in this country. The First and Third corps had been broken up, and distributed into the Second, Fifth and Sixth. The Second was commanded by Major General W. S. Hancock, the Fifth by Major General G. K. Warren, and the Sixth by Major General John Sedgwick. These officers had greatly distinguished themselves, and were recognized as three of the best corps commanders in the Union army. The cavalry was in command of Major General Sheridan, who was ordered from the West for that special purpose. Major General Burnside was in command of a force of about forty thousand men encamped at Annapolis, Maryland. This force was intended as a reserve corps for the Army of the Potomac, but was kept at Annapolis until the army was ready to move, evidently for the purpose of putting the rebel authorities under the impression that it was intended to strike some point along the Southern coast. Major General B. F. Butler was also in command of an army of about forty thousand men, with headquarters at Fortress Monroe. This body of men was called the Army of the James, and was intended to co-operate with the Army of the Potomac, by attacking Richmond via Bermuda Hundred and Petersburg. The combined force, whose objective point was the capture of Richmond, numbered, about 200,000 men. Major General Siegel was also in command of a considerable force in the

Shenandoah Valley. He was directed to move on Lynchburg at the same time Meade and Butler moved on Richmond. Grant made his headquarters with the army of the Potomac, and personally directed its movements. There can be no doubt but that this had much to do in detracting from the honor that really belonged to Meade. The army was constantly spoken of as Grant's army, and the fact that he was with the army would do much to produce the belief that he, more than Meade, deserved credit for compelling the surrender of the greatest chieftain in the Confederate army. Gen. Meade had saved the country in one of its greatest crises, and, judging from the military genius he displayed wherever in command, the impartial reader can come to no other conclusion but that, had he been in chief command, Lee's overthrow would have been just as certain, and as soon accomplished. General Grant, in a dispatch to the Government, said of Meade: "Commanding all the armies, as I did, I tried as far as possible to leave Gen. Meade in independent command of the Army of the Potomac. My instructions were all through him, and were general in their nature, leaving all the details and execution to him. The campaign that followed proved him to be the right man in the right place. His commanding always in the presence of an officer superior to him in rank has drawn from him much of the public attention which his zeal and ability entitled him to, and which he would have otherwise received."

The campaigns of General Siegel, and of his successor, Gen. Hunt, in the Shenandoah Valley where a series of blunders that resulted in the Union forces being driven from the valley with heavy loss. This campaign, in place of terminating in the capture of Lynchburg, and assisting Meade's forces in the capture of Richmond, endangered the Capital at Washington to such an extent as to necessitate the sending of a portion of the Army of the Potomac, under the gallant Sheridan, to the valley. Gen. Butler's campaign south of the James river was equally unfortunate, and only resulted in repeated disasters to his army. As these generals received all the odium connected with their respective campaigns, and their forces were under the command of the Lieutenant-General, as well as Meade's army, it would be but fair to suppose that Meede was equally entitled to the credit of conducting the campaign that ended in the surrender of the rebel army at Appomattox Court House. At the time Grant established his headquarters with the Army of the Potomac, our division (the Pennsylvania Reserves) was encamped along the line of the Orange and Alexandria railroad, our regiment (the First) being in camp at Bristow Station.

On the 29th of April we broke camp and marched to Warrenton, a distance of thirty miles, where we camped for the night. Early in the morning we continued our march, moving in the direction of Culpepper. We crossed the Rappahannock river at Rappahannock Station, and by evening had reached the army. We had been for some time separated from the main army, and were glad to get back to it again. We all knew that we were on the eve of an important campaign, and one that would in all probability close the war. The greatest enthusiasm existed throughout the entire camp, and all had the utmost confidence in the two great soldiers who were to lead us. On the 3d of May the camp was in a furor of excitement, and all anxiously waited for the orders to move. The army had been reinforced, and everything now appeared to be in readiness to commence the campaign that was to break the backbone of the rebellion.

General Meade during the day issued the following order, which was read to every regiment in the evening on dress parade:

HEADQUARTERS ARMY OF THE POTOMAC,
May 3, 1864.

SOLDIERS: Again you are called upon to advance on the enemies of your country. The time and the occasion are deemed opportune by your commanding General to address you a few words of confidence and caution. You have been reorganized, strengthened, and fully equipped in every respect. You form a part of the several armies of your country, the whole under an able and distinguished General, who enjoys the confidence of the government, the people, and the army. Your movement being in co-operation with others, it is of the utmost importance that no effort should be spared to make it successful. Soldiers, the eyes of the whole country are looking with anxious hope to the blow you are about to strike in the most sacred cause that ever called men to arms. Remember your homes, your wives, and your children, and bear in mind that the sooner your enemies are overcome, the sooner you will be returned to enjoy the blessings and benefits of peace. Bear with patience the hardships you will be called upon to endure. Have confidence in your officers and each other. Keep your ranks on the march and on the battle field, and let each man earnestly implore God's blessing, and endeavor by his thoughts and actions to render himself worthy of the favor he seeks. With clear conscience and strong arms, actuated by a high sense of duty, fighting to preserve the government and the institutions handed down to us by our forefathers, if true to ourselves, victory, under God's blessing, must and will attend our efforts.

GEORGE G. MEADE,
Major General Commanding.

Directly after midnight, May 4th, the reveille in the Union army was beaten. Soon after, the troops were marching from their camps, and the great movement against the rebel capital had begun. Our corps (the Fifth) marched out on the Fredericksburg plank-road, and some time in the forenoon crossed the Rapidan river at Germania Ford. We marched until about four o'clock in the afternoon, when we camped for the night, having gone a distance of thirty miles. Our camp for the night was in the vicinity of what is known as the Wilderness tavern. The Sixth corps had followed on the same road, and had also crossed the river, its left connecting with our right. General Hancock's corps crossed at Ely's ford, and marched to Chancellorsville. General Burnside, with the Ninth corps, had left Annapolis, Maryland, about a week before, and by forced marches, succeeded in getting into camp at Culpepper at about the time the movement begun. He was instructed to stay in camp twenty-four hours, and then follow the army. It does not appear to have been Grant's plan to fight the battle of the Wilderness, but to compel Lee to abandon his strong position by a movement on his right flank, thinking, no doubt, that if Lee would find his communications with Richmond in danger of being severed, he would withdraw from the Wilderness, and be compelled to fight on ground where the chances of success would be more favorable to the Union army. The tract of land known as the Wilderness is covered with "scrub oak, low pines, cedar, and brush." It is crossed in all directions by a number of narrow roads, and numerous foot or cattle paths. So dense was the undergrowth where the ground was wet and low, that it was almost impossible for troops to get through; and the entire nature of the ground was of such a description that it was almost impossible to bring cavalry or artillery into action. Lee, who was familiar with the country, and had beaten Hooker on nearly the same ground, had selected this wild and isolated place for a defensive position. He had added to its natural strength by a complete system of fortifications, which extended for twenty miles to the right and left of Orange Court House. Had Grant attacked him on his left or front, Lee's position would have given him all the advantage; but the weak point in his line was his right flank, and Grant and Meade seemed soon to have discovered it. Lee, who was undoubtedly deceived by Grant's movements, was unprepared to resist the passage of the Rapidan, and the movements of the Federal troops on the first day endangered his position to such an extent that immediate steps became necessary to prevent Grant from completely turning his right wing and cutting off his communications. But Lee was not the commander to be very long deceived by the movements of an opponent. He immediately commenced a movement on Grant's right flank, assuming an "offensive defensive" attitude that would compel Grant to give him battle on ground of his own choosing. In this movement Lee was entirely successful, and it soon became evident that Grant would have to fight him where the chances would be greatly against our side.

Lee's army had been strongly reinforced by Longstreet's corps, which had just arrived from the west, and as near as can be ascertained the two opposing armies were about equal in numbers when the fighting commenced. Lee had greatly the advantage in fighting in a country where he was familiar with every foot of the ground, and could resist almost every movement of his opponent with fortified positions. Grant, on the other hand, had the advantage during the campaign that followed in being strongly reinforced. It does not appear that Lee received any considerable number after the fighting commenced. Grant was strongly reinforced after the first battle. On the night of the 4th of May, when the Union army was resting in its camps waiting for the dawn to continue the movement on Lee's flank, that crafty commander was moving his army in two parallel lines on Grant's right flank. He had moved Gen. Ewell's corps on the turnpike and Gen. Hill's on the plank road, and before morning had them in position in front of the right wing of our army.

There was a strange analogy between the two opposing armies on the morning before the great battle; each commander had moved on the right flank of his opponent, and yet from somewhat different motives. Long before daylight, May 5th, the Union army was in line, waiting for the orders to advance. At about sunrise the march was continued, but we had not proceeded more than about one-half mile when information was received that the enemy was in our front. It was evidently somewhat of a surprise to our officers, as the appearance of the enemy was unexpected. Preparations were immediately made to give them battle. Our corps (the Fifth) was concentrated on the pike and ordered to attack the enemy in our front whenever an opportunity presented itself. The Sixth corps was ordered to move to the right of the Fifth and attack the rebels, who were moving in heavy columns in that direction, and endangering our line of communications. General Hancock was ordered to "deflect his line of march, and take position with his corps on the left of the Fifth." The position of our division (the Pennsylvania Reserve Corps) in the early part of the day was on Major Lacy's farm. At about ten o'clock we were ordered to move in the direction of Parker's store and form a line of battle. We moved along cautiously, meeting a few rebel skirmishers, who fled at our approach. We then formed in line of battle near the plank-road, our regiment (the First) and the Bucktails being on the extreme left. Directly after forming line, Capton Wasson, commanding our company, was ordered to take his command and move through the woods beyond for the purpose of reconnoitering the enemy's lines. This wood was a perfect wilderness, being composed of "low-limbed and scraggy pines, stiff-bristling chincapins," and brush of every description. Through it, however, were several foot or cattle paths, on one of which we took our line of march.

After proceeding about one-half mile, we came to an opening, or small tract of cleared land. Along the edge of the woods on the other side, we could see a line of troops, but could not at first determine to what army they belonged. When we started, we were cautioned to be careful about firing on any one, as Gen. Getty's division (which had been detached from the Sixth corps) was moving for position on our left. After discovering the presence of troops in our front, we came to a halt and tried to make out where they belonged. They had by this time became aware of our presence, and evidently were about as much perplexed about us as we were about them. We were, however, not to be left long in doubt as to what side they belonged; for one of them advanced a few steps from his line, and unfurled a large rebel flag. We could hardly be kept from firing on them; but as our captain had received instructions not to bring on an engagement, he would not let us fire. As we fell back, the rebels fired one shot at us, which passed harmlessly over our heads. We slowly fell back to the line. About an hour after, Lieut. Wilder and ten men from Company B were ordered to make a reconnoissance in the same direction. As our company had been over the ground, Col. Talley thought it would be best to send two men from it with the detail. The Colonel then asked for two volunteers from the company, and William Bruce and myself offered our services and accompanied the squad. We had proceeded but a short distance when we encountered the enemy, who had advanced and occupied the wood our company had just marched through. We were driven back to our regiment, making a narrow escape from death or captivity. Companies C and K were then sent out to dislodge them; but, finding the enemy in strong force, fell back in haste to our lines. The severe fighting did not commence, however, until about twelve o'clock, when the divisions of Griffin and Wadsworth, of our corps, which had position on the right of our division, met the enemy, and soon became hotly engaged. The rebels, who were commanded by Gen. Ewell, were driven back, and a decided advantage would have been gained, had the difficult nature of the ground not prevented the Sixth corps from getting into position in time to assist Griffin and Wadsworth. The advantage thus gained was unfortunate in the end, as it exposed the extreme right flank of our corps. The enemy soon took advantage of it, and attacking Griffin with great fury, succeeded in turning his right flank, and compelling him to fall back. The division of Wadsworth, after the most desperate fighting, was also compelled to give way, and the enemy succeeded in getting between his troops and our division. The right wing of our division was now in great peril, but bravely held its ground.

During this time the fighting on our left was also very severe. A. P. Hill's rebel corps had attacked and driven in the cavalry, when they encountered Getty's division of the Sixth corps. Getty, although outnumbered three to one, bravely held his ground until the arrival of General Hancock with the Second corps. Had Getty's command given way, our division would have been surrounded and cut off from the army. As stated before, Hancock had marched his command to Chancellorsville, where he was in camp on the morning the battle opened. When he received the order to deflect his march, he obeyed with his usual alacrity, and his arrival on the field was most fortunate. Hill's entire corps was contending with Getty's division, which could not much longer have held out against the tremendous odds it was fighting. Hancock promptly brought his corps into action, and for three hours the battle on this part of the field raged with the most intense fury. Directly after a gap was created between Wadsworth's command and our division on our right, and Getty's lines were threatened with destruction on our left, an aid rode up to Gen. Crawford, and informed him that his command was in danger of being surrounded, and if he did not withdraw immediately, his retreat would be cut off. Almost the entire Third brigade of our division was on the skirmish line. The Second brigade, under the command of Col.

McCandless, had been sent to support Wadsworth's hard-pressed troops. Our brigade was in line in the rear of the Third brigade. Gen. Crawford took immediate measures to withdraw his command from its dangerous position. To Col. Fisher, a most meritorious officer, was assigned the duty of withdrawing the skirmish line in our front. A messenger was sent to Col. McCandless, ordering him to return to the division. Col. Fisher, with great skill, succeeded in withdrawing the skirmish line, and the First and Second brigades were ordered to a position about one mile in the rear. The Second brigade was, however, not so fortunate. The messenger sent to inform McCandless of his danger, did not find him; the consequence was, his command was surrounded by the enemy, who had advanced rapidly over the ground vacated by the other two brigades. Col. McCandless was, however, too good a soldier to surrender his command without making a desperate effort to save it. Finding himself unsupported, and being surrounded, he ordered his command to "about-face," and endeavor to withdraw from a position he knew had become untenable. The movement was made none too soon, as a rebel column had formed in line in his rear to cut off his escape. He immediately ordered the Eleventh regiment to charge on this line and open the road. This command was obeyed in the most gallant style, the men

13.

charging with an impetuosity that scattered the rebels in every direction. The most of the Second, Sixth, and Eleventh regiments succeeded in escaping through the opening made by the charge, but lost severely in killed and wounded. The Seventh regiment, commanded by Col. Bollinger, had been advanced too far in the woods to be successfully withdrawn, and the Colonel, with almost his entire regiment, were captured and taken to Richmond as prisoners of war. During the fighting, the woods caught fire, and it is said "a number of the unfortunate wounded burned to death." Our division was re-formed on Lacy's farm, which position we held during the night. The Sixth corps, on the right, in moving for position, had encountered the enemy several times during the day, and had some severe fighting—but very little was accomplished in that direction. Owing to the difficult nature of the ground, Sedgwick did not get his entire corps into position during the day. A demonstration by Hancock's corps, supported by a portion of the Fifth, put an end to the fighting for the first day; but little was accomplished, however, by this, more than to get the lines into good position, to renew the conflict in the morning. Night had put an end to the fighting, and both armies rested on their arms, waiting anxiously for the dawning of another day. The desperate nature of the fighting, and indecisive results arising from it, were enough to convince us that terrible would be the carnage before the great battle was decided. Two armies, whose combined strength numbered fully one-fourth of a million men, commanded by the best military men of the age, had locked in a deadly embrace, and both would have to suffer severely before the contest was over. Only those who have been in like situations can fully appreciate the feelings of a soldier on the night after an indecisive battle. Many of his comrades have fallen, and he knows that before the setting of another sun, many more will be added to the "bivouac of the dead." He cannot avoid thinking that the chances are many that he, too, may be among the number; and how lovingly he thinks of the dear ones at home, and hopes and prays that he may meet them again. I have frequently heard men say that the soldiers who fought for the Union were prompted by selfish ends, and that men never go to war from patriotic motives. "They enlisted for the money," is a common expression made use of by that kind of people. No baser or more cowardly slander could be invented against the dead, who died to protect the lives and property of their slanderers. Had the men who whipped the rebel army at Gettysburg been moved by no other motive than the few paltry dollars they received for their services, the boast of the rebel General Toombs, that he would call the roll of his slaves on Bunker Hill, would have become a fact.

> "An honest soldier ne'er despise,
>   Or count him as a stranger;
> Remember, he's his country's stay
>   In hour and time of danger."

The first day's battle closed without any material advantage to either side; if any existed at all it was probably on the side of the rebels. The loss in killed and wounded was about equal; but the greater part of Warren's corps had been thrown into some confusion, and lost a considerable number of prisoners. No blame can, however, be attached to Gen. Warren and his corps. His attack at noon would undoubtedly have been a complete success, had not the want of roads and denseness of the thicket prevented Sedgwick from bringing his corps into action at the time. On the other hand, it may be said that Grant and Meade had received valuable information in regard to Lee's strength; and, although they had not driven the rebel army from its position, they had held their own against the fearful assaults made on them; and a reasonable hope might be entertained that a decided success could be achieved on the morrow. General Burnside, with the Ninth corps arrived on the field late in the evening, and was moved to the right and rear of Hancock's corps, where it became evident the brunt of the battle would fall in the morning. Subsequent events proved that the disposition of Burnside's corps was most fortunate. General

Longstreet's corps of the rebel army arrived on the field during the night, and re-inforced General Hill, whose corps held position in front of Hancock's lines.

At daylight, May 5th, Hancock opened the battle by a vigorous charge on the enemy in his front. The attack was at first successful, and Hill's rebel corps was compelled to give way, losing a large number of prisoners, and five stands of colors. Hill's hard-pressed troops were at this time re-inforced by Longstreet's corps, who, as yet, had not been in action. Longstreet and Hill succeeded in rallying Hill's broken divisions, and uniting them with Longstreet's corps. The combined rebel host pressed forward on Hancock's lines. Then issued one of the most terrible battles known in the annals of the war. Hancock was at last compelled to give way and fall back to the Brock road, where, being re-inforced by the Ninth and part of the Fifth corps, he succeeded in holding his position. It was in this action that the lamented General Wadsworth was killed and Getty severely wounded. On the right, Gen. Sedgwick's corps also became furiously engaged with Ewell's rebel corps, early in the morning. Ewell commenced the battle by a charge on the Union line, and was driven back with terrible slaughter. At about ten o'clock Ewell renewed the battle, but was again defeated. At about noon the fighting stopped entirely, and for four hours peace and quiet reigned along the entire front. During the heavy fighting on the right and left, our corps held the centre of the line, and with the exception of Wadsworth's division, was not severely engaged.

During the lull in the fighting, both armies made preparations for another test of strength. The rebels had again massed in front of Hancock's lines, and that part of the field was again to bear the brunt of the battle. Hancock's line advanced from the Brock road, and Stevenson's division, of Burnside's corps, was placed in position between the Second and Fifth corps. The balance of the Ninth corps was in position in the rear of the Second. At about four o'clock the cheering and rapid volleys of musketry announced the advance of the enemy. The two large corps of Longstreet and Hill, directed by Longstreet, who was known as the most rapid and desperate fighter in the rebel army, fell like a thunderbolt on the right of Hancock's corps and Stevenson's division of the Ninth. Birney's division of Hancock's corps was in position on the right, and it, with Stevenson's, received the brunt of the attack. After the most desperate fighting, these two divisions were compelled to fall back. The rebel troops rapidly advanced through the gap thus created, and penetrated to within a short distance of Meade's headquarters.

Their success was, however, short-lived. Gen.

Hancock ordered Gibbon's division of his corps to charge on the advancing rebel hosts, and after a terrible hand-to-hand conflict, first stayed the further advance of the enemy, and then drove them from the field, re-capturing Birney's entrenched position. The balance of the Second, Ninth, and Fifth corps were rapidly brought into action, and the battle raged with great fury until night. The rebels were defeated, and Lee's most desperate effort to cut through our lines was frustrated It is said when Lee saw his troops beaten back by our men, he rushed forward to lead a rebel brigade, but was prevented by his officers and men, who begged him not to expose himself in that way. During the heavy fighting on the left, our division became engaged with the enemy in our front, and defeated them. In the evening we marched to the assistance of Hancock's corps, but did not proceed far when we received word that the rebels were defeated; we then returned to our former position. During the day our brigade lost one of its best officers, Lieut. Col. Dare, of the Fifth regiment, who was killed at the head of his command.

To all appearance the fighting was over; not a shot was heard along the entire line, and we were thinking of getting a good night's rest. But in this we were greatly disappointed. Gen. Lee, after his terrible defeat in front of Hancock's lines, immediately made preparations to attack our right wing. Under cover of the night he rapidly moved a heavy column of troops, and hurled them on our extreme right. We had just finished our suppers and were congratulating ourselves that the day's work was over, when rapid firing on our right dispelled the delusion. The rebel attack was a complete surprise, and for sometime threatened a serious disaster to our army.

The rebels had succeeded in turning the right wing of the army, capturing two brigades of Sedgwick's corps, and getting possession of our line of communication by way of the Rapidan. Our division was ordered to fall in line and march to Sedgwick's support. Communications between the army and that corps had also been severed, and to our division was assigned the duty of opening them. "Guided by the roar of battle," we started on the march. As we did not know at what moment we might meet the enemy, we moved along with the utmost caution; after proceeding a short distance along the pike, we turned to the left, and followed a by-road down a hollow. As we marched through, we could distinctly hear the movements of a rebel battery on a hill to our left. With cautious steps and beating hearts, we worked our way slowly along, no one speaking above a whisper, and using the utmost care to prevent our tin-cups and equipments from clanging together or making any noise that would betray us to the enemy. After getting through the hollow, we continued our march through a wood until we reached Sedgwick's lines. The fighting was by this time over, and as Sedgwick had stopped the further advance of the rebels, our services were not needed, and we returned to our former position on Lacy's farm. The fighting on the right ended what is known in history as the battle of the Wilderness. In the morning, Sedgwick's batteries on the right opened fire, and as the rebels did not reply, skirmishers were advanced along the entire line, which demonstrated the fact that Lee had withdrawn his army, and was marching in the direction of North Anna river. The battle of the Wilderness was a drawn battle, and neither army could claim much advantage over the other. The loss was probably about equal in killed and wounded, but the rebels held the largest number of prisoners. Their getting possession of our line of communications, by way of the Rapidan, was a barren victory to them, as the day after the battle closed, the city of Fredericksburg was occupied by the Union forces, and communications opened with the army in that direction. Both armies lost severely in officers. On the Union side, Generals Wadsworth and Hayes were killed, and Generals Hancock, Getty, Gregg, Owen, Bartlett, and Carroll were wounded —Hancock but slightly, as he did not retire from the field.

The rebels lost in killed, Generals Jones, Jenkins and Stafford, and Generals Longstreet, Pegram, Rickett and Hunter were wounded. The wounding of Longstreet was a severe loss to the Rebel army, as it disabled him from further service during the war. He was, without doubt, one of the best commanders in the Southern army. With no disparagement to the other able corps commanders, it may be said, that to the great skill and bravery of General Hancock, more was due for the success that was achieved in this battle than to any other corps commander on the field.

As soon as it was fully ascertained that Lee was withdrawing entirely from the field, preparations were made to pursue him. The cavalry marched out on the Brock road, and our corps was ordered to move past the Second and join in the pursuit. As we marched well to the front, in passing Hancock's lines, we had a good opportunity of witnessing the terrible effects of the fighting on that part of the field. It was here that the colored troops received their first baptism of fire, and the large number of dead demonstrated how nobly they had sustained the ordeal. After we passed the Second corps, it fell in line and followed in our rear. The Sixth and Ninth corps marched on the Orange plank-road, "all converging to Spottsylvania Court House."

During the night we marched slowly and made frequent short stops; the cavalry being compelled to feel their way cautiously, as Lee was moving his army on a road parallel with the one we were on, and but a short distance from our column; and as he was familiar with the ground, he might at any time stop and give us a blow. After daylight we commenced to move along rapidly, and it soon became evident that we were racing with the rebel army for some object in our front. As we had a good rest the day before, and marched slowly during the night, we were in good marching condition, and all the men kept up to the work, and by nine o'clock the march became a double-quick, which was continued for nine or ten miles. The most of the men gave out, and, when we formed line of battle on the Po, the regiments were small indeed. Captain Wasson, commanding our company, had less than a dozen in line. Most of the men, however, succeeded in getting up during the afternoon and joining their companies. It appeared to have been a race between Grant and Lee for position at Spottsylvania Court House, and Lee was successful, as he had the start and the shortest route. We may console ourselves with the fact that it was not a fair race, anyhow. The cavalry struck the rebel column at Elsop's farm, and skirmished with the enemy until the arrival of Griffin's and Robinson's division of our corps, which soon became severely engaged. The rebels were com- to fall back, but, being re-inforced, they made a desperate charge on Robinson's troops, and succeeded in forcing his division from the field. Our division was at this time arriving on the field, and we were immediately ordered to form line, and charge on the advancing rebels. The troops on our left were fleeing from the field, and a rebel battery was pouring at short range volley after volley, in rapid succession, into their demoralized ranks. This battery our brigade was ordered to charge. As we were almost worn out by the marching, it was with some difficulty that the men could be brought into line. It was a critical moment. The rebels had attacked Griffin's division in overwhelming numbers, and it, with Robinson's division, was forced from the field with fearful loss. After we formed line to charge on the battery, it opened its fire on us, and for a short time the brigade hesitated about advancing. Fortunately, a band belonging to one of the cavalry regiments came to our rear, and commenced playing a national air. The effect was almost magical; the men commenced cheering, and dashed forward on the rebels. The battery was sending volley after volley of grape and canister into our ranks; but on pressed the brigade, reserving its fire until within short range, when, opening on them, it dislodged the battery, and drove its supports to the rear. The charge was made in the most gallant style, and was a decided success, as it enabled the retiring troops to re-form their lines, and stop the further advance of the enemy. In the impetuosity of the charge, we had, however, advanced too far, and being in imminent danger of being flanked, we were withdrawn to the main line. Re-inforcements were rapidly coming up, and a brisk skirmish was kept up all along the line during the afternoon; but there was no heavy fighting until about six o'clock in the evening.

In the meantime, we had refreshed ourselves with a good dinner; the most of the men had also succeeded in getting a little sleep. At about five o'clock we again formed line of battle. Meade's entire army was now on the field. His line extending from the north of Spottsylvania Court House along the Po river, our corps was again in the centre, the Sixth on our left, the Second on the right, and the Ninth in reserve. The marching of troops, the dashing back and forth of aids carrying dispatches, and more than all, the appearance of Meade and Grant on the field, inspecting the line, indicated that a great battle was again at hand. Directly after six o'clock the order was given to advance. As the mighty host moved forward, the loud cheering of the men indicated how little the hard fighting and severe marching of the campaign had dampened the ardor of the army. The rebels were driven back for a considerable distance, and their first line of intrenchments carried. They then fell back to a strongly fortified position, from which they successfully defended themselves from the furious assaults of the Union troops. About dark, our division held a position along the edge of a wood. We were soon after ordered to advance through it and attack the enemy in our front. We had gone but a short distance when we met the enemy, who held a strong intrenched position. They let us come close to their line, when they gave us a terrible volley of musketry. It was a complete surprise to us, and the line was thrown into some confusion; but order was soon restored, and we commenced to return the enemy's fire. Fortunately for us the rebels had directed their fire too high, a shower of bullets passing over our heads, cutting the leaves and small limbs of the trees like a hail storm.

Our brigade held its ground for some time; but owing to the troops on our left giving way, we were flanked and compelled to fall back. We, at first, retired slowly, keeping up a continuous fire on the enemy, but finally broke and fled. After retreating a short distance, Col. Talley, commanding the brigade, made a determined effort to rally his men and check the rebel advance. The result was, that he and about four hundred of his men were captured and marched to the rear. When the line broke I ran for the rear; but, after getting to the place where the Colonel was trying to make a stand, I fell in line again, but soon wished that I had continued in my flight. We made a short resistance, but found that certain death would be our fate if we did not surrender. The rebels had flanked us on the left, and were getting into our rear; discovering this, I came to the conclusion to attempt an escape by running to the right. In the confusion I had succeeded in getting away, and would, no doubt, have escaped, had I not become confused in regard to the course I should pursue after getting away from my comrades. Had I turned to the right after running a few hundred yards, I would, no doubt, have succeeded in getting to our lines; but I continued running until I came to a small opening or clearing in the wood. I stopped to consider what would be best to do. As I was almost played out, and had got away from the rebels, at least for the present, I came to the conclusion to lie down and take a rest, and watch for further developments. For a short time everything was as quiet as the grave; and tired and worn out as I was, rest was very sweet, and I could hardly make up my mind to move. As I had had very little sleep for the last two nights, I soon became, after lying down, very sleepy. I was almost asleep, when I was startled by a small animal that ran close by me. I jumped up, but discovering the object of my alarm, I lay down again. However, I soon concluded to move on, and was getting up to do so, when I heard a noise as if some one was coming through the wood in my rear. I walked back a few steps and listened, when I discovered that a rebel skirmish, line was moving through the woods. Taking my gun at a trail arms, I started to run across the clearing, and had almost reached the other side, when the word "Halt!" from a skirmisher at the edge of the wood, brought me to a sudden stop. Thinking, however, that I had reached the Union lines, I stopped but an instant, when I advanced, gun in hand, exclaiming, "Do not fire—I am a Union soldier!" The reply was, "Drop that gun and march in here, or I will put a ball through you." I again stopped, but did not drop the gun. The rebel repeated the order, when I threw down my gun and surrendered. My captors belonged to a North Carolina regiment, and were a gentlemanly, clever set of fellows, and as long as I was in their hands I was treated very kindly. After I was captured, one of them asked me where I had intended going. I told him I was trying to find the Union army. He replied, "O, never mind, you will soon find them, for in a few days we will have the rest of you." I could not help but tell him that, judging from the way they had kept up running since leaving the Wilderness, they, themselves, must have feared capture. Somewhat to my surprise the rest laughed heartily, evidently enjoying the discomfiture of their comrade, who was inclined to be a little cross at what I suppose he considered my impudence. "O, that's all right; we fell back to draw you on," he answered. Among my captors was a Sergeant Hill, who was especially kind to me. I had quite a chat with him, and, judging from what he told me, I do not think he was much of a rebel. During the night, my captors were relieved and sent to the rear, taking me with them. I was then given in charge of guards who proved themselves as mean as the others had been generous. As the sergeant left me, he bid me good-bye, and said he hoped I might soon be released and get home. We also exchanged addresses. I lost his soon after, and as I have never heard from him, I do not know whether he is living or dead. If he is living, I can assure him he will find the latch-string of my door on the outside at any time.

My captors had not searched or made any effort to take anything from me; but I was not so fortunate with the new guards. I had a fine, new hat, which a big, burly fellow took possession of before I was with them ten minutes. He was, however, generous enough to leave me his; but as I was not in the soap-fat business, I did not care much about it. It had brim enough to cover a small bake-oven, and looked as if it had been soaked in grease for a year or two. I attempted to remonstrate with the villain, but found the least said, the better for me. I here met Col. Talley and about three hundred and sixty men, who were captured after I left there.

"Misery," it is said, "loves company," but in this case, at least, it was not so. I was sorry to see our brave Colonel and so many men in the hands of the enemy. Early in the morning, May 9th, we started for Beaver Dam station, where the rebels intended to put us on the cars and send us to Richmond. Our guards were again changed—a company of cavalry taking charge of us. This change was very agreeable, as the new guards, with few exceptions, were a great improvement on the ones we had just left. The weather was very warm, and as we were tired out with marching, and received no food, we suffered very much during the day. Some of the men gave out entirely; what became of them, I could never ascertain. As we marched along, we were quite an object of curiosity to the natives, who gathered along the road to see the "Yankees." Some of them must have formed strange ideas about our appearance and looks, as one good woman exclaimed, "Why, they look just like our men." If the woman had the man in her mind who stole my hat when she made the comparison, I do not think it was much of a compliment. I did not care much about the opinion of most of them, but I could not help wishing that the few really pretty girls we passed would not despise us. When within a few miles of Beaver Dam station we passsed the house of a fellow who was terribly indignant, and had a great deal to say about what should be done with us for coming "down here and taking our niggers from us," as he expressed it to one of the boys, who gave him a clincher by telling him to do all of his "Secesh" talk now, as the Union troops would be along, and then he would be a good Union man. It was well-known to both armies that quite a number of citizens were rebels or Union men just as the occasion suited. The remark of the prisoner was greeted with hearty laughter by the guards and prisoners, much to the disgust of Mr. Civilian, who, no doubt, came to the conclusion that soldiers were a queer set. We had marched thirty miles, and were within a short distance of the station, when a strange rumbling sound in our rear attracted our attention. The hope had impressed itself on every mind during the day that we might be recaptured; and when I first heard the noise, I made the remark to one of my comrades, that I believed our cavalry was coming. One of the guards, who was riding close to me, overheard the remark, when, turning his horse, he rode to the other side and commenced talking to one of his officers. The officer put spurs to his horse and rode rapidly back to the top of the hill we had just crossed. The noise could be heard coming nearer and nearer, and I suppose from the top of the hill the officer could see the approaching column. If he did, he did not stay long to view the sight, as he came back as fast as his horse could carry him, shouting, "The Yankees are coming—the Yankees are coming!" We were now within a few hundred feet of the station, and the train that was to convey us to Richmond was standing on the track with steam up and ready for starting. The rebel officer who had charge of our guards, ordered us to double quick for the station; but instead of obeying, we came to a sudden halt. The rebels threatened, by saying, that if we did not move they would fire into us; but we stubbornly refused to move a step. Finding they could not compel us to move, they turned their attention to the approaching cavalry, and formed line of battle across the road, placing us in the rear. They had just about accomplished this, when the advance of the cavalry column burst over the hill. Gen. Sheridan, with almost the entire cavalry corps, had flanked Lee's army in the morning with the instructions to destroy his line of communications, burn his supplies at Beaver Dam, tear up the railroad, and then move on to Richmond. He first deceived the rebels by marching his command in the direction of Fredericksburg, when, turning suddenly to the right, he struck out boldly for the rear of Lee's army. He succeeded in passing the right wing of the rebel army, and, after severing Lee's communications, advanced rapidly in the pirection of Beaver Dam station. On the way, some colored people gave him the information that a rebel guard had passed along the road with a number of Union prisoners. He immediately ordered Gen. Custer with the Michigan Brigade to advance as fast as possible and endeavor to overtake us before the rebels could get us into cars. Some of his men, after the re-capture, informed us that Custer told them he would overtake us or kill every horse in his command. The horses were certainly in a fearful condition when they reached us. It was the advance of this column with the gallant Custer, the first man in front, that dashed down the hill to our rescue. As the road was narrow, with fence on one side and wood on the other, but a small portion of the advance could charge on our guards. This squad, as mentioned before, Custer led in person; and as he, with sword in hand, dashed on the rebels, we heard him shout, "Clear the way, boys!" We knew this was intended for us, who were directly in the rear of the rebels, and we did not stand long upon the order of our going, but went at once. Some of the prisoners fled into the woods, others jumped over the fence, and a few of us got on it, where we could have a better view of the fight. Among the number on the fence was our good, gallant Col. Talley, who was almost wild with excitement. The fight was soon over; a few of our guards who had fleet horses succeeded in escaping, but the most of them were cut down or captured. A number of rebel infantry were at the station guarding the supplies; they fled at the first alarm. The act was a cowardly one, and yet it was the part of wisdom, as Sheridan would have made short work with them after his arrival with the balance of his corps. The rebel guards who had charge of us were a brave set of fellows, and fought with a desperation worthy of a better cause. Among the number killed was one who had been very kind to us on the march, and I could not help but pity the fate of him who had been so brave and generous; several times during the day he dismounted and let some poor fellow who had given out ride his horse, he himself walking.

Among the number captured, was a young fellow of about sixteen or seventeen years of age, who took great delight in teasing us about our unfortunate condition. He had a peculiarly fine, squeaking voice, very much like an old woman's. Annoying as it was to us, it must, however, have been the sweetest music to himself, as he kept his tongue going all the time. One of his frequent expressions, and one that appeared to give him great delight, was "Well, boys, daddy Lee has got you!" and then he would laugh as if he considered it an immense joke. Several of his comrades during the day told him to shut up; but he paid no attention to them, evidently thinking the fun too good. One of our boys jokingly, and without the least idea that anything of the kind might happen, reminded him that the cards might be turned before the day was over, as our cavalry was in pursuit of them. Little did he think that in a few hours his prediction would come true. After the fight was over, we found our tormentor in the hands of the cavalry, and he was the most frightened man I ever saw. Some of our boys could not help but tease him about the change of affairs; one of them exclaimed, "Well, my lad, daddy Grant has got you!" at the same time imitating his voice and manner so perfectly as to raise a shout of laughter from the rest. The poor fellow begged piteously that his life might be spared. This was too much for the boys, who told him to rest easy, as he was entirely too innocent to be killed.

Immediately after the fight, Gen. Custer took possession of the station, where we found an immense amount of rebel supplies, consisting of flour, pork, cornmeal, fish, sugar, rum, and other rations. Two large trains of cars, one loaded with flour, and the other which was to take us to Richmond, were captured and destroyed. Fire was immediately applied to the station and buildings around it, and in a short time the entire amount of supplies, estimated by Gen. Sheridan to be worth two million of dollars, was totally consumed. The men, in helping themselves around the station, had found several barrels of whisky, and were going to fill their canteens, when

Gen. Sheridan, who had come on the ground, ordered the heads of the barrels to be knocked in. It was amusing to see the thirsty fellows run after the dirty stuff, and dip it up as fast as it flowed along the ground. Some of them succeeded in getting too much of it. Gen. Sheridan's arrival was greeted with three hearty cheers by the re-captured prisoners. He made us a short speech, in which he advised us to stick to his command, as we might be captured again by the rebels if we did not. He also told us to arm ourselves, but if we found the arms a burden, to throw them away, and by all means try to keep up with his command. He said, also, we should take any horse or mule we could find on the way. Some of the cavalry had lost their horses, and as they were on the hunt, we did not stand much of a chance of finding any.

The rebels had quite a number of colored men employed at the station. They did not imitate the examples of the whites by fleeing, but hid themselves about the station until they felt sure their masters were out of sight; which, by the way, did not take very long. Then they commenced to pop their heads out of every conceivable hiding place in the vicinity. They appeared to understand perfectly well from the first, that we were friends, and they were very demonstrative in their welcome. One big fellow knocked in the top of a sugar barrel, and, taking a tin-cup for a scoop, commenced to share out the sugar to all who would accept. He would frequently call out, "Fall in here, you Yanks, for your rations!" and his broad face would beam with pleasure, when some one would accept a dip. When we started for the James river, they all followed, and by the time we got there, hundreds of these poor, down-trodden people had joined us. I saw poor mothers, carrying their babes, and keeping up with the column all day. When asked where they intended going, they would reply, "I want to be free." After the destruction of everything at the station was fully assured, the line of march was resumed in the direction of Richmond. In the way of arms I succeeded in getting a fine carbine. I also loaded up as much provisions as I could well manage to carry, but had not gone very far on the march when I was compelled to throw the most of it away. I had delayed longer at the station than was prudent, for I had marched but a short distance, when the boom of cannon in the direction of the station announced the fact that the rebels had overtaken our rear guard. The quick moving of the cavalry indicated that it was not Sheridan's intention to stop and give them battle longer than he would be compelled to. He had succeeded in accomplishing all that he wanted at the station, and being in the rear of Lee's army, he of course would not stop longer than was absolutely necessary. The rebel Gen. Stuart, with the rebel cavalry corps, was in pursuit, and several times during the day had attacked Sheridan's rear, but was every time defeated. When the head of the column started we should have left with them, as it would have given us a much better chance of getting away; but in place of doing so, some of us stayed at the station until most of the cavalry had left, and as the rear regiment marched away more rapidly than the ones in the van, we had some difficulty in keeping up. The food and short rest I had taken at the station had refreshed me a little; but the strain on my system had been so severe for the last five days that it did not help me much. I had marched but a few miles after leaving the station, when I became very much exhausted, and found that I would have to unload. I threw away the most of my provisions, and gave my carbine to one of the cavalry, but it was no very great relief. We had proceeded but a short distance when my strength gave out entirely, and I sank down by the road almost unable to move. I wistfully watched the column as it passed along, hoping something would turn up to help me out of the miserable fix I was in. I had just made up my mind to crawl in the bushes and hide, so as to keep the pursuing rebels from finding me, when the van of the Eighth New York cavalry commenced passing. One of the officers ordered me to get up and move along, as the rebels would capture me. I told them that I was played out, and could go no farther. One of the men then left the ranks, and dismounting, helped me to mount his horse, at the same time remarking, "It would be too bad to leave you in the hands of the rebels again." The kind-hearted fellow marched on foot until we stopped for the night, and almost all of the next day. The company I was fortunate enough to get into was one of the most intelligent and gentlemanly set of soldiers I had ever met with, and I enjoyed their society very much. About midnight we stopped for the remainder of the night, and had a good rest until seven o'clock in the morning, when we again started on our journey. We marched a distance of about twenty-five miles during the day, and went into camp early in the evening. As we did not break camp again until about eight o'clock next morning, I had a splendid rest, and felt so much refreshed that I insisted on my friend taking his horse again.

On the morning of May 11th, Sheridan sent one brigade to Ashland Station to destroy the railroad and burn the depot. The brigade, after completely destroying the railroad station and bridges, returned to the main column, when the march was continued in the direction of Richmond. We marched until about three o'clock in the afternoon, and had reached the vicinity of Glenallen Station, when information was received that the rebels under Gen. Stuart were in force in our front, at a place called Yellow Tavern. The rebel cavalry, by hard marching, had succeeded in getting in position between us and Richmond, evidently for the purpose of cutting off Sheridan's advance on that city. As soon as the presence of the enemy became known, Sheridan made preparations to give them battle. Stuart, however, brought on the engagement by a fierce attack on Sheridan's advance brigade, commanded by Gen. Devens, and was successful in forcing it back. It was re-inforced by several other brigades, and a hotly-contested battle took place. The rebels were completely defeated, being driven from the field, and leaving a battery of artillery and a number of prisoners in the hands of the gallant Union troops. I was at Sheridan's headquarters during the battle, and had the pleasure of witnessing a most gallant cavalry charge, made by Custer's Michigan brigade, on a rebel battery. When Devens' brigade was compelled to fall back, the rebels succeeded in getting a battery into position that was doing terrible work in his ranks. This battery, Custer was ordered to charge. He rapidly formed his brigade, and ordered his advance regiment to charge. The rebel battery had directed its fire on them, and was cutting a swath through their ranks at every discharge; but on they rushed, until their glittering blades flashed over the heads of the rebel cannoneers. The men were cut down at their guns, which fell into the hands of the gallant troopers. It was in this battle that the rebels sustained a severe loss in the death of their greatest cavalry leader, Gen. J. E. B. Stuart, who was killed during the engagement. At three o'clock in the morning, Sheridan again resumed his march, and by daylight was within three miles of Richmond. He succeeded in getting possession of the outer line of intrenchments, and his intention was to attempt the capture of the city itself; but daylight revealed that the rebels had been re-inforced during the night so strongly as to make the capture of the city by cavalry and light artillery an impossibility. The forts and redoubts bristled with bayonets, and as we were in range of the heavy guns of some of the forts, Sheridan immediately commenced to withdraw his command, with the intention of crossing the Chickahominy river at Meadow Bridge. It soon became evident, however, that the enemy did not intend letting him get away without making a most desperate attempt to destroy his command. The rebel cavalry had succeeded in getting possession of and destroying part of the bridge on our line of retreat, and had a strong force of cavalry and infantry in position on the other side to oppose our crossing. At the same time we could see heavy columns of troops marching from the fortifications, for the purpose of attacking our rear. The situation now was a most critical one; the enemy had completely cut off our retreat, and could bring a greatly superior force to advance on our rear. Fortunately for the Union cause, the Federal force was in command of an officer who was known to be very fertile in resources; and, as the sequel showed, he was fully competent to extricate himself and command from the dangerous position they were placed in. He immediately formed the plan of repairing the bridge partly destroyed, at Meadow Bridge, over the Chickahominy, and escaping by the way of Mechanicsville. As mentioned before, the rebels had a strong force of men in position to oppose his crossing, and had also the advantage from the fact that the ground on this side of the river is very swampy, and difficult to move on. The reconstruction of the bridge was also a difficult matter, as it would have to be done under a severe fire from the rebel batteries. I was at headquarters during this time, and was perfectly astonished at the unshrinking bravery and self-possession of Gen. Sheridan during the terrible fighting that followed. Several times, when some of his men gave way, he exposed himself with a bravery that was extremely reckless; where the fighting was severest, and the danger the greatest, there was Sheridan, encouraging his men by talking in his social, familiar manner, that made him so famous afterwards in the Valley, where he turned a disastrous defeat into a glorious victory. As soon as it was ascertained that the object of the rebels was to surround his command, Sheridan ordered one of his divisions to attack them at the bridge. After the most desperate fighting, the enemy was forced back, and, although exposed to the most severe firing, our forces reconstructed the bridge. To repel the rebel assaults from the direction of Richmond, Sheridan had formed a line of all his artillery, supported by a division of cavalry dismounted and fighting as infantry. The balance of his men, not engaged at the bridge, he held well in hand, to reinforce any point where they would be the most needed. The rebels in strong column advanced to the assault, cheering loudly, and evidently expecting an easy victory. The Union troops reserved their fire until the enemy was within short range of their guns, when they received them with a terrible discharge of grape and canister, which tore horrible gashes through their ranks. The line reeled and commenced to give way; but the rebel officers succeeded in getting their line reformed and again advanced to the assault. Again and again the artillery poured volleys of double-shotted grape and canister into their ranks; but they pressed forward until they came within range of the carbines in the hands of the cavalry, when they received a storm of bullets that shattered their ranks, and drove the entire line in the utmost confusion back towards Richmond. In a short time, however, the rebels again advanced with a column stronger than the defeated one, to renew the conflict. Every discharge from the Union guns made terrible gaps through their lines, but on they pressed, determined to carry the Union position. This time, Gen. Sheridan met them with a fierce counter-charge, and a terrific conflict ensued, which resulted in the enemy being again compelled to retire from the field. I was watching the flight of the demoralized enemy in the direction of Richmond, when loud cheering in the direction of the bridge announced the fact that our men had succeeded in getting possession of it, and were forcing the enemy from their position on the opposite side. The enemy, however, fell back but a short distance, when they made the most determined resistance to the further advance, or rather retreat, of our forces. The bridge had, however, been gained, and Sheridan made immediate preparations for crossing his train. His command was still, however, in a perilous situation. The rebels were re-forming their lines for another assault on his rear and flanks, and the position they still held near the bridge would enable them to concentrate a severe fire on the Union troops as they crossed it. The crossing of the ammunition train, in the face of the fire, was a dangerous undertaking, as the explosion of it would in all probability have insured the destruction of Sheridan's entire command. After the train was ready to move, he placed himself at the head of one of his brigades, and led a charge against the enemy's lines in person. The men who were fighting under the eye of their great leader charged with an impetuosity that drove the enemy from the field, and the ammunition train crossed in safety. After the train was all over, the balance of the troops crossed rapidly, and the rebels pursued in the direction of Mechanicsville. Here they made a stand, but were soon put to flight. We then marched to the vicinity of Gaines Mill, where we camped for the night. Continuing our march, by evening of May 4th, we arrived on the banks of James river, where we camped for the night. Directly after, a Union gunboat, that mistook us for rebels, opened fire on us, and a shell exploded in rather close proximity to where I was sitting making supper. I had a large tin-cup on the fire full of boiling coffee, and not wishing to lose the best of my supper, I grasped it, and ran behind a tree for protection. I succeeded in saving the coffee, but burned my fingers severely in doing so. The unexpected fire from the vessel created considerable alarm; but the mistake was soon discovered, and the firing ceased. On the following morning we bade our cavalry friends farewell, they marching to rejoin the Army of the Potomac, and we leaving on the steamship John Tucker for Fortress Monroe.

Here we changed vessels, and were put on the steamship Baltimore, bound for Alexandria, Virginia, where we arrived at two o'clock p. m., May 17th. We stopped at the Soldier's Rest over night, and in the morning marched to Camp Distribution, where we stayed until Friday, May 20th, when we were shipped to Belle Plains. At this place we were organized into a battalion, Col. Talley in command, and ordered to guard a wagon-train to the front. We marched to Fredericksburg, where we stayed all night. On the following day we continued our march, and by evening had reached Bowling Green, a distance of twenty-five miles, where we camped for the night. We again continued our march at daylight, and by evening, May 24th, we reached the army, then in line of battle on the North Anna river. We were informed that in the morning our battalion would be broken up, and we would be sent to our respective regiments. I was so anxious to get back to the boys, that I could not resist the temptation to slip out of camp as soon at it was dark, and make an effort to find them. After a good deal of hunting along the line, I succeded in finding the regiment. The boys had just finished their supper, and were lying on the ground taking a good rest. As it was quite dark, I walked in among them without being noticed. My brother Frank, who was a member of the company, was sitting on the ground, and in earnest conversation with one of the men. I was trying to get quite close to him without being discovered, so as to give him a pleasant surprise, when, hearing my name mentioned by one of the boys, I stopped to listen, and heard the remark, "I guess Urban's gone up this time;" before the other could reply, I remarked, "I suppose not," and commenced to laugh. Brother Frank, who had recognized my voice, jumped up, and the remembrance of the look of pleasure and surprise depicted on his countenance will ever be a green spot in my memory. I had the glad tidings to tell to the boys that our gallant Colonel and some of the men, who were supposed to be killed, were returning to the regiment, and would be with them on the following day.

It was like coming home, to get back to the old regiment again; and I was as happy as man could be. Little did I think, however, that in a few days the fortunes of war would again find me in the hands of the enemy, and that for seven long months I would have to suffer all the pain and misery that could be inflicted on me, and the effects of which would leave my body a physical wreck, and all through life would cause a thrill of horror to pass through me at the recollections of prison life in the South.

CHAPTER VIII.

Advance of Grant's Forces from the North Anna—Battle of Bethesda Church—My Third Capture by the Enemy—Entrance into Libby Prison—Pemberton Prison—Departure from Richmond—Arrival at Andersonville.

AFTER the great battle of Spottsylvania Court House, Gen. Lee withdrew his army to a strong position south of the North Anna river, and along a stream known as Little river. His left extended for some distance along this stream, and his right to Sexton's Junction on the Fredericksburg railroad. Immediately after his retreat from the former place, Gen. Grant marched in pursuit, and after some slight fighting, succeeded in crossing the North Anna, and getting his army into position in front of the Rebel army.

It does not appear reasonable to suppose that Grant could have crossed this stream without severe loss, had Lee wished to prevent it. His strongly intrenched position, but a short distance from that stream, made it desirable for him that the Union forces should cross it. The rebel position, strong by nature, had been greatly strengthened by long lines of intrenchements and other fortifications; and should the Union forces attack this position and be defeated, the crossing of the steam in their rear might have become a difficult matter. Lee's position would have given him almost all the chances of success, and in case of defeat, his position would not have been as dangerous as Grant's under like circumstances, for the stream in his rear was a small, insignificant affair, and would, to no great extent, have embarrassed his retreat. After crossing his army, Grant spent three days in reconnoitering the position of the enemy's lines, and evidently came to the conclusion that it was too strong to carry by direct assault, for he again resorted to his flanking tactics to compel Lee to withdraw from his chosen ground.

The movement was entirely successful, and Lee was compelled to abandon his intrenchments, and march to intercept the Federal army before it reached the rebel capital.. Lee succeeded, however, in getting his army into position at Cold Harbor, thus getting a position as strong as the one he had evacuated, and interposed his army between Grant's forces and Richmond. The Union army crossed the Pamunky river on the twenty-eighth of May, the Fifth and Ninth corps crossing at Hanover Ferry, and the other corps at a ford further up the river. Communications were now opened with the White House Landing on the Pamunky river, and it again became the base of supplies for the Union army. Gen. Grant had now succeeded in getting on Gen. McClellan's old fighting-ground, and it would certainly be a stretch of the hyperbole to claim that any great advantage had been gained thus far.

The loss of the Union army at this period of the campaign exceeded forty thousand men in killed, wounded, and missing; and although Lee was compelled to evacuate his strong position at the Wilderness, Spottysylvania, and the North Anna river, he was not driven from any of them by direct assault, and the position he secured at Cold Harbor was fully as strong, and better adapted for the defence of the rebel capital than any of the positions he had abandoned. It is true, Grant again flanked this position, and compelled Lee to march to the south of Richmond — but not until he had in vain assaulted it, and added ten thousand more to the Union loss, and inflicted a comparatively small loss on the enemy.

The crossing of the James river by both armies was only a change of base that again gave the enemy all the advantages in regard to position. That the advantages gained so far by the Union forces compensated for the loss of more than fifty thousand men, is believing more than the facts in the case warrant.

On Monday, May 13th, our corps crossed the Tolapotomy river, and our division moved forward on the Mechanicsville road. We marched until two o'clock p. m., when we met a rebel skirmish line, which fled at our approach. Our brigade was ordered to move rapidly on Mechanicsville, and hold the Mechanicsville road until the arrival of re-inforcements. Col. Harding, commanding the brigade, moved us rapidly forward, and we soon encountered a strong line of rebel skirmishers, and drove them across a small stream of water and a swamp bordering on it. We crossed and advanced a short distance, when we found that the enemy was in strong force in our front. As we were some distance from our supports, the brigade should have been withdrawn immediately across the swamp; but instead of doing so, our officers ordered us to barricade by piling up rails and logs, and endeavor to hold our position. We were working away like beavers to get our position as strong as possible, when the enemy, which numbered a full division of Gen. Ewell's corps, made a desperate charge on us. We sprang to arms, and formed line of battle behind our half-finished breast-works, and when the enemy came within short range of our rifles, we gave them a deadly volley, which shattered their ranks, and compelled them to fall back in confusion. They, however, soon rallied, and again advanced to the assault. We poured volley after volley into them, and succeeded in holding them at bay in our front; but their line being much longer than ours, they soon outflanked our position, and compelled us to fall back.

Capt. Wasson, who did not hear or understand

the command, and seeing the regiment giving way, called to his company to stick to the pit and hold their position, and the most of the company jumped back to the rifle pit. The Captain had, however, by this time noticed that the entire line was giving way, and that further resistance would be useless, so he told us to save ourselves as best we could. When we reached the swamp, the most available places for crossing were crowded and jammed with men. The rebels had advanced rapidly in pursuit, and were sending a shower of bullets into the struggling mass in the swamp. I stopped for a moment to survey the situation, and then ran to the right for a short distance, and made an attempt to cross. I jumped for what I believed to be a firm spot of ground, but it proved to be anything but solid, for I sank into the mire almost to my knees. Thinking I could not get across, I worked myself back, and ran still farther up to the right, looking for a better place to get over. I had lost considerable time in extricating myself from the mire; and as the rebel line, which had extended a considerable distance past our left, had advanced and taken possession of the ground on the other side, I found my retreat cut off, and was taken prisoner.

After my capture, I made a narrow escape from being killed by one of my captors. I had dropped my gun and was entirely disarmed, when the cowardly scoundrel thrust his bayonet almost into my face, and swore that he would blow the Yankee head clean off me. Most of the men who had succeeded in getting over the swamp made their escape, and as they ran over the hill they turned and fired into the pursuing enemy. Fortunately, about the time the rebel was threatening to kill me, several balls came in pretty close proximity to where we were standing, and it probably reminded him that the fighting was not over, and that he would perhaps better let me go and pay more attention to the Yankees who were still armed. A few moments after my capture, the color-bearer of an Alabama regiment was killed close by me, by a shot from one of our men who had escaped over the hill. The rebel column formed on the other side of the swamp, but did not advance until after we were taken to the rear. As we were gathered together for that purpose, I looked around among the captives to see what kind of company I was going to have The first person I recognized was Aaron Fralich, who was captured almost buried in the mud; then my old chum, John E. Gilbert, who had been captured with me on McClellan's peninsula campaign, and then William Allison and Jack Wilhelm, all members of my company. Wilhelm had succeded in getting over the swamp, when he was struck by a rifle-ball on the head, which knocked him over. He was not injured very severely, the ball scarcely burying itself, but as he afterwards expressed it, "When I came to, the blasted 'rebs' had me."

The rebels had captured between three and four hundred prisoners, and as they marched us to the rear we were cursed and abused to such an extent, that some of the prisoners commenced to entertain the thought that we would all be murdered after they got us back into the wood. They certainly were the most enraged set of rebels I had ever met with, and I confess I was glad when we were placed under other guards. I suppose the fact that they had been compelled to fall back day after day had something to do with their ill nature. As bad as we felt at our own capture, we could not help feeling amused at Wilhelm's doleful appearance. Slowly drawing his hand over his head to wipe off the blood, he looked at us with an expression both comical and pitiful, at the same time cursing both his bad luck and the rebels, and caring very little if they heard him or not.

After my release from rebel prisons—seven months afterward—I was pleased to learn that the rebels who had captured us received a terrible beating the following evening after our capture. After the repulse at the swamp, the brigade fell back about one-half mile, when being re-inforced by the remainder of the division, they re-formed line at the edge of the wood, and waited the attack of the enemy. The rebels fortunately did not take advantage of their success by immediately pressing forward and pursuing our fleeing troops, but made the mistake of stopping long enough after crossing the swamp to enable our troops to re-form their lines, and to make preparations to receive them. The nature of the ground was such that our line of battle, composed of our division, one brigade of Tyler's, and several batteries of artillery were almost entirely hid from the enemy, and from their sheltered position calmly awaited the rebel assault. They did not have to wait very long, however, as the rebels, after re-forming and strengthening their line, boldly advanced to storm their position. The Union troops reserved their fire until the rebels were within a hundred yards of their line, when the batteries and regiments poured into the advancing line a terrific volley of grape, canister, and rifle balls, which completely broke the rebel column, and sent it flying to the rear. The enemy again, however, re-formed and advanced to the attack, but were received with a storm of bullets, grape, and canister, which swept their line like a storm of fire. The rebels gave way completely, and fled in the utmost disorder, leaving the ground covered with killed and wounded. The Reserves now advanced from their position, and, charging after the fleeing enemy, succeeded in capturing a large number of prisoners, and drove the entire rebel line in great confusion from the field. The term of service of this division expired on this day, and the boys evidently wanted to give the rebels a good trimming before leaving the army. It is a strange fact that the division fought its last battle on about the same ground upon which most of it had fought its first one. Parts of the division had been engaged in several actions before, but Mechanicsville was the first battle that the entire division was engaged in. The day after the last battle, the division organization was broken up. The men who had not re-enlisted were sent to their homes, and seventeen hundred and fifty-nine, who had re-enlisted as veterans, were organized into two regiments, known as the One Hundred and Ninetieth, and One Hundred and Ninety-First Pennsylvania Volunteers. These two regiments served with the army until the close of the war.

Among the captured were a large number who had not re-enlisted, and would have left for home the following day. Some of them died in rebel prisons, and their fate was a peculiarly sad one. They had served their country faithfully and well, and had looked anxiously forward to the day when they would be permitted to return to their homes and loved ones; but to be captured just as their hopes were to be realized, and compelled to suffer untold misery, and then death, was a sad fate indeed.

After being taken to the rear, we were marched

into a field close to the road, and given in charge of other guards, who were more friendly, and in every respect an improvement on those who had captured us. During the night, a large train of ambulances, loaded with wounded, passed us, going in the direction of Richmond. They were wounded during the afternoon, and the large number convinced us that the rebel loss was very great. As the train conveying them passed, we could hear groans from the inmates in almost every wagon. Among our guards was one who was very social and friendly with us from the first, and Gilbert became impressed with the belief that he was a Union man, and could be persuaded, if an opportunity occurred, to let a few of us slip off. He succeeded in getting close to this guard, and had a long talk with him, and found that his first opinion was correct. He informed Gilbert that he was a Union man, but was compelled to enter the rebel service. Gilbert then told him that if he would let us slip off after dark, we would give him what money we had, and his (Gilbert's) watch. He also told him that if he ever came to his (Gilbert's) home, he would reward him handsomely. The guard told him that he was willing to let us off if he possibly could, but did not wish to be rewarded for it. He also informed Gilbert which would be the best way to get to our lines, if we succeeded in escaping. We expected the guard to come again on post at about midnight, and we waited anxiously for the appearance of our friend, but did not get to see him again; whether he regretted his promise or was suspected by his officers and kept away, we could not ascertain. The plan would not have been a success, anyhow, as the rebels, after dark, built large fires around us, which lit up the ground to such an extent, that getting away without being noticed by the other guards, would have been an impossibility.

As soon as we discovered that all hope of escape during the night was cut off, Gilbert Fralich and myself lay down to sleep. It would have been pleasant indeed to lose ourselves in grateful unconsciousness of our unfortunate condition for a short time, but I found it impossible to do so. Although weary in body, my mind was in such a disturbed condition that I found it impossible to fall asleep. But a few days before I was so happy in the thought that I was delivered from a terrible captivity, and I could hardly realize that I was again in the hands of the enemy. My thoughts continually went back to the company, and wondering how many of our brave boys had fallen in the battle after I was captured. The last I had seen of my brother Frank was in line of battle, where he was fighting close by my side, and I felt very uneasy about him. After my release from my long captivity, I was rejoiced to hear that he was one of the fortunate ones who escaped. I was also happy to hear that comrade

Lindley McClune, whom I had seen fall shot through the neck, and supposed to be dead, had recovered and was doing well. I felt very sad, however, to hear that Jacob Crummel, a member of Company E, a neighbor at home, and an intimate friend in the army, was numbered with the slain. Poor Crummel, wounded nigh unto death in the Seven Days' fight before Richmond, and again wounded at Gettysburg, where I stood close to him on the skirmish line, he being detailed from Company E, and I from Company D, to dislodge a number of rebel sharpshooters, and then to fall dead on the last day of his three years service! A braver or truer soldier never wore the uniform of the Government.

> "Far away in humble cottage
> Sits his mother sad and lone,
> And her eyes are red with weeping
> Thinking of her absent son."

In the morning we were taken to Richmond, and, as we marched through the principal part of the city on our way to Libby, we had a good opportunity of seeing the famous, or I might say infamous Capital of the Southern Confederacy. I could not help noticing the difference in regard to the feelings of the people and appearance of the city, compared to what it was two years before, when I was marched through its streets as a prisoner of war. Then the people were demonstrative and loud in their boasts of what they would do, and how soon the Northern invaders would be driven from Southern soil—the city then had an animated and lively appearance; but now everything looked gloomy and despondent, and the boastful spirit of the people appeared to be broken.

The papers still kept up the cry that Grant was accomplishing nothing and getting his men all butchered; but the people evidently realized the fact that somehow or other the enemy was getting nearer and nearer to their Capital, and that the prospects of Southern independence were not very bright. While the papers kept up the cry of "Grant the butcher," they no doubt wished the butcher a great deal farther off.

In the afternoon we were lodged in the notorious Libby prison, and searched for our valuables. Two men acted as searchers, and we were taken two at a time, before them to be robbed. This gave the boys a chance to hide their valuables, and Yankee ingenuity prevented the rebels from getting a good part of them. One of the searchers was an old man, who, for low villany would easily have taken the premium at a world's fair. He took all he could find, even the pictures the soldiers had of loved ones at home. The other one was a young man, who was much more considerate, and I do not think took more than he was compelled to. I was fortunate enough to be searched by this one, and he told me he was ordered to search for side-arms and money. I had a few things which I prized very highly, not from any intrinsic value, but from associations connected with them; these he made no effort to take. As he took a rather long look at a lot of photographs I had, I was beginning to feel a little uneasy, thinking that he might keep them, but after examining them closely, he handed them back with the remark that "we appeared to have pretty girls in the North, anyhow." All the money I had I succeeded in hiding by rolling it up and keeping it in my mouth until he was through with me.

While I was being searched I had a good opportunity to see how the old gentleman who was searching near me was doing business. In searching a prisoner he found an ambrotype picture, and was going to appropriate it to his own use when the prisoner commenced begging for it, telling the rebel that it was a picture of his wife. The rebel, with a malignity that would disgrace a South Sea heathen, dropped it on the floor and stamped it to pieces. The prisoner's face was livid with rage and indignation, but he was powerless to prevent it. He declared afterward that if he had had a knife in his possession, he would have stabbed the villain dead on the spot.

Some of the boys had very clever plans to hide their money, but did not always succeed in keeping it from the old reprobate. I saw one of the prisoners take a fifty-dollar note and put it in a large pipe, and then fill it with tobacco; when his turn came to be examined, he lit it and commenced to take a smoke. The old searcher, however, suspected the pipe, and emptying it, found the money. Some of the prisoners destroyed their greenbacks, saying they would save the Government the expense of redeeming them before they would let the rebels have them.

On the following day we received our first rations from the rebels. It consisted of a small piece of corn-bread, and quite a small piece of pork. The following day the weather was quite cool and pleasant, and I succeeded in putting in almost the whole forenoon in sleep.

About noon we again received our day's ration, which was so small that we consumed it all in one meal. Fralich and myself had our knapsacks taken from us when captured, and did not have overcoat or blanket. Gilbert succeeded in keeping his blanket, and also getting it into prison. He kindly offered to share it with us, and in the long imprisonment which followed we used it in common.

On the following day, we were informed that we might write to our friends if we wished to, but that our letters would be examined by the Confederate authorities before they were sent North. We gladly availed ourselves of the privilege, and in a short time the most of us were busy penning messages to our friends. We of course knew that it would not not do for us to write anything detrimental to our enemies, so we merely wrote that we were captives, and doing well. I wrote one to my parents, and another to a dear friend; but as one never reached its destination, and the other did not until after my release, I might as well have left them unwritten.

The following day, June 5th, was the Sabbath. It was our first Sabbath in a rebel prison, and it was a most gloomy one, indeed, to all of us. We could not help contrasting our miserable condition with the one we enjoyed a few days before. Then we were free—now in a rebel dungeon, and the prospect of getting out, slim indeed. We commenced to suffer severely from hunger, and could hardly wait until two o'clock, when we received our mite again. When it did come, we had a little change; a small amount of bean soup in addition to the corn bread and pork. But the entire amount was so small that we again consumed it at one meal, and felt hungry when we had it eaten.

Wednesday, June 8th, we left Libby prison, and were put into Pemberton, a short distance from Libby. This place was even worse than Libby, being more filthy and gloomy. Our stay, however, in this place was only a short one, as we left it in the morning; and, although we knew that it was only for the purpose of being sent to some other prison, we were heartily glad to leave. We did not think it possible that our enemies could find a more terrible place than the one we were leaving; but then we did not know anything of the horrors of Andersonville, and it was fortunate for us that we did not, and that the terrible future was hidden from us; for, could we have foreseen the horror and misery of the prisons that were to receive us, we would have given up in utter despair. It was only the continuous hope of a speedy release that enabled us to live through it.

After leaving the prison we crossed the James river to Manchester—a town directly opposite Richmond—where we were loaded on the cars as so much inanimate freight, and at eight o'clock A. M. we started on our long journey for Andersonville, Georgia. We did not know at the time where we were going to, but from what we learned from the guards, we supposed our next prison would be somewhere in the far South. The distance from Pemberton to the place where we entered the cars is hardly more than one and a half miles; but so weak had I become in the few days that I was in prison, that I could hardly stand in line when we reached the train, and I was glad when we received the orders to get on board. We found the accommodations, however, were very wretched. The cars were common box freight cars, without seats, and the rebels crowded so many of us into them that we could not all sit down at the same time on the floor. Gilbert,

Fralich, and myself, succeeded in getting together in a corner of the car, and in getting seats side by side on the floor; but as "eternal vigilance is the price of liberty," so, in our position continual watching was necessary to hold the corner. The train moved along slowly all day and the following night, and by morning we had reached the city of Danville, about one hundred and forty miles from Richmond. At this place we changed cars, and also received one day's rations. At eight o'clock A. M. we again resumed our journey, and by one P. M. arrived at the beautiful little town of Greensborough, North Carolina, where we again changed cars.

We arrived at Charlottesville, North Carolina, early on Sunday morning, June 12th. Directly after, we were taken from the cars, and marched into a wood about one mile from town, where we were kept under a strong guard until the next morning. As the weather had been extremely warm since we left Richmond, and we were most of the time without water, we had suffered very much; and the change from the filthy cars to the pleasant, cool wood, was a most agreeable one to us during the day, but in the evening it began to rain, and continued raining very fast all night; consequently we had a miserable night of it, and bad as the cars were, we wished ourselves back in them again. During the day a large number of men, women, and children gathered together to see the "Yankees." It being Sunday, had, no doubt, the effect of greatly increasing the number of our visitors, they using this day for visiting and recreation. We were evidently objects of great curiosity to them, as they stood around and watched us for hours. As the weather was quite pleasant during the day we enjoyed a splendid rest, and stretched out in the shade, watching our visitors was quite a pleasant pastime to us; and as by far most of our visitors belonged to the feminine gender, and some of the children and young women were really good looking, that did not, of course, detract from our pleasure in watching them. Some of the women were anything else but good-looking, however, being lean and lank, and as one of the boys expressed it, "as ugly as a mud fence." But if the day was pleasant, the night was certainly not, as we were without shelter and exposed to the rain all night. About midnight I was taken quite sick and suffered terribly until morning.

At six o'clock in the morning we were ordered to fall into line and march back to the town, where we were again put on the cars, and our journey was continued southward. While we were in the wood the day before, a few of the prisoners formed a plan to overpower the guards and make an attempt to escape. The attempt was not to be made until we were on the railroad, and at some lonely place. After discussing the matter among ourselves, we came to the conclusion that it would be folly to attempt anything of the kind. The guards might possibly have been overcome, but it is not likely that any of us would have succeeded in escaping to our lines, as we were right in the heart of the Confederacy, and notice of our escape would have been telegraphed all over the South in a few hours, and at the first alarm, horsemen and bloodhounds would have been in pursuit. The chances of getting away would have been distressingly small, and I have no doubt that it was well for us that better judgment prevailed, and the plan of trying to escape in a body was abandoned.

We left Charlotte at seven o'clock A. M., and arrived at Columbia, South Carolina, in the evening, where we stopped for the night. We remained on the cars all night, and suffered very much for the want of water. What excuse our enemies could make for not furnishing us with it, with plenty all around them, would be hard to conjecture, if it was not for the purpose of torturing us. In the morning we again changed cars and continued our journey, and arrived at Augusta, Georgia, late in the evening. We were furnished with two days' rations at this place, consisting of corn-bread almost as hard as a brick, and a piece of pork hardly fit to eat; but as we were almost starved we made short work of it, however, eating nearly all of it at one meal. We stayed all night, and were again kept in the cars but as the night was cooler and more pleasant than the previous one, we did not suffer so much. In the morning we again changed cars, and left for Andersonville, Georgia.

We had by this time found out that Andersonville was to be our place of imprisonment, and various were the conjectures as to what kind of a place it was, and what kind of treatment we would receive from our new jailers. Surely in our case "ignorance was bliss." We were informed by some of the guards that it was a camp in the woods, and *that* alone made the impression that it would be a better place than prison-life in buildings like Libby. The descriptions we received of the place were not unfavorable, and the rebels assured us that the treatment we would receive would be much better than that which we experienced in Richmond.

Whether they did this from ignorance, or from a desire to keep the truth from us until they had us safely inclosed in the pen, or from a fiendish desire to increase our torture by disappointment, we could not find out; but we did discover that they were either liars or ignorant of what they were talking about, and that all our former experiences and sufferings in rebel prisons were but an intimation of what was still in store for us.

We arrived at Andersonville at two o'clock P. M., June 16th, and as the train stopped we looked

PRISONERS ENTERING ANDERSONVILLE PRISON-PEN

around anxiously to see what kind of a place it was. We were somewhat surprised to find that it was only a small way station, with few houses in sight. Directly after our arrival we were ordered to get out of the cars and form in line for the purpose of marching to the prison, which was about one mile from the station. It was raining very fast at the time, and, as we were in a country almost entirely covered with timber, we expected to find some kind of shelter in our new prison; but as we marched from the station, and caught a sight of the prison, our hearts sank within us, for inside of the large inclosure we saw a living mass of prisoners, the most of them being wholly without shelter, standing around in the rain and mud, presenting an appearance no words can describe. It was so crowded that we could not at first believe it possible for them to put all of us into the inclosure. As we came near the gate we noticed that a regiment of rebel soldiers were drawn up in line to the right of us, and were kept in that position until we were inside of the prison.

We were afterward informed by the prisoners that this was done every time a large number of new prisoners arrived, and that they were kept there for the purpose of guarding against an outbreak when the gates were open, and perhaps thinking that when the new arrivals discovered the hell-hole that was open to receive them, they would, in their despair and madness, make an attempt to overcome their fiendish jailers and escape. As we entered the prison a muleteam that was coming from the gate got in position between us and the line of rebel troops. Capt. Wirz, who was riding to and fro, making as much fuss and putting on as much style as if he were in command of an army of fifty thousand men, discovered the team, and thinking his precious mules in danger should his captives make an attempt to escape, yelled out, "Take them aisels away!" The Captain got his Dutch and English frightfully mixed when excited.

This act proved at least that the Captain was not entirely without feelings—that is, for his mules, anyhow. How much he had for the poor wretches who were placed in his charge to be starved and murdered, was a question easily answered. I do not suppose that Jeff. Davis and his advisers could have found a human being on the face of the earth who would have carried out their hellish plans better than this Dutchman, who was sent to Andersonville to reduce our armies.

CHAPTER IX.

ANDERSONVILLE.

> "But that I am forbid
> To tell the secrets of my prison-house,
> I could a tale unfold, whose lightest word
> Would harrow up thy soul; freeze thy young blood;
> Make thy two eyes, like stars, start from their spheres;
> Thy knotted and combined locks to part,
> And each particular hair to stand on end,
> Like quills upon the fretful porcupine."

ON my way home, after being released from rebel prisons, I was in company with a sergeant of a New Jersey regiment, who had also been a prisoner of war in Andersonville prison. We occupied a seat together, and the seat in front of us was occupied by two gentlemen, who, on finding that we had been prisoners of war in the South, became very sociable, and endeavored to engage us in conversation in regard to the treatment we had received. My friend was an intelligent and fluent conversationalist, and for some time related to them incidents of prison-life that had came under his own observation. As I felt very weary and ill, I remained a quiet listener; but I knew from my own experiences that all my friend was relating was true. After finishing their conversation, the sergeant left the car for a short time, going to the car in front, and I nestled down in the corner of the seat for the purpose of taking a nap.

The two gentlemen, who had been the most respectful listeners, and were loud in their demonstrations of pity for the prisoners, and bitter in denouncing the course of treatment pursued by the rebel authorities toward us, evidently did not believe all the sergeant told them to be the truth. Thinking, I suppose, that I could not overhear them, the one remarked to the other, "What do you think of that?" The one addressed shook his head and replied, "Well, I have no doubt it was a terrible place; but I suppose he was stretching it a little." I could not help feeling indignant at them for doubting my friend's veracity; and as any other soldier would be under the same circumstances, I was somewhat sensitive on that particular point; so getting up, I remarked to the last speaker that I was sorry that he doubted my friend's word, and that I could assure them that all the sergeant told them was the truth. They did not like it very much that I had heard them, and the one I had spoken to, hastened to reply, and said, "O, I beg your pardon. I did not mean to hurt your feelings or your friend's; but it really does appear somewhat hard to believe that so many died in that one prison in so short a time. Your friend may possibly have been mistaken as to the numbers."

After the gentlemen left the car, and my friend returned to his seat, I said, "Sergeant, I think I shall be very careful in the future what I say about the treatment we received from the rebels when in Southern prisons." "Why?" he asked. "Well, the truth of the matter is," I answered, "we have witnessed and experienced a good many things that any one not acquainted with the facts could hardly believe." After considering a few moments, he replied, "Well, Urban, I think you are right; for had I not experienced it myself, it would be impossible for me to believe the half I know to be facts."

In writing the following description of Andersonville, I do not intend to describe the horrors of that place more than is absolutely necessary to set forth the scenes enacted; and in writing this entire volume, I do not expect to produce much of a literary work, but merely a simple, truthful story of life in Southern prisons. I claim but one merit for this narration—Truth—and I shall not relate anything but what I know to be the truth, and that I will be willing to answer for on the great day of final account. If things should appear that may seem incredible to you, kind reader, please remember that comparatively little is known of the sufferings of our soldiers in the South; if much has been said, much more has been left unsaid, and a great deal will remain "with the secrets of unwritten history." No tongue can express, no pen can describe, the terrible sufferings of the inmates of the prisons of the South; and it is only through the experience given to the public by the survivors, that this thrilling part of the history of the war can become known.

Andersonville prison, where the climax of rebel atrocity was reached, is located in Sumter county, Georgia, about one mile from Andersonville, a small station on the Georgia Central Railroad, sixty-two miles southeast of Macon, Georgia, and about fifty or sixty miles from the Alabama state line. This station of itself is a small, insignificant, unimportant place; and were it not for the fact that the prison was in such close proximity to it, very few persons outside of its immediate locality would ever have heard of its existence. The land for a considerable distance around it was almost entirely covered with forests, which consisted principally of oak and pine. The surface of the land is in some places low and swampy, and at others rolling, forming a scenery picturesque and pleasing to the eye. The general appearance of the place, however, is wild and desolate. It is very thinly settled, and was well calculated for the purpose it was intended for. Situated as it was, in a country where the timber was so valueless that large quantities of it were destroyed for the purpose of clearing the land, it can readily be understood by the reader how easily the rebel authorities could have furnished shelter for the prisoners. The extent of ground inclosed by the stockade has been a subject of considerable difference of opinion, as it was somewhat difficult to form an opinion, owing to the crowded state of the prison; but I suppose after the enlargement of the pen in July, it contained about twenty-five acres. Of this, four or five acres were swampy, and could not be occupied. A small stream of water, about five or six inches deep, and several feet wide, entered the east side of the prison, and ran through it. This stream had its origin in a swamp a short distance from the stockade, and the water was warm and impure. To add to its natural filthiness, the rebels had built their cook-house directly across the stream on the side where it entered the prison, and the water was often covered with filth and grease. The rebels also washed their dirty, lousy clothes in the stream. On almost every clear day we could see dozens of them sitting along its banks for that purpose; and thirsty as the poor prisoners were, they could hardly make use of the water. The entire prison was inclosed with a high stockade made of pine logs. These logs were about sixteen feet long, and were put into the ground about four feet, thus making a fence twelve feet high. As some of the prisoners succeeded in tunneling out, the rebels built a second stockade a short distance from the first one, and the intervening space they kept lit up during the night with large fires, to prevent the prisoners who might succeed in getting out from escaping. Sentinel boxes were built on top of the stockade; these were about fifty feet apart, and were reached by steps from the ground on the outside. On the inside, about thirty or thirty-five feet from the stockade, was a small railing, fastened on stakes about two feet high. This was called the "Dead Line," and woe to the poor prisoner, whether ignorant of its terrible meaning or not, who crossed, or even reached under it, for instant death was sure.

The rebels, in building this terrible prison, cut down all the trees in the inside with the exception of two, which stood in the northeast corner of the prison, and in such a position that the shade fell on the *outside* of the inclosure. The earth, with the exception of the swamp, was of hard, red clay, with a slight covering of soil almost as light as sand. Lying and starving on this unmerciful, unyielding earth; dying from exposure, hunger and thirst; the sun beating on them until in many cases the hands and neck were burned to blisters —what would not these suffering and dying men have given for the tempering shade of the trees, which the rebels so cruelly and ruthlessly cut away?

Since the close of the war, some of the rebels and apologists of the South have endeavored to prove to the world that the course of treatment pursued by the Southern authorities was as humane as the circumstances connected with the case would allow. What plea of justification can they give for the fact that thousands of men died in this pen, with the hot, scorching sun beating on their faces with an intensity that alone was enough to kill them, and after the rebels had purposely cut down the shade-trees that would have been so grateful, and in some measure have eased their sufferings?

Inside of this inclosure, thirteen thousand two hundred and fifty-three Union soldiers perished, averaging more than one thousand deaths to every month that the prison existed. There is no spot on the face of the earth where "man's inhumanity to man" was more fully demonstrated than in this terrible place, and the name of Andersonville will be a dark spot on American civilization for centuries to come.

As mentioned at the close of the preceding chapter, we had now reached the gate of the prison which was to receive us, and which was to be a Confederate executioner to almost one-half of the entire number who entered its inclosure. As we marched through the gate I could hardly believe it to be possible that this horrible place was to contain us even for a few days, and my blood almost froze with horror as I looked around and saw men who but a short time before enjoyed health and strength, worn down by suffering and disease, until they hardly looked like human beings. Some of them were almost naked, and were all covered with dirt and vermin, presenting an appearance that made our hearts sink within us as we looked upon them; and the terrible thought would continually force itself into my mind, How can I ever expect to live in this horrible place? After the gates closed on us, we stood around for a short time, dumbfounded, and did not know what to do. Around us was a huge wall of pine logs, effectually shutting us from the outer world. On top of this wall was a line of guards, who, with rifle in hand, were only too willing to end our mortal career by sending a ball through us for the least violation of the rules imposed upon us.

The rain was pouring down in torrents, and as it had been raining several days before our arrival, the mud was almost ankle deep, and we could not even see a place to sit down without getting right into it. Night was fast approaching, without a dry stitch of clothing on us, and we were getting chilly and cold. We anxiously inquired of the prisoners if no part of the prison contained sheds, tents, or shelter for us. The reply was, "No, you will find none." One of my comrades, with a groan of despair, exclaimed "My God, can this be hell?" Gilbert finally suggested that we explore the prison and endeavor to find a spot where at least the mud was not so deep, and where we could lie down. We tramped through the mud for a short time, trying to find a spot we could claim for that purpose, but in vain; wherever we stopped, we found that some one else had already claimed the place. We were commencing to fear that we would not even have room enough to lie down on, when finally we came to where several prisoners, who belonged to a West Virginia regiment, had quartered. They were some of the first inmates of the prison, and had succeeded in getting a pretty good shelter. They also possessed a small log or piece of wood, which they kindly offered to us to sit on. Close to them was a small spot of ground not occupied, which we succeeded in getting possession of, and, moving the log on it, we at last succeeded in getting a good seat, and it kept us, at least for a short time, from the necessity of lying down in the mud. Valueless as this piece of wood would have been on the outside of the prison, it was a great treasure to us. I should perhaps mention that at no period of the history of Andersonville was the prison quite so crowded as at the time of our arrival.

The rebels shortly after built an addition to the prison, and in regard to room it was somewhat more comfortable. In our wanderings around the prison I had made a narrow escape from being killed by a rebel guard. I had not as yet heard about the terrible dead-line, and was in the act of crossing it, when a prisoner cautioned me not to do it. Had I done so, my life in Andersonville would have been of short duration. In the evening, our old friend, Amos M. Sourbeer, who had formerly belonged to our company, but was now a member of the One Hundred and Eighteenth regiment, found us. He had been here a few weeks before our arrival, and gave us a terrible account of his experiences. He also informed us that the prisoners were dying at the rate of sixty per day. After the shadows of night had gathered around us, Gilbert, Fralich and myself seated ourselves on our log, and, spreading Gilbert's blanket over our shoulders, endeavored to get some sleep. It was long in the night, however, before sweet, welcome slumber closed our senses in unconsciousness of our helpless condition and misery. We talked long about our unfortunate condition, and pledged ourselves anew to stick together, and, as best we could, help each other. We tried to console ourselves with the hope that our Government would find out the terrible condition of our prison, and some measures be taken to release us.

It rained all night, and as it was quite cold, we suffered terribly, and were thankful when daylight appeared. In the morning it cleared off, and the sun shone brightly for several hours, when it again became cloudy, and rained almost all the time until Sunday morning—two days after. I spent most of the first day in moving around among the prisoners and examining the prison. I was surprised to find from information given me by some of the prisoners, that the prison was infested with a gang of lawless characters, who were adding to the horrors of the place by practicing a system of robbery on the new arrivals to better their own condition. I could not at first but believe that the reports about them had been exaggerated; but I was only a short time in prison when I was fully persuaded that the half had not been told.

Tuesday we received our first day's rations in Andersonville, which consisted of one pint of cornmeal, a small piece of pork, and about a spoonful of cooked rice. After the close of the day we again took possession of our log, or "chicken roost," as Fralich called it, and had another most miserable night of it. Miserable, however, as our condition was, we had accustomed ourselves a little to our surroundings, and were not quite as despondent as the day before. We even laughed when Fralich, who had been in vain trying to sleep, and becoming impressed with the similarity between our resting-place and a chicken-roost, commenced to imitate a rooster by crowing. Some of the prisoners who had no shelter, and not wishing to lie down in the mud, conceived the plan of making what they called a sleeping-post. A number of them got close together, and after forming a centre-post, would get around it one against the other, and try to sleep. Fralich, after watching the proceedings for a short time, informed us that he would try that plan, too. He had hardly got his position when the centre gave way, and the sleepy fellows fell, a confused mass, into the mud. Fralich came back thoroughly disgusted, and said he preferred a log to sleep on to that kind of a sleeping-post. On the following night we again resumed our position on the log, but did not occupy it long, when Gilbert suggested that we lie down in the mud, and endeavor to sleep in that way. Our position on the log had become very tiresome, and we longed to have a place to lie down and rest. So lying down side by side, we soon, in spite of our miserable condition, fell asleep, and slept until late in the morning. After getting up, the impressions of our bodies were stamped on the ground several inches deep. We felt stiff and sore for a short time after getting up, but on the whole felt much refreshed after our long sleep. It also stopped raining, and the sun coming out very warm, our clothing became dry, and we felt more comfortable than we had been for some time. In the afternoon we had, however, a very severe thunder-storm and heavy rain, and again received a complete drenching, which compelled us again to sleep in clothing as wet as it could be. On the following day the weather was an exact repetition of that of the day previous, being clear and very hot until some time in the afternoon, when a severe rain and thunder storm passed over us, and left us in a condition to at least sleep cool during the night.

I had now been six days in Andersonville, and as it had been raining almost all the time since my arrival, I commenced to wonder if there was any prospect of it letting up, or if it rained all the time in that country. In conversation with some of the prisoners who had been inmates of the prison for some time before our arrival, I learned that it had been raining almost every day for two weeks before we came in. Most of the old prisoners preferred rain to sunshine, as it was so hot when it did not rain for a few days that the men who had no shelter almost perished of the heat.

The next day, June 22d, the sun shone brightly, and it was the most terribly hot season I ever experienced in my life. It really appeared as if we would have to suffocate with heat. I actually found myself wishing it would commence to rain again. We succeeded in getting a few short sticks, on which we put Gilbert's blanket, and in that way formed a screen to protect us a little. It did not, however, help much, as the sun was so terribly hot that it almost appeared as if it would burn the blanket. Directly after the middle of the day I became quite sick, but after sundown the weather became cooler, and I felt better again.

The hot sun had at least brought us some comfort, as it had dried up the mud, and we could, for the first time since our arrival in Andersonville, lie down to sleep without getting into it. The six following days the sun beat down on us with the same terrible intensity, and it really appeared sometimes as if it would sink us into the ground. The nights, however, were quite cool, and were a great relief to us, although the mosquitoes were a source of considerable annoyance, they being both numerous and large.

About this time a considerable number of new prisoners arrived, and we eagerly scanned every face and form as they entered, hoping and praying that none of our friends might be among the number. Under any other circumstances, or at any other place, we would have been glad to see them, but we could not but tremble at the thought of any of them coming to our miserable abode. Two hundred and fifty prisoners arrived from the Army of the Potomac on Friday, June 23d, who reported General Grant and his army at Petersburg, Virginia, and that the capture of Richmond was sure to take place in a short time. On the following day a small number arrived from Sherman's army, and reported him within twenty miles of Atlanta. This was glorious news, and created a strong hope within us that the cruel war would soon be over, and we be released from our terrible sufferings. Rumors of a parole or exchange were also being spread among us, and were the subject of considerable controversy. Some believed them to be true, and others contended that they were only rebel lies got up to deceive us.

These frequent reports about being exchanged, although, containing no truth, were, nevertheless, the means of doing some good, as it to some extent kept up the spirits of the men, and diverted their minds from the terrible scenes daily enacted before them. I have already referred to the fact that our prison-pen was infested with a gang of lawless roughs, and on the 28th of May I met with an adventure with them in going through the prison, which was the means of raising intense excitement among the prisoners; and as it differs somewhat from the remainder of my prison-life, and has been a subject of considerable controversy, I will devote the following chapter entirely to a fair, impartial statement of the affair.

CHAPTER X.

HANGING OF THE THIEVES.

PERHAPS one of the strangest chapters in the history of Andersonville is the one relating to the hanging of six of the inmates by their own comrades. It has been a subject of much comment, and persons who are not familiar with all the facts connected with the case would naturally look at it as a cruel and barbarous act, with no justification whatever. It would naturally be supposed that these men, who were suffering for the same cause, would be bound together by the strongest ties of sympathy. Among the better class of prisoners it would undoubtedly have been so; but we must not forget that, under all circumstances, where so many men are gathered together, we will find a great diversity of character, and of course Andersonville was no exception to the rule. There will be no doubt in any intelligent, unbiased mind, that by far the most of the men who served in the Union army were men who acted from purely patriotic motives; and in the ranks could be found some of the best citizens in the country. But it is also true, that quite a number went into the army more for the purpose of plunder than for any love they had for the conntry. This class of men came as a general thing from the large cities, and most of them were not native born.

When this class of men became prisoners of war, and were compelled to suffer for want of the necessaries of life, it was but natural that they would try to secure their own comfort, although it should be at the expense of their more patriotic and honest companions. To what extremes bad men will go to secure their own comfort was fully illustrated in the doings of a band of robbers in Andersonville, or "Mosby's Marauders," as the rest of the prisoners call them. The old adage, "birds of a feather will flock together," was fully verified in this case. To be more fully enabled to carry on their nefarious business, and protect themselves from punishment, the villains had congregated themselves, as much as they possibly could, together. Their rendezvous was near the southwest end of the prison. So bold and defiant did the gang become, that they soon got to be the terror of the entire prison, and actually at one time appeared to rule it. At least one poor fellow's death was traced to their hands; others were terribly beaten because they would not submit to their demands. But little did they dream of the terrible retribution they were bringing on their own heads—that the men who appeared to so tamely submit to their despotic sway would rise in their might and crush them. The prison was at this time in a horrible condition. It was before the grounds were enlarged, and we were literally crowded into the inclosure. The number of inmates was not less than fifteen thousand. Sickness was increasing at a fearful rate, the number of deaths averaging sixty per day. The poor prisoners, who were starving and lying on the ground exposed to the weather, were suffering in a terrible manner, and were in no mood to endure tyranny from those who should have been their friends. The prisoners organized a company of *Regulators* to enforce law and order. The leader was a man by the name of Key, from the State of Illinois.

He was a man of gigantic stature and immense strength, and was well fitted to command the determined men who had organized for the purpose of protecting the respectable inmates from the assaults of the low and vicious.

For some time the robbers appeared to have things all their own way; but a storm was brewing. Had they been wise they would have averted the consequences by stopping their miserable system of robbery and oppression. But very little, however, appeared to be accomplished towards suppressing the raiders, until at length an event occurred that in the end put a stop to their deviltry.

Robert H. Kellogg, Sergeant-major of the Sixteenth Regiment Connecticut Volunteers, who was in the prison at the time, and is the author of the interesting work called "Life and Death in Rebel Prisons," writes of that affair in the following words:

"These new-comers afforded the raiders, or camp robbers, fresh opportunities to continue their work. They seized upon one of these, and it soon proved to be a robbery in earnest. After severely beating and cutting his head, they took his watch and $175 in money. He entered a complaint to Captain Wirz, and the whole camp being completely aroused, collected around with clubs, and began to arrest the gang as fast as possible," etc.

I was the soldier the Sergeant refers to as being robbed and beaten by the raiders. Mr. Kellogg is correct in his statement, with the exception of the taking of the money. I had none at the time of the assault, so could not have been robbed of any. In justice to the Sergeant, I will say that I have carefully read his book, and the work is a faithful, reliable account of the terrible sufferings of the prisoners; and he deserves the thanks of every survivor of rebel prisons for the truthful manner in which he has shown their friends the terrible course of treatment the rebel authorities adopted, as they themselves acknowledged, for the purpose of reducing our armies.

Gilbert was the owner of a small silver watch. When searched by the rebel authorities at Richmond, after his capture, he somehow succeeded in hiding it, and was successful in getting it into Andersonville prison. As the pockets were torn out of his jacket, he requested me to carry it. It was a source of some comfort to us; but it was not destined to stay with us very long. In the afternoon I went to the brook to get a drink of water, when noticing that some rebel soldiers were drilling on the ground outside of the stockade, I went to the south end of the prison, where I could get a better view of them. Having been but a short time in the prison, I knew nothing about the locality where the raiders had their quarters, and so, unconsciously, got right in among them. I was looking at the rebel soldiers drilling, when I noticed a stranger who had come close to my left side, and was apparently looking at the same object. Directly after a second came to my rear, and another to my right side. The three coming so close, aroused my suspicions, and I was thinking about moving away from the place, when I felt a hand lift the watch from my pocket. Turning suddenly, I grasped the thief by the throat; I succeeded in getting a very good hold, and as he was quite a small man, I soon had the best of him. In the scuffle some one tripped me and I fell to the ground. I, however, kept my hold on his throat, and was giving him a severe choking when some one, to compel me to let go, commenced to give me a terrible beating, Being now thoroughly alarmed, I cried "Murder!" as loud as I could. Some one then, to stop my cries, commenced to choke me; and I have no doubt that they would soon have finished me, had my cries not been heard by the Regulators and my friends, who came to the rescue. The fellow whom I had taken by the throat was a New York ruffian by the name of Crowly. He was a small, villainous-looking, pock-marked fellow, and was no doubt one of the light-fingered gentry who are so numerous in that city. I had succeeded in giving him a severe punishment, the marks of my fingers being visible on his neck; and had the rest let me alone, I don't think he would have been in a very good condition to carry on his business for some time after.

At the first alarm, the robbers crowded around us, and in that way tried to cover their tracks by keeping the Regulators and prisoners not belonging to their gang back until it was over. Had they succeeded in knocking me insensible, they probably would have lied themselves out of the crime; for had I recovered, I could not have identified more than the one I had taken hold of, and he loudly proclaimed his innocence. The disturbance was heard by the rebels, and a sergeant, with several guards, came in to see what was the matter. Crowly then made the most pitiful plea to the rebels, even shedding tears, and charging me with making an attempt to kill him. I then told the rebel sergeant that Crowly had taken my watch, and that I was the aggrieved party. The rebels, no doubt expecting to make a watch by the operation, took Crowly and me outside of the prison. On the way going out, the miscreant again, in the most earnest way, protested his innocence, and loudly demanded to be searched. After we got outside the prison, the sergeant proceeded to search him, but no watch appeared. The sergeant, who was evidently disappointed in not finding one, then told me I should have been more careful before I made the assault, and that I must have been mistaken in my man. I told him I could not possibly be mistaken; that the man I had seized by the throat was the owner of the hand that took the watch out of my pocket, and that I did not expect him to have the watch at this stage of the proceedings. We were then sent back to the prison. On the way coming in, Crowly commenced to threaten me; but after we got in, he found he had trouble enough on hand without disturbing me any further. The most intense excitement existed in the prison among the prisoners. The Regulators, who had had their suspicions aroused for some time in regard to the character of the men who had gathered together on this spot, commenced a furious assault on them. Crowly and about fifty of his comrades were soon under arrest. Hid in the ground where the villains stayed, were found watches, money and different kinds of weapons; also the body of a man the miscreants had worked out of the way. The valuables were taken possession of by the rebels, who no doubt rejoiced at these proceedings, as it not only enriched themselves, but also weakened their enemies. During the next day, the hunt for the raiders was kept up. Quite a number were added to the arrested number. As fast as captured, they were turned over to the rebels, who were to keep them until we were ready to try them. A jury of twelve was taken from the new arrivals to try them, and after a fair, impartial trial, six of the ringleaders were found guilty of murder and robbery, and were sentenced to death. A large number of the rest were compelled to run a gauntlet of enraged men, who had formed two lines outside of the prison, and were prepared to give them blows as they passed through; most of them got off with a few blows, but several were terribly punished, and one was beaten to death.

On the 11th of July a gallows was built on the south side of the pen, and the six who had been sentenced to death were hung. As they were taken to the gallows, one of them broke loose from his guard, and made a vain attempt to get away; he was soon re-captured, and with the rest put on the platform. Meal-bags were finally put over their heads at the last moment, and then the drop fell; the rope around the neck of one of them broke, but he was again taken up, and in a few moments they were in the eternal world. The wretches at first seemed to be unable to understand that they would have to pay the penalty of death for their crimes, and I do not think that any of them believed that they would have to die until within a very short time before their execution. When, however, they found it was to be a terrible reality, their firmness commenced to give way, and the look of helpless despair on their countenances, as they looked on the mass of men around them, was sad to see. When asked if they had anything to say before being put to death, one of them requested a comrade to go to his friends in New York, and tell them of his sad fate; all of them requested their comrades to take warning by their death. A Catholic priest, who very frequently paid us a visit, begged hard that their lives might be spared; but finding he could not change the purpose of the men who were determined to carry out the sentence, he endeavored to get the doomed men to realize the awful position they were in. Let us hope that the prayers of this good man prevailed on them to look to Him who will finally judge us all, and who never judges unrighteously.

It was a sad sight to see six of our own men, who were fellow-prisoners, suffer death in such

HANGING OF SIX THIEVES BY THE REGULATORS IN ANDERSONVILLE PRISON.

an ignominious manner; but their crimes were great, and we felt that the punishment was just. Their crimes had been carried on with such total disregard of the rights of others, and so reckless of human life had they become, that there can be no doubt but that the sentence of death inflicted on them saved the lives of others, who were of more service to their country, and better members of society. The prisoners at Andersonville were of all classes of men; you would find there the most earnest Christian, as well as the most depraved villain. New arrivals were coming in almost every day, and we were compelled to have some system of law that would protect the respectable class of prisoners from the low and vicious. Of course, this very bad element was comparatively small; but a few determined bad characters can do a great deal of evil among a very large class of respectable people, and in this case we felt that severe measures alone would keep in subordination the bad element among us.

The same view was evidently taken by our captors, who sent an officer and a squad of soldiers to maintain order at the execution.

CHAPTER XI.

ENLARGEMENT OF OUR PRISON.

ON the first day of July the rebels completed the addition to our prison-pen, and a number of us were ordered to gather up our movables and go over into the new part of the inclosure. As the property of our trio did not consist of more than one blanket and a few short sticks of wood, it did not take us very long to get ready. About ten feet of the stockade standing between the two sections of the prison had been removed for the purpose of letting us through; and as we all felt anxious to get on the ground first, so as to get the most desirable places to camp on, there was quite a stampede to the new portion.

Captain Wirz, who, I suppose, wanted a little amusement, issued an order that all of the prisoners who had been ordered to move, and who would not be through this small opening in two hours, should have their blankets, and whatever property they might possess, confiscated. In a short time the old part of the prison was thinned out, and made more comfortable in regard to room than it had been for some time. We succeeded in getting possession of a good dry spot in the northeast corner of the prison, and marking four by six feet of ground, we squatted on it, and bravely held the fort until the rest of the prisoners had located their ground and settled down.

Some of the soil close to us was composed of brick clay, and we found that by mixing it up with water, and letting it dry, it would get almost as hard as a stone. To make our title stronger, we gathered a lot of this clay, and built a wall about six inches high around our lot. After being in possession of our new quarters for a few days, we gathered more clay, and, at first only for amusement and pastime, commenced to build our wall higher and stronger. We then discovered that when exposed to the sun for several days it would become very hard, and we commenced to think that we might secure some kind of a shelter by raising the wall higher and arching it part way in. We built the two sides and one gable end of our house about three and one-half feet high, and taking Gilbert's blanket for a roof, we had a pretty good protection against the heavy dews so prevalent after night in that part of the country.

We found before our removal from Andersonville that even in the very warmest weather the nights were sometimes quite disagreeable, and the dew so heavy as to give us a thorough wetting. When it rained hard our roof did not amount to much; nevertheless, we were in a more comfortable condition, and felt considerably richer than when in the old part of the prison. The reader may, perhaps, think that this was a small matter, but to us it was one of the greatest importance, and we prized our mud-house very highly; more so, no doubt, than some men do their brown-stone fronts. It is said, "necessity is the mother of invention," and our prison life fully demonstrated that to be a fact. Some of the mud-houses and stoves were quite a novelty, and required considerable skill in constructing them.

Among the inmates of the prison were quite a number of men who were members of churches at home. These men were desirous of forming some system of holding religious meetings, but the terribly crowded condition of the prison had prevented much action being taken in the matter. A few would sometimes get together and have a prayer-meeting, but it was only after the enlargement of the stockade that much attention was paid to this important movement. A prisoner by the name of Shepard, a native of Ohio, and a member of the Ninety-seventh regiment of the Ohio Volunteers, who had been a minister at home, and Boston Corbett, a native of New Jersey, and whose name become so famous after the close of the war on account of his shooting John Wilkes Booth, the assassin of the lamented President Lincoln, were recognized as leaders in these religious movements. They preached to us frequently, and their preaching was no doubt the means of accomplishing much good. They were, indeed, nature's truest noblemen, perfect gentlemen, and earnest true Christians. They devoted almost all their time to giving spiritual consolation and advice to their fellow-prisoners. They appeared never to weary of doing good, and could frequently be found at the side of the dying, and entreating them to look to Him who would deliver them from all their misery and suffering, and receive them to a better and brighter world above. These poor, dying soldiers, away from loved ones at home, separated from all their comforts, tormented with vermin, dying from exposure, hunger and thirst, these martyrs to "man's inhumanity," had nowhere to look for deliverance but to Him who had created them, and without whose notice no sparrow shall fall to the ground. How sweet and welcome the words of these holy men of God when they proclaimed to them the words of our Saviour, "But even the very hairs of your head are numbered. Fear not, therefore. Ye are of more value than many sparrows." And again, "Be not afraid of them that kill the body, and after that have no more that they can do." Yes; the enemies of these poor dying men might torture them to death, but when the breath had left their poor emaciated bodies, they could do no more.

It is said that "man's extremity is God's opportunity," and it was surely so with these poor dying ones. Cut off from all earthly hope, they received the word eagerly and gladly, and who can doubt that the Recording Angel carried the glad tidings "*Saved*" from this terrible spot when the spirits of these poor soldiers passed away.

The leaders of the "*Praying Band*," that being the name these men were known by in prison, succeeded in getting possession of a spot of ground in the new part of the prison for the purpose of holding religious meetings, and on this spot for some time every evening these men came together and worshiped God. The meetings were well attended, and accomplished much good. What a contrast between these meetings and the ones our friends enjoyed at home! No ringing of bells announced to us the solemn hour that called the people of God together to raise their hearts and voices in praise and thanksgiving unto Him for His mercies. No happy family groups of fathers, mothers, and children, stepping along with light hearts to large, commodious buildings dedicated to God's service, and where were comfortable seats and eloquent sermons, and where swelling anthems, lifting the soul upward from earth, came flowing through these sanctuaries. None of these blessings were enjoyed by the men who gathered together in this terrible place to thank God for His past mercy, implore His protection in the future, and beg His forgiveness for past shortcomings. These men enjoyed these blessings in their happy homes before they entered the service of their country. But how changed their circumstances now! When they gathered together to worship their Maker, they came covered with rags, mud, and vermin, and some of them had suffered from disease and starvation, until they presented an appearance so wretched that their best friends would not have recognized them.

When they reached the spot of ground set apart for worship, instead of seating themselves in good comfortable pews, they sat close together on the ground, and quietly waited for the meeting to commence. After a sufficient number had gathered together, some one opened with prayer, and then one of the leaders preached a short sermon or exhortation, which was again followed by prayer and singing. An invitation was also given to those who desired to be prayed for to come forward into the circle and kneel in a row on the ground. Sometimes five or six penitents would be found at one time in that position, imploring God's mercy. It was a strange, solemn sight to see these men kneel side by side on the ground enjoying this great privilege in so terrible a place; but they felt the need of Divine assistance even more in their deplorable condition than they would have felt it if surrounded by the comforts of home, and God would hear their humble petitions here as well as anywhere else.

One Sabbath evening, Elder Shepard preached a sermon from the sixth verse, fiftieth chapter of Isaiah: "I gave my back to the smiters, and my cheeks to them that plucked off the hair. I hid not my face from shame and spitting." The subject was handled in an able manner, disclosing the fact that our comrade was not only a good and pious man, but one who was fully competent to expound to us the teaching of the Holy Bible.

On one occasion, when we had received no rations at all during the day, and it appeared as if we would all have to die of starvation, Elder Shepard prayed most earnestly in the evening that God would not forsake us altogether, and that we would again receive our humble rations in the morning. On the following day we again received our rations, and they were a trifle better than we had received for some time. Whether it was the result of the prayer of our comrade or not, I do not know; but it was accepted as such by a considerable number of the prisoners, and as

> "More things are wrought by prayer
> Than this world dreams of,"

it may have had something to do with it. Some of the prisoners, who perhaps depended more on the efficiency of the prayers of their more pious comrades than on their own, said, rather irreverently, that they thought Shepard might pray more earnestly that God would release us altogether from our dungeon.

I am sorry to be compelled to relate that amidst all the suffering, misery, and death surrounding us, there were a few among us who could so far forget the common demands of decency, as to annoy and disturb these religious meetings; but, as already mentioned in the preceding chapter, our prison-pen contained the most vicious characters to be found anywhere, as well as some of the best. The reader will, no doubt, suppose that where disease and death held such high carnival, at least no attempt would be made to disturb those who were making an effort to prepare for the summons that will finally call us all to "that bourne from whence no traveler returns." But such was the case, and as I intend to give a description of our prison life as it really was, I am compelled to state this fact. It gives me pleasure, however, to be enabled to say that this very bad element was comparatively small, and these disturbances did not last long.

McKey, the leader of the gang of Regulators, hearing of this state of affairs, issued an order that any one found disturbing a religious meeting would be punished by a number of lashes on the bare back, which effectually put an end to that kind of business for the future. Whipping on the bare back was the mode of punishment generally inflicted by the Regulators. It was about this time that I saw my old enemy, Crowley, taken to the place of punishment and receive ten strokes well laid on for stealing a fellow-prisoner's tin-cup. I always did think he got off too easy when he stole our watch, and I am afraid I was uncharitable enough to wish the number of lashes twenty instead of only ten.

It was a strange fact that, situated as our prison was, in a State where several prominent Protestant churches were very strong, no minister (with the exception of one, who was a chaplain in the rebel army) ever entered the prison to administer spiritual consolation to the many who belonged to their own churches. The rebel chaplain referred to came in on one occasion, and read an extract from some Northern paper in regard to an exchange of prisoners, and then held a short religious service. This was the only time during my stay in Andersonville that a Protestant minister from the outside came into the prison. A priest belonging to the Catholic church was almost daily among us, and worked faithfully among the sick and dying members of his own church. He had also always a kind word for all of us. We sometimes tried to find out through him what the prospects of being exchanged were, but he told us that he was on his word and honor not to disclose anything to us that was going on outside of our prison

Capt. Wirz, commanding the prison, was a member of the Catholic church, and it was said that he would allow none but Catholic priests to enter the prison for the purpose of administering spiritual consolation to the dying. I do not know if this was the case or not; but, if true, it was only in accord with his general principles. He really appeared to delight in inflicting pain and disappointment on us, and it seems hard to believe that any one could have so fiendish a hate toward human beings as he had toward the helpless captives who were in his power.

The night after entering the new part of the prison, some of the prisoners carried away part of the old stockade left standing between the old and new ground, for fuel. Wirz immediately issued an order that if the timber was not returned, he would punish the whole of us by stopping our rations altogether. We received most of our food at this time in a raw condition, and, although wood was so plenty on the outside as to be almost valueless, we could hardly get enough of it to cook our scanty food. Our rations consisted at this time principally of corn meal, of which we got a cup—holding a little more than a pint—full per day, and a small piece of beef or pork, often covered with vermin. Sometimes we received rice instead of cornmeal, and for quite a time, beans were the principal diet. These we generally got in a cooked, or at least half-cooked, condition and filthy beyond description. This bean, or pea, as it was called by the rebels, is grown in the South for cattle; and I suppose, when purchased by the rebel government for the purpose of feeding their captives, was stored up in old barns and sheds, and left to become so unclean and filthy that it was not fit for human beings to use; but I suppose they thought it good enough for the "d——d Yankees," as they called us. Some of the men found the excrement of fowls in their soup; and as that was a little more than even starving men would want to eat, careful investigation of that kind of food became the order of the day. Under any other circumstances it might have been amusing to see the boys carefully, with stick in hand, examining the soup to find things indigestible; but when the finding involved the loss of the most of that day's rations, it was no laughing matter, at least not to the unhappy finder. The finding of sand, feathers, pods, and even small things which looked suspiciously like as if rats and mice had gamboled over these beans for a month or two, was not uncommon. This was too insignificant to compel the most fastidious of us to do without our daily food; but the finding of the first-named article was too much even for men in our hungry condition. Salt must have been a very scarce article in the South, or they did not care about giving us any of it, as sometimes we received none with our food for several days. Sorghum molasses was given in place of meat for a considerable time. This stuff was of the very poorest quality, and almost always sour or in a damaged condition. What article of food the rebels could have selected that would have been a poorer substitute for meat, would be hard to find out. As an article of food to men in our condition it was almost entirely worthless, and in fact it was to the men who were sick with the various bowel comlaints, a positive injury.

We came to the conclusion that a little "lasses" might be good, but when it was substituted for substantials, it became a positive nuisance. Some of the prisoners declared the rebels had given it for the purpose of killing us, and it was the only article of diet of which they ever complained of receiving too much.

On Monday was the glorious 4th of July, but we had a poor opportunity to celebrate our country's natal day. About noon we had a severe thunder-storm and rain, which continued until evening. To add to our misery, we did not receive any rations that day, Wirz evidently being determined to make us as miserable and unhappy as he possibly could on this particular occasion.

We could not help wondering why it was that we appeared to be so forgotten by the Government we had enlisted to save, and that it could be so indifferent to our fate. We tried, however, to comfort ourselves with the hope that perhaps very little of the true state of affairs was known in the North, and consequently it was not because of neglect on the part of the Government that we had to suffer so long. The rebels endeavored to make us believe that this was so, but we did not pay much attention to what they said. Hungry, wet, and miserable as we were, yet we had not lost all feelings of patriotism; and when in the morning we heard the rumor that Richmond had fallen and Sherman's army was whipping the rebels at Atlanta, we rejoiced heartily. In regard to the capture of Richmond, we soon found that it was not true, as a large number of prisoners arriving a few days later from the Army of the Potomac, informed us that Grant was not in possession of the rebel capital, but that he had gained some decided advantages over Lee, and that the capture of the city was only a matter of time. Some prisoners also arrived from Sherman's army, who reported him within three miles of the city and severe fighting going on; so with all our suffering we were still enabled to rejoice at the continued success of our armies, and entertain the hope that the Rebellion would soon be crushed out.

About this time we could also see that something of great importance was going on on the outside of our prison. We observed a great commotion among our enemies, and we were somewhat excited with the hope that perhaps our men were advancing on our prison, and our day of deliverance was not far off. A large number of men were busily employed in throwing up intrenchments and building forts, not even stopping their work on Sunday. A number more were employed in cutting down trees, no doubt for the purpose of sweeping the country with the fire from the artillery on the forts. Everything indicated that the rebels were in a great state of alarm, and that they apprehended an attack on them for the purpose of releasing us. We felt sure they could not be making all this preparation merely for the purpose of guarding against an attempt to break out by their captives. The manner in which the intrenchments were built indicated that they were intended to resist foes from the outside, and the cutting away of the trees in the direction of the station, that they expected to turn their cannon on armed enemies instead of helpless prisoners. Several rebels came into the prison to try to induce us to go out and work on the fortifications. They promised us good shelter and plenty of food if we would do so; but almost all of the prisoners indignantly rejected all their offers to tempt them to betray the country they had sworn to defend. This act of the rebels was, however, the means of creating a great deal of controversy among us; some contending that it would not be wrong to go and work for them, but the most of us stoutly maintained that no true Union soldier could think of doing anything of the kind, and that he could not do so without committing perjury and being guilty of treason.

Perhaps no one among the prisoners opposed this movement more earnestly, or exerted a greater influence for good in persuading men not to forget themselves so far as to assist our enemies, than comrade John E. Gilbert. He argued, begged, and, if necessary, fought with those who were in favor of going out to work. "What!" he would say, "go out and help to build forts to enable the rebels to kill the men who may be sent here to release us! Before I would throw one shovelful of dirt for a purpose so low and mean, I would die a dozen times." Those of his comrades who know "Shorty," as we called him in the army, will have no trouble in believing him perfectly sincere in what he then so stoutly maintained.

As already stated, the rebels tried hard to create the impression on our minds that our Government did not care for us; but we soon came to the conclusion that they did this not from any sympathy they had for us, but from hatred to the Government we loved, and for the purpose of getting us to assist them. A few, however, whose love for the Union was but slight, and some perhaps who had better never entered the army, accepted the rebel offer, and were taken out and put to work on the intrenchments and forts from which the rebels expected to slay our soldiers, should an attempt be made to recapture us. Some of the new prisoners coming in informed us that a cavalry expedition had really been fitted out, and was then on its way to attempt our recapture. The news created a great deal of joy throughout the prison, but we felt highly indignant at the base conduct of the few of our comrades who were working on the forts, and we could not help wonder how they would feel if our men were to come and find them engaged in such work.

About this time the number of prisoners arriving was very great, some coming in almost every day. On the 9th and 10th about three hundred arrived from the Army of the Potomac; and although the number of deaths was fearful, the influx was so great that the prospect was that the prison would soon be as crowded as it was before the enlargement of the stockade. The arrival of so many prisoners, and the necessity of having the gates open so often, convinced the brave captain that it would be necessary to intimidate us a little by making a great military display of his forces, and showing how soon he could annihilate us, should we attempt to escape. We were suddenly startled, and somewhat alarmed, by seeing several of the guns from the forts which pointed on our prison flash fire, and apparently pour their contents into our prison. Our first impression was that the rebels had opened fire on us, and we looked anxiously around to see the effects of it; but we soon discovered that the guns were loaded with blank cartridges, and no harm was done beyond giving us a good scare. Immediately after the discharge of the cannon, a great commotion was visible in the rebel camp. The infantry fell into line in double-quick, and all the artillery was manned, with its frowning guns trained on the inmates of the prison. It appeared as if certain death was to be the fate of us all; but after they had succeeded in giving us what I suppose they considered a great fright, they marched back to their quarters, no doubt fully satisfied in their minds that we would not again, after witnessing so terrible a demonstration, think of escape.

In the early history of the prison, the men, finding that the water of the small stream which flowed through the prison was very warm, and made very impure by the rebels building their cook-house over it, commenced to dig for water close to the stream. Much better water could be obtained in this way, by digging a few feet in the ground; but the unfortunate situation of these springs or wells was such that they soon became in a terrible condition. The prisoners, in obeying the calls of nature, were compelled to go to the swamp bordering on the stream, and the frequent rains washed much of the filth from the sides of the prison on the swamp, where it lodged. This part of the prison became so terribly filthy that it is impossible to give a perfect description of it. The rains, carrying down the sewage of the prison-pen on the filth-covered swamp, made it a mass of putrefaction where the hot sun, beating upon it, soon bred into life millions of loathsome maggots, which spread themselves all over this part of the prison. These tumbled in countless numbers into the new-made springs, making it, with the filth that washed into them, as impure as the horrid stream itself. The lower part of the stream especially received almost all the time a drainage of this hideous spume from the swamp.

The prisoners, who were seeking for water to quench their thirst, would crowd to the upper side of the prison, and as close to the dead-line as possible, so as to get the water a little more palatable. On one occasion I went to this place for water, when, finding a crowd at the upper end of the stream, which had gathered for the same purpose, I kept back for a few moments to let it thin out, when my attention was drawn to the nearest guard, who, with rifle in hand, was watching the men getting water. His countenance displayed about as much eagerness and expectation as that of the hunter when he discovers his game, and expects to have a good shot. I was watching the demon, and wondering whether it was really possible that he contemplated firing at the men who had gathered there for no other purpose than to get water, when I was horrified to see him deliberately raise his gun and fire into the crowd. I turned in the direction of the crowd, and screamed, "Look out!" but too late, as the ball had sped on its deadly mission, and the soul of one more poor unfortunate had left its earthly abode, and one more murder was added to the already long list in Andersonville.

One of the prisoners, in his eagerness to get clean water, had dipped through under the dead line, when the guard, who had been watching and waiting for just such a chance to give him some kind of an excuse for his inhumanity, and an opportunity to display his bravery and chivalry, fired at him. The ball missed the mark it was intended for, but unfortunately hit one of the others who was in the act of stooping for water in the rear of the one shot at. The ball passed through his head, and the poor unfortunate soldier fell dead alongside of the stream. After the cruel shot was fired, the comrades of the dead prisoner fled, leaving his dead body lying where he fell. Almost riveted to the spot with horror and indignation, I could not run, but, turning around, I took a long look at the monster who could murder a fellow-being for so slight an offense, if an offense it could be called at all. He

PRISONER SHOT FOR DIPPING WATER TOO NEAR THE DEAD LINE

coolly proceeded to load his gun, turning himself, however, so that he could not see the dead body of his victim. A few prisoners gathered around me, and we commenced to express indignation at the cowardly act. One prisoner exclaimed, "I want just one good look at him, and then one chance to meet him in this world, and I think I will know him if ever I do meet him."

After the guard had finished loading his gun, he noticed that we were watching him and expressing indignation; he raised his gun to his shoulder, and yelled out, "Scatter thar, or I will blow some more of you over." I do not think I ever in all my life felt quite as I did when I walked from that spot. I felt as if I would have to cry out, "My God, how long must we endure this?" I really believe that I would have been willing to give my life for one chance at him.

A few of the friends of the dead soldier had gathered around his body, and I went up to see if he was really dead. Some of them were shedding tears, and all expressing the deepest horror at his sad taking off. His blood had formed a small rivulet that flowed into the foul stream, which of itself had been a terrible rebel executioner to a large number of our brave soldiers. We had become accustomed to seeing the sight of death in all of its horrible aspects; we saw men dying almost every hour: but this terrible death moved me more than anything I had yet witnessed. It appeared to me so sad that he had to suffer death for trying to get a drink of water. "Vengeance is mine; I will repay,' saith the Lord." And who can doubt that the blood of the thousands of slain soldiers who were murdered in Southern prisons, has cried aloud to high Heaven —not unheard, but God has or will yet inflict punishment on these murderous oppressors.

It was said, and never denied by the rebels, that a guard on post who shot a prisoner when trying to escape, or in the act of crossing the dead-line, got a thirty-day furlough as his reward. As the miscreant did not again appear on post, I suppose he was thus rewarded for his courageous act. It was a rule of the prison that no prisoners were allowed to cross the dead-line; but in the case of this poor soldier it could not have been taken for any violation of this order, as the prisoner had made no attempt to escape or cross it.

It is but fair to state that not all of our guards were that kind of characters. Almost all of them were either boys or old men, who were unfit to be sent to the front. In justice to the old men, I will say that all the shooting was done by the boys, and at least a few of those old men denounced the shooting as an outrage. I remember hearing one who was on guard, and was speaking to some prisoners on the inside, say that "God would not prosper a nation or people who used human beings as we were being treated."

After the water became so impure in the streams and springs along the swamp that we could not use it, or only when positively compelled to, some of the prisoners commenced to dig wells on the high ground farther from the stream. Some of these wells were dug quite deep, and when completed contained good water. The nature of the ground was of such a description, however, that they sometimes caved in almost as soon as finished; and even when they did not, the getting up of the water was a very difficult matter.

Directly after moving into the new part of the prison, a few of us concluded to dig one in our part, but the difficulty in getting tools prevented us for some time from commencing it. We at last succeeded in getting a spade, an old rope, and a common wooden water-pail, and with these implements commenced operations. The ground, with the exception of a few feet of soft soapstone, was of a soft, loose, sandy nature, and we made considerable progress in sinking it. As the rope was old and unsafe, only small men could be let down to dig. We had succeeded in digging about forty feet when we came to water, but of so small a quantity that it did not amount to much; so we dug down about six feet more, when we struck a good stream of water. I was in the well digging about the time it was finished, and I noticed that at the place where we first found water, small quantities of sand would be continually working out of the wall or side of the well, and fall to the bottom. It soon made quite an opening, and commenced to look dangerous. We, however, finished it, and congratulated ourselves that we would have at least good, pure water. Great was our disappointment, however, when we looked down the well a few days after, and discovered that it had caved in in such a manner as to make it useless for us to think of working at it any longer. During the digging the rope broke, and let one of the boys fall about twelve or fifteen feet, but he was not hurt much. Several of these wells were used by the prisoners as a screen to cover their attempts to tunnel out. Under the pretence of digging a well for water, they dug into the earth for a considerable distance; and then, abandoning it, would start a few feet from the top, and commence tunneling for freedom. This work had to be done entirely after night, as the rebels were always on the watch; and even among us there were a few who, for a paltry amount of victuals or tobacco, were willing to betray their comrades.

Just before my arrival in prison, the prisoners had made a most determined effort to tunnel and undermine the stockade. The plan was to weaken the stockade by tunneling under at five or six places, and then make a rush against it and push it over. They then intended to charge the rebel batteries, and try to capture them and turn the cannon on the rebels. The plan was well arranged, and as a large number of the most desperate men had organized and sworn to break out and get their freedom or die in the attempt, it might have been successful, at least so far as the overthrowing of the stockade was concerned, had not a traitor disclosed the plot to the enemy, who came in and had the tunnels shut up, and took the most vigorous measures to prevent an outbreak. The miserable traitor was taken out of the prison, and no doubt received a reward for his treachery.

As already mentioned, the stockade had been undermined in five or six places, and the determined men who had accomplished the work had high hopes that the attempt to escape would be a success. When they found themselves betrayed by one who had assisted in the work, and whom they had not suspected of being capable of such meanness, their indignation was very great, and it was no doubt well for the miscreant that his stay in the prison came to an abrupt determination, for his betrayed and outraged comrades would have torn him to pieces. It is not probable, however, even had the effort to overthrow the stockade been successful, that any considerable number of the prisoners would have succeeded in getting to the Union lines; and there can be no doubt that most of them would have been recaptured or killed. The rebel guard was very strongly reinforced, and the stockade strengthened, and everything indicated that the prisoners had at least succeeded in giving the rebels a good scare.

Tunneling was frequently attempted after this failure, but only in one or two instances did any succeed in getting away, and then almost all were killed or recaptured. The rebels kept a pack of bloodhounds, and as soon as the discovery was made that any of the prisoners had escaped, these hounds were put on their track, and fortunate indeed were the poor fugitives if they escaped death. We could hear the yelping of these furious dogs as they were unchained and sent in pursuit of our comrades, and our sympathy was aroused to its utmost extent for the unfortunate objects of their pursuit. At one time three prisoners succeeded in somehow getting away from the guard who accompanied them to the dead-house, and in a short time the yelping of the dogs announced to us that they were being pursued. A few days after this occurred one of the guards informed us that they had met with a terrible death at the hands of their pursuers. The guard stated that the prisoners, finding themselves pursued, and that they would surely be overtaken, climbed on trees to escape the attack of the dogs. The rebels, who were on horseback, and but a short distance in the rear of the dogs, soon came up, and ordered the men to come down. As soon as they reached the ground these chivalrous sons of the South put the dogs on them, who tore them to pieces. This is the story as given by one of their own men, whether truly or not I do not know; but as the escaped prisoners were not returned to the prison, it was no doubt true. The guard who gave us the information declared it was an outrage, and denounced it in the most bitter terms.

On the 22d of July a report reached us that Gen. Grant was killed in front of Petersburg. It created quite a sensation throughout the prison, and much anxiety in regard to the truth of the report. The arrival of a number of prisoners from the Army of the Potomac a few days later dispelled the fear, as they declared the report to be untrue.

We almost always had some excitement to divert our minds from the terrible transactions going on around us. On the following day I went to the far end of the prison to see a friend, and on coming back I found the prisoners in our part of the prison in a great state of excitement. Some of the men had about finished a tunnel, and expected to pass in a short time through it to freedom; but the rebels discovered it, and had come into the prison for the purpose of shutting it up. The rebels intimated very plainly that they had received the information of its existence from one of our own men, and it created a terrible excitement and anxiety to find out who was the culprit. Suspicion at last rested on an Irishman known among us as "Big Tom." He was a man of immense stature, and was as good, honest, and warm-hearted a son of Erin as could be found anywhere. For some unaccountable reason, a few of the prisoners suspected him of disclosing the tunnel to the rebels, and in a short time he was in the hands of a crowd of infuriated men, who charged him with the crime. He earnestly denied the charge; but the maddened men would not listen to him or give him a chance to defend himself. A considerable number of those who believed Tom innocent, gathered together and made an effort to get him out of the hands of the mob. After considerable trouble we succeeded in doing this, but not until the poor fellow was in a sad plight. His hair was cut off on one side of his head, and he had received a terrible beating. One of the enraged men had struck him over his left eye with a stick of wood, inflicting a severe wound. During the terrible trial he passed through, and when his life was in the most imminent danger, the brave Irishman kept as cool and collected as possible for any one to be under such circumstances; and although protesting his innocence in the most earnest manner, he did not betray any indications of fear.

After we succeeded in getting him away from

his tormentors, he requested me to dress the wound on his face and clip the balance of his hair, "so as to look more respectable," as he expressed it. I cut off his hair and fixed up his wound as best I could; and during the remainder of my prison life I do not think I had a better or warmer friend than "Big Tom." I could not help noticing that he enjoyed my company perhaps a little better than he did that of any one else in the prison; and when on one occasion he said to me, "Urban, I hope the day may come when I can do you a favor," I felt that the wish came from the warm-hearted man's heart, and should I ever need a friend, with Tom in call, he would not be found wanting.

In a few hours after we had got Tom out of the hands of the mob, the excitement was renewed in the central part of the prison; and on going there I found that the prisoners, who had kept on hunting for the guilty party, had arrested another man on suspicion of disclosing the tunnel to the enemy. This time, however, they succeeded in getting the right one. His base conduct was found out from the fact that he had a considerable quantity of food and tobacco; and on being questioned in regard to where he received it, he could give no satisfactory answer, and his fear disclosed the fact that he was the guilty party. His demeanor was just the opposite of that of the one who was first arrested.

His face was as pale as death, and his limbs shook with terror, as he confessed that he was guilty of the deed, and he begged most piteously that his life might be spared. His captors had succeeded in getting possession of an old well-rope, by which they intended to hang him in one of the wells; and they would have succeeded in accomplishing their object, had not Wirz found out the state of affairs, and sent in a squad of men to rescue him. He was taken outside, but did not fare as well as the traitor who had disclosed the first tunnel. Instead of protecting him, and keeping him out of the prison, as they in honor were bound to do, Capt. Wirz had him sent back into prison again. He issued an order, however, before doing so, that he would stop our rations if we killed the traitor.

The poor miserable wretch, almost dead with fright, was sent back to us again, where he knew that almost every one's hand would be turned against him. He no doubt bitterly regretted serving masters who so illy repaid him. He did not live long after being sent back by the rebels. He was abused by some and shunned by all, and in a short time his body was carried to the

DEAD HOUSE.

This place was only a short distance from the prison, and was constructed of pine limbs and brush, which formed a kind of a cover or screen to keep off the sun. To this horrid spot more than thirteen thousand dead prisoners of war were carried during the history of this one Southern prison. After the death of the prisoner, his comrades would write his name, company, and regiment on a piece of paper, and then pin it on his clothing. If his name was not known, as was sometimes the case, the single word "Unknown" was written on the paper. They were then carried to the Dead House, and laid side by side on the ground. Sometimes more than one hundred bodies would be lying in a row at one time, awaiting burial.

When the prison was first established, the rebels furnished plain pine coffins for the dead; but that was soon abandoned, and they commenced burying in long trenches, in which the bodies of the men were laid side by side, covering them with earth. They then drove a stake into the ground at the head of each body, and numbered it. A record of the dead was kept by a Union soldier, who had been paroled for that purpose. His duty was to enter the name, company, and regiment, of the dead soldier, in a book called the "dead-list." These names were all numbered, and corresponded with the numbers on the stakes in the cemetery. The soldier thus employed kept a secret list of the dead, and after the close of the war he gave it to the Government. This enabled the Government to take up all the dead and re-bury them with coffins, and furnish tomb-stones with the respective names, companies, and regiments, on them. The cemetery is located one mile from the prison, on high dry ground, surrounded with pine trees, making it a pleasant place, and well adapted for a burying-ground.

A considerable number of men were employed to remove the corpses from the Dead House to the cemetery, and bury them. It was said these men received large quantities of whisky to enable them to do this horrid work—and horrid it was in the extreme, for some of the bodies had become so decomposed as to almost fall to pieces when taken from the Dead House. It may perhaps seem incredible to the reader, but it is nevertheless a fact, that it was considered quite a privilege among the prisoners inside of the stockade to carry out the dead, and some of the men even quarreled for the privilege. The principal reason was the hope that they might be allowed to get some wood on the way back, which was very scarce and valuable with us. It was also pleasant to get out into the woods, and away from our horrible abode, even if it was only for a few moments. A few also succeeded in making their escape while engaged in this work; and no doubt the hope that some such opportunity might recur was a strong inducement with the men who helped in this horrible work.

One of the prisoners managed to escape by

playing a clever trick on the rebels, which was accomplished in this manner: He feigned death, and then had several of his comrades to carry him to the Dead House, and place him in line with the dead. In the morning the burying party found his place vacant. He had no doubt struck a "bee-line" for the Union lines, and I hope the clever fellow succeeded in finding them. The rebels after this kept a watch over the dead, for the purpose of preventing any more such "Yankee tricks." It was, however, but a short time after this that at least one tried the same game; but he was not so successful. His comrades, who were in the secret, carried him to the gate, expecting to pass the guards and deposit him in the Dead House. With his name, company, and regiment pinned on his clothing, and his hands crossed over his breast, he looked indeed as if he were dead; and they no doubt would have been successful in passing through the gate with the pretended corpse, had not an accident occurred that revealed the true state of affairs to the guards. The gate was thrown open, and the stretcher-bearers proceeded to pass through, when unfortunately the pretended dead man let one of his arms fall to his side in such a limp manner as to arouse the suspicions of the rebels, who ordered the men to stop, and then proceeded to examine their load. When they found that he was alive they laughed heartily, and declared that nothing was equal to the "d——d Yankees." They did not, however, punish him, but sent him back to his fellows again. I suppose it is not necessary to state that he was not carried back. His comrades were too much disgusted with him for making the awkward mistake to do anything of that kind.

From the 20th of July to the last of the month, the arrival of prisoners was very great. A considerable number arrived from the Army of the Potomac on the 23d, and over two thousand from Sherman's army came in on the 28th and 29th of the month. About five hundred came in on the 27th, who were captured on the Monocacy creek in Maryland, which proved conclusively that the rebels had again invaded the North. This last lot of prisoners were ninety-day men, and were just fresh from home, and presented an appearance so healthy and fresh as to form a strong contrast between them and the old prisoners. They had been left in possession of their blankets and knapsacks, and as we watched them coming in I remarked to a companion that I considered them the best-looking men I had ever seen. "Yes," he replied, "they should be able to stand it for awhile." A few weeks, however, demonstrated the fact that they could not endure as much as the old soldiers, and the mortality soon became very great among them. Some of them died in less than two weeks after their arrival.

It was the same with the men who belonged to the heavy artillery regiments in the Army of the Potomac. These men had been stationed in the forts in and around Washington, and knew comparatively nothing of the hardships of a soldier's life. When Grant received the command of the armies he had these soldiers armed with rifles, organized into infantry régiments, and sent to the front. The name "heavy artillery" clung to them, it being the name they were known by in the army. A considerable number of them were captured in the campaign from the Rapidan to the James river, and of those sent to Andersonville almost all died. The mortality among them in a short time after their arrival was terrible in the extreme. Close to our quarters twelve of them, belonging to one regiment, quartered. They dug a hole in the ground about eighteen inches deep, and banked up the loose earth to keep the water from flowing into it. They had been left in possession of a few blankets, and with these they formed a roof. After it was finished it looked comfortable compared to some of the lodging places which the other boys had, but it was undoubtedly a mistake in them to dig in the ground as they did. Death soon came among them, and one by one they fell victims to the fell destroyer, until only one remained of the twelve stout, hearty men, who less than three months before had entered the prison; and he was so sick when we were removed to Millen prison that he could not go along. Thinking we were going home, he made frantic efforts to get up and accompany us, but all in vain; he was too far gone, and I have no doubt he too very soon after fell a victim to rebel brutality.

The name of this poor unfortunate, I think, was William Langdon, and he was from the interior of New York State. He had been in the army but a few short months when he was captured and taken to Andersonville. In conversation with him one day, he informed me that he had received a letter from home a few days before his capture, informing him that he was the father of twin daughters; and he often talked about them, and told us how anxious he was to get home to see them. When we left he wept and begged piteously to be taken along, but we were obliged to leave him.

The arrival of so many prisoners made us feel somewhat anxious in regard to the Union cause, especially when we knew that some were captured so far North. The most of them, however, gave us a cheerful account of the situation, and declared the Southern Confederacy almost played out. They also assured us that if the number of prisoners arriving was large, the number of rebel soldiers being sent North was larger. As the prisoners who were captured in Maryland came into the prison, we crowded toward the gate for the purpose of getting a talk with them, when the rebels, who, I suppose, thought we intended making an attempt to escape, fired a cannon-ball directly over our heads. We at first believed that they intended to open fire on the prison, and some of the prisoners threw themselves in terror on the ground; but from the throats of thousands of the doomed men inside of the prison arose such a howl of derision and defiance as was perhaps never before heard on the face of the earth. No tongue can express, nor pen describe, the intensity of that cry. It appeared as if on the instant that the cannon flashed fire, every mind was moved with the same impulse, and the thunder of human voices all came as from one great mighty throat. I have heard the mighty shouts of thousands of men when charging on each other in mortal combat; I have heard the cheering of legions of men flushed with joy at the announcement of a great victory, or when some famous commander rode along the line; but I have never heard a cry or cheer to compare with the one that sprang simultaneously from the throats of the doomed men at Andersonville prison. One poor fellow, who was almost dead, made an effort to get up, at the same time exclaiming, "My God, why do they not continue firing, and end our misery?"

After the gates were closed, several rebels came in and planted a line of poles through the prison, on which were placed small white flags. This was intended to warn us not to approach or gather in crowds nearer to the gate than the poles when prisoners were being marched in. Capt. Wirz declared that if we did he would open fire on us, and fire away as long as any one was "left kicking."

All of this time the rebels worked like beavers on their fortifications, and in cutting down trees. Almost every train brought in reinforcements for the rebels, and the ground in the direction of the station became white with tents. On the arrival of some of the trains we could hear the rebels cheering loudly, and we felt anxious to find out the nature of the news they received. The prison was now again in a fearfully crowded condition, and, although death was carrying off the prisoners at the rate of almost one hundred per day, the new arrivals were much in excess of the number carried out.

The weather for the last three weeks had been warm and dry, with the exception of two or three days, and consequently the prison was again in a dreadfully filthy condition. Some of the men were giving up all hope of ever being released, and some became so despondent that they became insane. The ravings, prayers and curses of these men added much to the horrors of the prison. Some of them wandered around the prison in the most helpless manner, and begged piteously for something to eat. Some of the poor wretches imagined themselves animals, and moved around on their hands and knees, hunting for something to eat. Some of them gathered the undigested beans lying around on the ground, and ate them. The number of these poor unfortunates who were becoming idiotic was fearfully on the increase, and this had now become the worst feature of our prison-life. On one occasion I was going through the prison when my attention was attracted by the cries of some one, and going in the direction from which it proceeded, I found one of these poor unfortunate ones, who although in a dying condition was trying to make a speech to a few men who had gathered around him. He was entirely out of his mind, and I am sorry to say that some of the men around him were making a jest of it. The poor fellow was reclining against the side of a mud-house, and made frantic efforts to get up, but was unable to do so. Finding he could not get on his feet, he proceeded with his remarks in a reclining position. Judging from his language and the excellent quotations he made, he must have been a man who had read extensively; but it was a strange mixture of broken remarks which made up his discourse. He appeared to think, however, that his speech was making a great impression on his hearers, and was entirely unconscious of the fact that some of them were ridiculing him. He would commence in quite a grand style on the greatness and prosperity of the country, but in a few moments he would change his discourse, and dwell on the inhumanity of man; and rebels, devils, and starvation would be so mixed up with it, that no intelligent sentence could be taken out of it. Some of his hearers conducted themselves in a manner that proved pretty conclusively that good sense and good manners were none of their qualifications, one of them exclaiming, "Go on, old fellow, we will carry you out in the morning, and trade you off for wood." The poor fellow appeared to think they were complimenting him on his oratory, and it only encouraged him to greater efforts. I could not conceal my disgust at the want of feeling displayed by a few of the men, and I told them pretty plainly what I thought of them. One of them replied, "Well, he don't know what we are saying, and he will soon be better off than we are, anyhow." I left the spot thoroughly disgusted with them, but I could not but think how indifferent we all were becoming in regard to death. Men were dying all around us every hour of the day, but we had become so accustomed to such scenes that they had ceased to make much impression on us. How shocked we would have been at home, or even in the army, to be compelled to witness a scene such as we here witnessed every day. A few hours after leaving the dying man, I went back to see if he was still living, but found that he had passed over the dark river. His clouded mind had left the poor emaciated body, and winged its way to a fairer, brighter home, where sorrow, pain and death can come no more.

As I looked at the dead bodies of our comrades, I could not help wishing that the men who were at the head of the Government could look into our prison-pen, and see the condition we were in. I thought surely if they could but know the true state of affairs, some great effort would be made to release us. In spite of the many rumors of exchange, a large number of the prisoners were fast sinking into the belief that we would all have to perish. We had been disappointed so often by these reports, that we had lost all faith in them.

We sometimes got a chance to talk with some of our guards, and as we were very anxious to find out all we could in regard to what was going on in the outside world, we took the privilege whenever an opportunity occurred. These guards, as a general thing, boasted of their victories; but some would occasionally admit that things looked a little blue for them—that, in fact, the Confederacy was about played out. Occasionally we met with one who informed us that he was a Union man, and was in the rebel army only because he was compelled to be. The rebels boasted that our prison contained prisoners from almost all the States in the Union, including the states they called the "Southern Confederacy," and this was no doubt true; but we could not understand on what special grounds they made this boast, as it revealed the fact that the love for the glorious Union was not crushed out entirely even in this section of the country, which they claimed as exclusively their own. That men who were born and reared in the South would suffer the agony and misery of living and even dying in a hell like Andersonville before they would enter the rebel army, is a high tribute to the glorious character and unflinching loyalty of the Union men of the South. All honor to them; and may the day hasten when their services will be more fully recognized everywhere! There can be no doubt that thousands of the men in the South, and even a considerable number in the rebel army, had no heart in the rebellion, and were secretly wishing for the restoration of the Union. We noticed that the rebel flag was very little displayed in the South. In going through the towns and cities in our travels through the South, we would rarely get to see one; while we remembered with pride that in our Northern homes almost every house contained the dear starry emblem of our country. We remembered with pleasure the countless number of flags which decorated the streets when we left home to fight the battles of our country, and that even the little children were loud in the demonstration of their patriotic feelings for the old flag. It was not so in the South, and it would indeed have been strange if it had been. The people had lived long under the protection of the Stars and Stripes, and it was hard to obliterate from their hearts all love and respect for the old flag.

The common class of people, or at least the more intelligent part of them, commenced to understand that the new flag had no tendency to better their own condition. The corner-stone of the Government the leaders in the South endeavored to establish was slavery, and by far the majority of the people of the South had really no interest in that institution. Slavery was a curse to the common, or most numerous, class of people in the South. In fact, the South contained a large number of poor whites who were even in a worse condition than the slaves; and the light of the present day has revealed the fact that not only this class, but almost the entire population of the South, was benefited by the abolishment of that great curse, human slavery, in the South.

The only exception may be the very wealthy aristocratic slaveholders, who became rich by the sweat of others, and who looked upon the poor "white trash," as they were pleased to call them, as even below slaves, and entitled to less consideration at their hands than the blacks received.

Unfortunately, ignorance was so general among the poor class of people that the rich slaveholders, who, as a rule, were the intelligent class, could make them believe just what suited them. I have frequently met and conversed with rebel soldiers in regard to the war, and almost always found them commencing with the inquiry, "What do you 'uns' come down 'ere and fight we 'uns' for?" To one who had thus interrogated me, I replied, "We have come to suppress rebellion in the South and save the Union." "No sir; you have come here to take away our slaves," he answered. Thinking it a waste of words to try to explain to him the true state of affairs, I concluded to cut the conversation short by asking him how many slaves he was the owner of. He answered, "I do not own any." "Is your father a slaveholder?" "No sir." "Will you please state to me what benefit slavery has been to you or your family?" He frankly admitted that he did not know of any, but still persisted that we had come down to steal their slaves and carry off their women and children. He was a fair sample of thousands of soldiers in the Southern army. Too ignorant to understand anything of the real cause of the war, they blindly followed the leadership of men who cared less for them than they did for the blacks on their plantations.

Had free schools and education been as general in the South as they were in the North, the great rebellion would never have occurred. I met with one rebel soldier, however, who appeared to have his eyes open to the true state of affairs. "I can tell you," he said, "we poor people are a set of fools for fighting to build up a slaveholders' Government in the South." "What did you enlist for?" I asked. "Oh well," he replied, "I was made to believe that you 'uns' in the North would come down 'ere and destroy our homes and carry off our people." "Well," I asked, "did you find these reports about us to be true?" "Oh no," he frankly answered, "your men are just about as we are. I suppose we have as bad among our soldiers as you have among yours. Some of your soldiers camped right close to my house, and I must say my family was treated very kindly by them."

I noticed that in speaking of the treatment that their men received when prisoners of war in the North, they never claimed that any injustice or cruelty was practiced on them. Some of them had friends who had been prisoners of war, and they were compelled to admit that there was a wide difference between the treatment they received and that which we were compelled to endure. Some of them even spoke in the warmest praise of the generosity of our Government toward their captives.

We could not help contrasting this with our miserable condition; and is it strange that we sometimes felt embittered against the Government for not making a greater effort to release us? But as true as the needle to the north pole so were the most of the Union soldiers confined in Southern prisons to the Government they had sworn to defend. They might feel themselves slighted, neglected, or even deserted, by the Government, and among themselves be tempted to say some bitter things; but a word or insinuation to that effect from their enemies would excite their ire and indignation to the utmost, and they were always ready to defend the Government from the charge that it was not doing all it could to release them. It was, however, a sad fact that hundreds died with the fear haunting them that it was so. Men who had cheerfully faced death on many a battle-field, lay down and died broken-hearted, as the terrible suspicion forced itself into their minds that the Government they loved so well, and had fought so hard to save, was indifferent to their sad fate.

That thirty thousand men suffered all the horrors of a living death, and that more than thirteen thousand died from exposure and starvation, rather than betray their country, established the fact that there is no spot on the face of the earth where greater heroism or loyalty was displayed than in this horrid prison-pen. These men, exposed to the rays of a Southern sun by day, to rain and storm by night, suffering from maddening thirst and gnawing hunger, consumed by lice, fleas, mosquitoes, and maggots, suffering from scurvy until the teeth dropped from the gums, enduring all the pain, agony, and misery that could be inflicted on them, and dying at the rate of more than one hundred per day, unflinchingly remained faithful to their flag, and, although food, clothing, and life were offered them to betray their country, less than five per cent. accepted the rebels' offers; and it is but justice to them to say that some of these fled to the Union lines at the first opportunity that presented itself. I think it but just to say that no blame can be attached to the most of the people of the South in regard to the course of treatment adopted by the rebel authorities. Only those living in the immediate vicinity of the prison probably knew much about it, and they were in a position where they could not have prevented it. But to Jeff. Davis, his Cabinet, and such tools as Gen. Winder, Capt. Wirz, and Lieut. Davis, belongs the infamy of destroying thousands of Union prisoners, contrary to the rules of war.

Capt. Wirz and Lieut. Davis paid the penalty of their crimes by death on the scaffold; but the big sinners, President Davis, Winder & Company, went "scot free." On what principles of justice the Government hung the old Dutch Captain and his Lieutenant, and let the men who were in authority, and were responsible for it all, go unpunished, is one of the things which are past finding out. It would surely not be very creditable to the intelligence of the Confederate authorities at Richmond to assume that they were not aware that thousands of their captives were dying of starvation and exposure in their prisons. It is worse than useless for them to try to defend themselves on the plea of inability to prevent it. Permitted to starve in a country where at least corn was very abundant; suffering for water with Sweetbrier Creek, a pure stream, but one mile from the prison; lying and dying on the ground exposed to the terrible rays of the sun until, as in many instances, the hands and face had burned to blisters; shelterless during the most terrific storms, with forests and lumber piles all around them; compelled frequently to eat their scanty rations raw, for the want of a little wood, at the same time that their enemies were destroying the timber outside of the stockade for the purpose of getting it out of the way; does it seem probable that the rebels were doing all they could to prevent the fearful mortality in Andersonville? No; there are too many links in the impregnable chain of evidence to prove that it was a fully-premeditated, devilish plan to reduce the Union armies. When we remember the fearfully large number that perished in the different Southern prisons, we may well believe the boast of Gen. Winder, that he was destroying more Yankees than Lee was by fighting in the front. Is not the fact that more than thirteen thousand able-bodied died in one Southern prison alone, sufficient argument to convince any one that it was a plot of Davis and his advisers to destroy the troops of the Government they were trying to overthrow? Is it reasonable to suppose that with proper shelter and sufficient food, ten per cent. of the number that were in prison would have died? Take the same number of men in the United States army that were in Andersonville, and in the time that the thirteen thousand perished, the mortality from disease could not have been five per cent. But, allowing that ten per cent. of the prisoners would have died had they been properly taken care of, the fact remains that about ten thousand fell victims to rebel brutality. And then, let it be remembered that at Fort Delaware and Johnson's Island, two of the prominent prisons where rebel prisoners were confined, the mortality was only two per cent. of the number confined for the same length of time as those at Andersonville.

Look upon the two pictures, reader, and then say if there was no design to murder the poor Union soldiers who fell into their hands! The mind of the person not believing it must indeed be warped in "treason and treasonable sympathies," and they belong to that class of people mentioned in Holy Writ, "They have ears but they hear not, and eyes but they see not." No, kind reader, it was not as counsel for Wirz claimed when he made his plea for the life of the monster whose catalogue of crimes was as long and black as the worst demon that was ever arraigned before a legal tribunal to answer for his horrible deeds—it was not "a fantasy of the brain, a wild chimera as unsubstantial as the baseless fabric of a dream." It was a terrible fact, and one that will hand down the names of the perpetrators to endless infamy.

Time has done, and will yet do, much to heal up the wounds created by the war. This is as it should be; we all belong to one brotherhood, and should glory in the fact of a united Nation. But after centuries have passed away the name of Andersonville will be a reproach and a by-word to the civilization of the nineteenth century. The time is fast coming when every intelligent citizen of the country will wish, but in vain, that the name of every Southern military prison could be erased from our country's history, and the recollections of them from the minds of the people.

That the United States authorities hung two miserable tools, and let the head and front of the conspirators, Jefferson Davis and Gen. Winder, escape punishment for their crimes, will ever be a reproach to the "Temple of Justice," and a stigma on the Government which failed to protect its sworn subjects. True, Wirz and his lieutenant richly deserved the punishment they received, for they were the willing tools of their superiors, and so were alike guilty; and again, a "superior officer cannot order a subordinate to do an unlawful act; and if a subordinate obey such an order, both are guilty." But these two men, with all their guilt, might have said to Jefferson Davis as Herbert said to King John: "Here is your hand and seal for all I did, and in the winking of authority did we understand a law."

CHAPTER XII.

The Great Mortality in August—The Great Storm—Providential Spring—Departure from Andersonville—Arrival at Savannah—Departure for Millen Prison.

IT was now the first of August, and almost two months of our prison-life, with all of its pain, sorrow, and disappointments, had been endured; and when I remembered the terrible suffering we had lived through, and the large number that had miserably perished, I felt indeed that I was fortunate in still being in the land of the living. The hope that had never entirely forsaken me of a speedy release, had kept me up so far, and it was indeed well that a wise Providence hid from me the future; for, could I have foreseen the fact that, although much as we had already endured, it was not equal in intensity of suffering to what was yet to come, I would, no doubt, have given up in despair.

During this month more than three thousand Union prisoners perished in this one Southern prison, being an average of about one hundred deaths for every day in the month. Of these about one-half perished in the first ten days of the month, when an event occurred which greatly benefited the sanitary condition of the prison, and lessened the mortality. These ten days were undoubtedly the most terrible in the history of this notorious prison. The weather was the warmest we had yet experienced, and the rains had not been sufficient to wash much of the filth away, and most of it that did wash from the hillsides of the prison lodged on the swamp. Terrible as was the prison on the high ground, it was much worse on the latter-named place. This place had become very filthy in the early history of the prison, but it was now in a condition which threatened to destroy every one of us. The filth which had washed from the hills, with the excrement of thousands of prisoners, had now become so putrid and full of vermin, that to stand on the banks and look upon it, it would seem as if the entire swamp was a living mass of insect life. From this large body of rottenness, and of pestilence, came millions of maggots, worms, and other vermin, which spread themselves all over the prison. These loathsome things had at first confined themselves almost entirely to that part of the prison; but at this time I do not believe that there was one foot of ground in the entire prison which did not contain some of them. Many of the prisoners, who had become too weak to help themselves, were covered with them, and were literally eaten up. To look upon these poor tortured ones, too far gone to get up or lift a hand to help themselves, or to keep off the lice, maggots, and worms that were devouring them, and in some cases could be seen issuing from their eyes, ears, and mouth—befouled with filth, writhing in helpless agony, and praying that God would release them from their terrible condition and awful misery—was a sight so sickening, and a sound so horrible, that it was enough to shock the beholder insane with terror.

The stench arising from the rotting matter had become almost unendurable. Pestilent vapors loaded the air with deadly poison, which found an easy lodging place on the half-starved beings inside of the prison. The water had now become so impure that it was almost impossible to get a drink of it that was palatable inside of the stockade. Not only the stream and springs along its banks were impure, but even the few deep wells had become so from vermin dropping into them. I have walked along the stream, and examined spring after spring to get a cup of water that was a little better than the rest, and would at last be compelled to dip it from some spring, the bottom of which would be white with maggots. A large stream of pure water ran within a few hundred yards of us, and we were compelled to drink of this horrid stuff!

Scurvy, the most destructive disease that afflicted us, was now becoming fearfully prevalent, and more than one-half of the prisoners were more or less afflicted with it. More than one-half of the number that died perished of this dreaded disease. This disease is the result of impure air, bad water and improper food, and as we had the two first-named articles in abundance, and what we did have of the third was of the improper kind, the result was, of course, scurvy. The first indication of its dreaded approach was almost always at the gums, or about the mouth. The gums became soft and ulcerated, and in a short time, if the disease was not checked, the teeth became loose, and in many cases dropped out. In some cases the body became covered with scaly, yellowish spots, and these soon developed into running ulcers, and the entire body of the poor victim was soon in the most horrible condition. In some cases the limbs swelled and face puffed up until the skin burst. It sometimes appeared as if the afflicted party was suffering with dropsy, but it was no doubt scurvy in its worst form that was doing it all. A most painful diarrhœa or discharge from the bowels, largely composed of blood, almost always accompanied it, and added to the suffering of the victim. Often the lower limbs became full of holes, and in some cases almost rotted off. Streams of offensive blood poured from the nose, mouth, and different parts of the body. Gangrene also often got into these sores, and finally mortification took place, and ended the terrible sufferings of the poor victims.

Terrible as this disease was, it could be easily checked when it first made its appearance, if the afflicted one could get potatoes, onions, or any kind of fruit or vegetables. Raw potatoes and onions were especially beneficial. When in its first stages, I have known it to be checked by the use of one raw potato. With us this disease was undoubtedly caused by the want of good water, wholesome food, and pure air; and had these things been given us by our enemies, this loathsome disease would soon have disappeared from our midst. The prisoner who found himself attacked with this disease would trade off anything he might have in his possession, so as to get something to check it.

A rebel sutler furnished such things as would supply our wants, but at such prices that what little the new prisoners succeeded in getting into prison with them would soon be in his possession. One dollar for a small potato, and the same for an onion, was about a fair sample of the prices charged by the rebels to get what money they could not steal from us when captured. Almost every prisoner had succeeded in getting some little money, or other small valuables, into prison with them, and quite a trade sprung up between them and the rebel guards. Our brass buttons especially were prized quite highly among our enemies, and they were almost all the time ready for a trade for them. I had traded off everything that I could possibly give, with the exception of several rings and my coat buttons. The rings I prized so highly from associations connected with them, that I could not make up my mind to let them go; but as the coat was in danger of going to pieces anyhow, I concluded to trade off the buttons.

Gilbert and Fralich were both showing symptoms of getting scurvy, and we began to anxiously consider what we could do to prevent it from getting worse. One of the sentry-boxes was directly opposite to us, and as only the small space of ground between the dead-line and the stockade separated us, we had a good opportunity of conversing with the guards who would get on this post. We hailed several of them in regard to a trade for our buttons, but were unsuccessful until a guard came on post who wanted a dozen of New York State buttons. The rebels appeared to value that kind of button very highly, and would pay more for them than for the common United States Regulation button. We did not have any of the former kind; but as our necessity was great, and believing that the end justified the means, we concluded to play a trick on the rebel by giving him United States buttons in place of the ones he wanted. After some little bargaining, he promised to furnish us with two quarts of corn meal, three pounds of pork, three potatoes, and three onions, providing that we got him one dozen New York State buttons—the exchange to be after dark. Watching that he did not notice what we were doing, we cut off a dozen of our buttons, and after rubbing them until they shone like gold, we strung them on a string, and held them up for his inspection. He was pleased, and remarked, "All right, boys; I will be ready for you when I get on post to-night." We waited anxiously for his appearance, nine o'clock being the time we expected to make the trade. We were already enjoying the anticipation of the good meal we would have, and we were heartily glad when the guard made his appearance and informed us that he was ready for the trade. He requested one of us to cross the dead-line, and come to the stockade and throw up the buttons. As a guard was but a short distance on each side of him, we felt a little suspicious about doing so, and asked him what guarantee we would have that they would not fire on the one crossing. He then told us that he had made arrangements with the other guards about that, and we would be in no danger. We, however, still felt somewhat timorous about crossing, as we thought it might possibly be a trap to get us over the dead-line; so we hesitated for a few moments, and talked the matter over among ourselves, when Fralich, who was getting impatient, grabbed the buttons, and stepping over the dead-line, ran to the stockade with them. He threw them up to the guard, and catching the bag that the guard dropped containing the victuals, he safely returned to us. The guard had, however, missed catching the buttons, which dropped to the ground, thus compelling Fralich to go back again and give them to him. We watched him examining the buttons, but as he said nothing, we supposed he could not discover the difference in the dark. In the morning when he came on post he told us that we had cheated him. We told him that no New York buttons could be found, and as we were very hungry, we concluded to fool him a little. He did not, however, appear to care much, and laughed over the matter, saying that we were up to all kinds of "Yankee tricks." The guard had given us fully as much as he had promised, and we had a glorious feast that night. The potatoes and onions especially were most welcome, and I have no doubt they did us much good. I do not think I ever in all my life enjoyed the meal as I did the one that night. We had enough to eat all the next day, and felt much refreshed, and our fortunate trade was quite a blessing to us.

On the afternoon of the 2d we had a severe thunder-storm, but not much rain, which we regretted, as it was not enough to wash away the filth, and the terrible amount of it that had accumulated made us wish for a severe rain to carry some of it away. On the 3d, four hundred and forty-two prisoners arrived from Gen. Stoneman's command, captured the day before at Macon, Georgia. On the following day about five hundred more arrived from Gen. McCook's command, captured south of Atlanta.

It appears that after the great battle of Peach Tree Creek, in which the noble Gen. McPherson lost his life, Gen. Sherman ordered Gen. Stoneman to move with a force of about five thousand mounted men around the left flank of the rebel army, and Gen. McCook with a force of about four thousand around their right flank, both commands to march on and destroy the Macon railroad. This road was the only one in possession of the rebels that could furnish Atlanta with supplies. Gen. Stoneman requested and received permission to move with his force on Macon and Andersonville, and attempt the recapture of the Union prisoners confined at those places. The two commands were to destroy the railroads at different places, and then form a junction at Lovejoy Station. Gen. Stoneman diverged from the assigned plan, and in place of meeting McCook's command at Lovejoy Station, he sent a small portion of his command under Gen. Garrard to Flat Rock to cover his movements, and then advanced with the others on Macon. His conduct was strange, to say the least about it. He succeeded in cutting the railroad and in destroying a considerable amount of rebel supplies before getting to Macon, which place he attacked, but did not succeed in capturing. The few prisoners who had been confined in the place were removed by the rebels when they heard of his approach. He made no attempt to move on Andersonville, but tarried some time at Macon until the rebel cavalry under the command of Gen. Iverson threatened his retreat, and finally succeeded in surrounding his command. He then held a council of war, and proposed to his officers to surrender his command to the enemy. His brigade commanders demurred against this, and proposed that an attempt be made to cut through the enemy's lines and escape. Gen. Stoneman then consented that two brigades of his command should make an effort to escape, while he with his remaining brigade would endeavor to hold the enemy in check. On what principles of military tactics he considered that one brigade could successfully resist the attack of the enemy, when he a few hours before proposed to surrender his entire command, does not appear; but perhaps the gallant General intended to offer himself as a sacrifice for the purpose of letting the most of his command escape, for escape they almost all did.

That one brigade succeeded in escaping entirely demonstrated the fact that the rebel line was but a weak one, and could not have prevented Stoneman from proceeding on his journey, much less to surround his command and capture it, as he believed it would. The second brigade was handled pretty roughly, but it too succeeded in escaping almost intact to the Union army. Gen. Stoneman, after a most desperate fight, surrendered the balance of his command, who were marched into our prison, the crossest and saddest crew I ever saw. Gen. McCook's command succeeded in carrying out its part of the programme, and at Fayetteville he destroyed a large amount of rebel supplies, and captured a considerable number of prisoners. He then moved on Lovejoy Station, at which place he arrived at the appointed time. He succeeded in destroying the station and a considerable amount of supplies, but being attacked by a large force of rebels, and hearing nothing from Stoneman's command, he was compelled to retreat. He moved his command to Newman, where he was attacked by a large force of rebel infantry. This body of troops were being conveyed by rail from Mississippi to reinforce the rebel army at Atlanta, and were stopped on their way on account of the destruction of the railroad. A fierce engagement took place, and McCook was compelled to withdraw, losing a considerable number of his men. He succeeded, however, in escaping with most of his men, and rejoined Sherman's army at Marietta.

The prisoners belonging to these commands

had been robbed of everything, as was almost always the case with cavalrymen when captured by the rebels. We had been informed by some newly-arrived prisoners that an effort was being made to recapture us; and as we had high hopes that it might be successful, we now suffered a terrible disappointment in finding out that it was an utter failure. Gen. Stoneman was bitterly denounced by all, but more especially by his own men, who blamed him for their unfortunate condition, and some of them charged him with treason or cowardice.

The truth of the matter probably is, that he overestimated the number of his opponents, and so concluded it useless to make the attempt to escape. Subsequent events, however, revealed the fact that his entire command might have escaped had they left with the other two brigades.

During the night of the 4th we had quite an excitement in our part of the prison, from the fact that one of our comrades made a desperate attempt to destroy himself. He first made an attempt to accomplish his object by trying to jump into one of the wells, but was prevented by a fellow-prisoner, who caught him. The poor fellow was no doubt out of his mind; and directly after he was taken from the well, he made a desperate attempt to cross the dead-line and let the guards shoot him, but was prevented by his companions. The excitement caused quite a number of prisoners to gather around him, and as his crossing the dead-line would endanger the lives of some of the rest, it was decided to frighten him out of it by making him believe that we intended to kill him—thinking that perhaps if he would get a taste of death, he would give up the notion of self-destruction. We got the old well-rope, and Gilbert fastened it around his neck, at the same time saying, "All right, if you want to die, we'll soon put you out of the way." We then drew the rope pretty tight, to see if he would give up or not, when, finding that he would not, we commenced to pull, and actually slid his body several feet along the ground. But he was evidently determined to die, and we found that we could not frighten him in that way; so we tied his arms and legs tightly, and left him in charge of the Regulators. Sometime during the day he pretended to be very penitent, and begged to be let go, saying that he had given up the notion of self-destruction, and that he would behave himself. He was then untied and left go. He kept quiet for a short time, when he suddenly jumped up, and before any one could prevent him, jumped over the dead-line, and folding his arms across his breast, he looked up at the guard and told him to fire. It created a great deal of excitement, and several of the men would have jumped after him and made an effort to save the poor fellow, had not their comrades prevented them, telling them that they would also be shot for their trouble.

The guard, who was only too willing to comply with the crazy man's request, and who no doubt rejoiced to get this chance to shoot a "Yankee," raised his rifle to his shoulder, and taking a deliberate aim, pulled the trigger. His gun missed fire, and for a moment we stood in terrible suspense, hoping that he would order the poor wretch back, who was standing as immovable as a statue, awaiting his doom. But that hope was soon dispelled, for the brute, with as little display of humanity as if he were preparing to shoot a dog, put a fresh cap on his gun, and then taking aim, shot him dead. A groan of horror escaped from some of the men as the body of their comrade sank in death to the ground; but accustomed as we were to seeing death in all of its horrible forms, this terrible affair did not make the impression on us that the reader might naturally suppose that it would. In the almost certain doom that appeared soon to await us all, the fate of our poor comrade was soon almost forgotten. The sad expressions heard in connection with it revealed the fact that almost all of the prisoners were settling down in utter despair. I heard one man say, "Oh well, we must all go the same road; it is only a question of time; and after all, he took the best way of getting out of his trouble." The murdered man was a sergeant in a German regiment, and was a man of education, and before his suffering drove him out of his mind, was a very companionable sort of a man.

Close to us two brothers by the name of Wallace, in company with two other members of their company, quartered. They had succeeded in getting several blankets into prison with them, and were more comfortably fixed than the most of the prisoners. The two brothers were intelligent, agreeable young men, and very fond of each other. They were well-bred and quiet in their demeanor, and belonged to the better class of prisoners, who would suffer the most keenly from their terrible surroundings. In the morning after the affair of the German sergeant, I was informed that one of them had died during the night; and I went to see them. Some of the comrades of the dead prisoner were preparing to carry him to the Dead House, and it was distressing to witness the sorrow of the brother. He was not demonstrative in his grief, but his countenance indicated that he was suffering intensely; and when his comrades lifted the body of his dead brother to take it away, he quietly kissed it, and then lay down with his face to the ground, and remained in that position for some time. A few days after, he too died, and his spirit had joined that of his brother in a better land to be united forever. He went up from a place of sorrow, to one of eternal rest.

They have met

> "—— beyond the river,
> Where the surges cease to roll;
> Where in all the bright forever
> Sorrow ne'er shall press the soul."

For a short time after we had occupied the new part of the prison, we had succeeded in keeping our corner pretty clean, and the number of deaths was not as large as in some parts of the prison, but it was now getting to be almost as bad as the old part of the prison. A number of prisoners from the vicinity of the swamp, in their desire to get away from that place, had commenced to move among us; and as they were all in the most horrible condition, some of them being compelled to crawl on their hands and knees, it greatly added to the unpleasant condition of our quarters.

Close to us on our right was a small piece of ground a few feet square, and on this could be found almost all the time one of these poor beings, who had crawled there to die. They belonged to that class who had no special friends or companions, and consequently were the most unfortunate class of all in prison. When a few who belonged to one company, or became intimate friends, kept together, and endeavored to cheer and help each other, they always got along much better than the unfortunates who were without friends or close companions.

As mentioned before, the prisoners who crept to this spot to die belonged to the first-named class; and as they were in the most wretched condition, it of course was very unpleasant to us; but they had no place to go to, and it was certainly unkind to ill-treat them, as several German Wisconsin soldiers did. These men had their quarters close to the spot, and it was a source of great annoyance to them; but they displayed a want of feeling for their companions that was contemptible. They often ordered them away when the poor fellows were beyond the power of obeying. One who was thus spoken to, asked, "Where do you expect me to go to?" "To where you came from; you are too filthy to be here," was the brutal reply. The dying man told them that he would not trouble them long; and so it proved, for on the following morning he was carried to the Dead House.

On another occasion, a soldier belonging to a Maryland regiment crawled to this spot to die. He was a mere boy, and his emaciated body and pain-pinched face did not altogether hide the fact that he had been remarkably handsome; and not only his physiognomy, but his conduct, gave strong indication of a pure moral character. Being very sick, and unable to keep himself clean, he of course was very filthy; and his general appearance was in strange contrast to his gentle, pure-looking face. One of these Wisconsin soldiers, who, as Gilbert expressed it, had as little humanity as the rebels, ordered him to move away; and weak as he was, he would have made an effort to do so, had some of us not interfered and told him to stay. His look of gratitude was surely enough to compensate for the short time we were annoyed by his presence. A few hours after, as gently and quietly as falls the autumn leaf, his pure spirit left his tortured body, and winged its way to a better land.

> "Matted and damp are the curls of gold,
>   Kissing the snow of the fair young brow,
> Pale are the lips of delicate mould—
>   Somebody's darling is dying now.
> Back from the beautiful blue-veined brow,
>   Brush all the wandering waves of gold;
> Cross his hands on his bosom now—
>   Somebody's darling is still and cold."

Some of the prisoners died so suddenly that we could hardly realize that they had passed away. They appeared to be as well as the rest of us up to within a few hours of their departure, when they would expire, sometimes without a groan. The hope of getting out had no doubt kept them up until almost every spark of life had left them, and death was creeping upon them in such a manner that they did not know that they were dying, and then, when they would finally give up hope, death was sure and sudden. An Irish soldier died in this manner close to us, on the day the Maryland boy died. He and an Englishman kept close together, and were evidently intimate friends. On the day he died we received molasses instead of meat, and the Englishman was offering his friend his portion and urging him to eat; but finding that he made no effort to take it, he sat down and rested his friend's head on his lap. He, however, soon after again commenced to urge him to eat his rations, holding the molasses to his lips and telling him to take it, saying it would do him good. Sergeant Bradbury and myself were passing them at the time, and noticing the deathly appearance of the sick man, we went close up to them, and Bradbury told the Englishman that his friend was dying, to which he replied, "Oh, I guess not," but immediately made an effort to lay him down. He died, however, before he could do so.

Thus we saw men dying every day, and the conviction was fast stealing upon us that we all would have to perish. The terrible condition of the prison, the large number of dying, and failure of the expedition sent to recapture us, had so settled the inmates of the prison in gloom and despair that even the little gatherings in different parts of the prison were given up. On the 7th, the rebel quartermaster came into the prison and informed us that Gen. Winder had received a dispatch from the rebel authorities at Richmond, informing him that he was to commence paroling us at once. This at first created a little excitement, and a hope that our day of deliverance was nigh; but it did not last long, for it soon proved to be another rebel lie. We had been deceived so often that we could hardly believe anything our jailers told us; but this last story was so well got up that it deceived some of us for a day or two, and the fact of it being another deception only sunk us deeper in despair.

On the 7th, 8th and 9th, the weather was so awfully hot that it really appeared as if the heat would kill us all; those were the most terrible days in the history of our prison. On the 9th, one hundred and seventy-five prisoners died, and the mortality in the three days was nearly five hundred. I have not the least doubt that had not a kind Providence interfered and sent the great rain-storm on the 9th, death would have swept all of us away inside of sixty days. This may be considered a wild estimate by those who have never experienced prison-life in the South, but I feel sure that at least those who remember Andersonville as it was at that time will not consider this is an unlikely statement. The terrible condition of the water we were compelled to drink, the fearful stench arising from the putrid filth that now covered the entire camp, was enough of itself to sweep the prison of every living thing.

Directly after noon on the 9th, the rain-storm already spoken of commenced, and this event will be remembered by those who witnessed it as long as their memory lasts. The large ink-black clouds approaching from the West, the constant vivid flashes of lightning, and sharp, quick claps of thunder, which reminded us of a heavy cannonade, all indicated that a fearful storm was approaching, and we watched its approach with a great deal of interest and anxiety. It was not pleasant in our unsheltered condition to be exposed to such a terrible storm as this threatened to be, but then we needed a heavy rain so badly that we were rather glad to see its approach. It soon burst over us with a fury that was appalling, and the rain poured down as if all the flood-gates of the heavens had opened. The deluge of water, the terrific flashes of lightning, the crashes of thunder and roaring of the storm, made a scene awful and grand; and it seemed as if all the elements of heaven were combining to set us free. The lightning struck into the stockade, and several times into the trees that surrounded our prison in rapid succession, and the prisoners to shut out the terrible sight sat down on the ground and covered their faces with their hands. Consequently we did not notice that the small stream through our prison had become a raging torrent, and was threatening to sweep away part of the stockade, when the boom of a cannon from one of the forts announced the fact that the rebels were alarmed about something, and getting on our feet we discovered that the stockade was being swept away at both sides of the prison. The greatest excitement now existed among the rebels, who were falling into line, and marching to the place where the break in the stockade had occurred, for the purpose of preventing us from making our escape.

Although the storm was still raging with great fury, and the rain pouring down in torrents, we commenced to crowd toward the stream, hoping some chance of escaping would present itself. The rebels had, however, formed a strong line to prevent this; but it was some satisfaction to us to know that our enemies had to leave their snug quarters and be exposed to the storm as well as we. After the storm subsided, some of the prisoners jumped into the still raging stream, and caught some of the wood floating down; but Wirz, with the devilish cruelty so characteristic of the man, ordered them not to use it, threatening that if we did he would stop our rations for five days. No rations were issued on this day, and hungry and wet, we passed a most miserable night. Whether Wirz did this from a desire to show us that he was in earnest about stopping our rations for five days if we used the wood, or from a desire to take the spite out of us for the trouble the elements had made for him, we could not tell, but one or the other must have been the cause for it; probably the latter, for the captain was in a terrible rage with every one until the break was fixed.

The rebels worked like beavers all night and the following day, to replace the stockade washed away. It was also weakened at different places, and a large number of blacks were sent inside of the prison to fix and strengthen it. These poor people were very friendly to us, and would watch every opportunity to show their sympathy in some substantial manner. They would keep a close watch on the guards, and at every opportunity slip to the prisoners tobacco or some articles of food. A squad of these people were at work close to us, and we were watching them working, when one of them suddenly slipped his hand in his pocket, and taking out a piece of tobacco, flung it to us; the next instant he had resumed his work. This was repeated several times by the generous fellow, who had no doubt amply supplied himself with the weed for the purpose of sharing it out to us. He was, however, at last caught in the act, and a stop put to it. As he threw the last piece the guard saw the action, and yelled out, "Look out thar, or I will blow your brains out!" The poor fellow was almost frightened to death; but the guard no doubt only intended to give him a good scare.

On the 10th, the day after the great flood, it

was very warm until noon, when it again rained until night. The next morning it was clear, cool and pleasant, and we had a chance to dry off and look around and see what the storm had done for us; and we found that it had indeed worked for our good. It had undoubtedly hastened the death of the very sickest men, but it had immensely bettered the condition of those who were still living. The entire prison, including the swamp, was swept in such a manner as to be quite clean compared to its former condition. Almost all the filth and vermin on the ground was swept away, and the atmosphere was quite pure, and in strange contrast to its terrible condition a few days before.

This was not the only great blessing the storm had conferred on us, and which was to greatly improve the condition of our prison; for it was soon discovered that a strong, pure spring of water had burst out right beneath the dead-line, alongside of the hill, and about one hundred feet from the brook. The water was cool and pure, and was in great contrast to the filthy stuff we had been using. The rebels, perhaps awe-stricken at this providential interference with their plans to destroy us, made a trough so that we could better get the water, and the rush soon became so great to get to this life-giving stream, that the Regulators to preserve order made the men who were crowding up to get water fall into line and take their turn to receive it. A long line of prisoners could be seen continually going and coming from this place, and for the remainder of our prison-life in Andersonville we had at least this one great blessing, pure water. If an all-wise Providence guides the destiny of nations and protects God's people, who can doubt but that this spring was sent by the Giver of all good for the purpose of bettering the condition of the inmates of our prison?

> "At his command the lurid lightning flies,
> Shakes the firm globe, and fires the vaulted skies."

On the 11th, John Robinson, one of my near comrades, passed away. He was a member of the Ninety-ninth Pennsylvania Volunteers, and quite an old man. It was often a matter of surprise to me as to how he succeeded in getting into the army, as he certainly could not have been less than fifty-five years of age. He had been ailing for some time, but considering his age he had kept up wonderfully well to within about a week of his death, when the terribly warm weather we had just before the great storm broke him down completely, and he fell one more victim to rebel brutality. Had this old man been furnished with such shelter as any human being under the circumstances might have reasonably expected, he would in all probability have lived to return to his friends; for his death was the result of his exposed condition. He possessed a great deal of vitality, and his death was one of the most lingering and wretched I witnessed in all of our imprisonment. We had all been as kind and attentive to the old man as we under the circumstances could be, and in every way endeavored to keep him from giving up hope. Life in our abode had taught us before this that to become despondent and give up in despair was a short but sure road to the Dead House, and those who could put on the boldest face would be the least likely to go there.

When we found that he was losing hope, we would gather around him and try to cheer him up by relating to him all the rumors we had heard about being exchanged, and tell him we had the strongest hopes of soon being sent home. It would always greatly enliven him, and sometimes his countenance would beam with pleasure at the renewed hope of soon meeting his wife and children again. Sergeant Bradbury, a member of Robinson's company, who had the happy and fortunate felicity of being able, under all circumstances, of looking on the bright side of life, and who I believe did more to keep up the spirits of his fellow-prisoners than any other man in prison, took a very great interest in his old comrade; and as he had a strong influence over him, he no doubt was the means of keeping him from giving up and dying before he did. The condition of our prison, and the intense heat in the early part of the month, were too severe on him, and it became evident to us that he could not much longer endure his sufferings. The sun had burnt his hands, feet and neck into blisters; and to add to his misery, his eyes commenced to fail so badly that he could not protect himself from the vermin that like a plague infested the prison, and his condition became wretched and miserable in the extreme. Sergeant Bradbury suggested that it might help the old man if we would trim his hair and give him a good washing, and requested me to help to do it. The old man gladly consented, and procuring the loan of a pair of scissors from one of the prisoners, we trimmed his hair and beard quite short, and then gave him a good washing. This appeared to help him a little for a day or two, but it soon became evident that his stay with us would be short.

On the forenoon of the 9th, and just before the great storm came up, he was standing near the dead-line, and I saw that he was trembling and keeping his feet with a great deal of difficulty. I was in the act of walking up to him when he fell on the dead-line, exclaiming, "Oh, Urban, help me!" I sprang forward and caught him, and with the assistance of several of the men who had gathered around, laid him down. He appeared to be so nearly gone that we expected him to expire in a few moments; but he lived for two days longer, and during the terrible storm and rain which followed, he was lying on the ground in a condition so wretched and miserable that it was a great relief to us when we found that his spirit had left the tortured body, and was at rest. It was a sad sight for us to look upon the dead body of this old man, and to think of his death so far away from his wife and children, who, unconscious of his sad fate, were still waiting and hoping for his safe return; but we could not help but think how great and happy the exchange was for him. His poor, emaciated, pain-racked form was with us, but his immortal spirit had fled to that "bourne from whence no traveler e'er returns," and where pain and sorrow could not reach him again.

Four of us carried him to the Dead House. When we reached that place we found eighty lying in a row, who had already during the day been carried out for burial. It would be impossible to describe the horrible appearance of these victims of rebel cruelty; some of the bodies appeared as if they would fall to pieces, and the stench was so sickening that we as quickly as possible discharged our duty, and hastened away from the place. Our guard consented to our request to take some wood with us back into prison, and also gave us the privilege of sitting down on the way going in for a rest, and to enjoy the pure air for a short time.

This was the first time since my imprisonment

in Andersonville that I had been in the woods, and oh! how I longed that I might not have to return to the prison-pen again. The trees with their cool, inviting shade, that would have so mercifully protected us from the hot, sultry sun by day and the dew by night—the beautiful flowers that looked so sweet and pure compared with our filthy surroundings in the prison—the birds singing in blissful glee around and over us —all these beautiful things in nature under different circumstances we might have enjoyed and admired; but now they only reminded us of our miserable condition, and made our hearts ache for the freedom we had so long hoped and prayed for. We could not help but wonder what chance there might be of escaping, could we overpower the guard that was with us; but the chances would have been slim, as rebel soldiers could be seen prowling around in every direction, and even could we have succeeded in getting away from them, the dreaded bloodhounds would soon have been on our track, and recapture or death almost a certainty.

We did not, however, have much time to contemplate either the beauties of nature or the chances of escape, for our guard after a short rest informed us that he would have to return with us to the prison, and that he had already indulged us longer than might be good for himself. We had, however, the satisfaction of having secured quite a load of wood, and as we were at this time receiving most of our rations raw, and often had no fuel at all, we felt quite fortunate in having secured this supply.

Early on the following day, Pond and French, two more of our comrades, passed away, and later in the day a comrade whose full name I do not remember, but who was known by the name of "Straney," also died.

Thus day after day we saw our comrades dying all around us, and we could not help but feel that if deliverance did not soon come, it would only be a short time before we would all perish.

On Sunday and Monday following, the weather was again most fearfully warm, and the number of deaths from the effects of the heat was very great. The total number of deaths on Sunday was 119, and on Monday 136. It was well indeed that the great flood had swept the greater part of the filth from the prison; for had the former condition of the prison remained, with the intense heat which prevailed all of the month, we all would certainly have perished. It was also most fortunate that we now at least had plenty of pure cold water, for our rations were so small that it appeared as if we would certainly all have to starve outright. Our daily rations often consisted of only one pint of corn-meal and a few raw beans; and as we often had to prepare this without salt, the reader can imagine how palatable it was. I felt the need of having this last-named article so much, that I came to the conclusion to make an effort to trade off my jacket for some of it. It was quite new when I was captured, and was still in pretty good condition, and I knew how much I would need it should I be so unfortunate as to be a prisoner during the fall and winter; but my present necessities were so great that I came to the conclusion to let it go. I also thought that if I was not released before that time I would not live to need it. After looking around a little, I finally struck up a trade with a guard, and received a pint of salt in exchange for it.

During the later part of the month, a considerable number of prisoners arrived from the Army of the Potomac and Sherman's forces, and we received plenty of news. Although it was, in some respects, not such as we had hoped to hear, yet taking it all together, they gave a cheerful account of the situation; and they also claimed to have positive information that we would soon be exchanged or paroled, and in spite of the fact that we had been fooled so often, we felt quite cheered up, and had a renewed hope that our day of deliverance was not far off.

On the 1st of September we had a very disagreeable change in the weather, and consequently the mortality again increased fearfully. The days were terribly hot, and the nights so cold that we shivered in agony. I bitterly regretted parting with any of my clothing, and I found to my dismay that I was going to be sick. I could now more than ever realize the unfortunate condition of some of the prisoners who had no friends or comrades to take care of them; for had I been in that condition, surely death would have been my fate. Attended by my comrades to the best of their ability, and the rumors that now so positively indicated that we would soon be released, kept me up, and in a few days I was better again. The sergeant who had charge of the detachment I belonged to suggested that I be sent to the hospital; but as I had never heard of any one who had been sent to that place leaving it alive, I came to the conclusion that if I had to die, I would do so surrounded by my comrades.

This so-called hospital was situated a few hundred feet from the entrance into the prison, and was inclosed with a high board fence. It was pleasantly located, and had a few shade trees standing inside of it; but few of the prisoners would, however, enter it voluntarily during the latter part of our imprisonment, for the impression among them was general that once in that place, death was certain. So, when taken sick, they preferred to stay and die with their comrades. The consequence was, that most of those who did get there were already in a very low condition, and with the terrible treatment they had no chance of recovery. There can be no doubt, however, but that with proper care and attention some of them at least might have been restored to health; but what single condition was there in this horrible place that would have a tendency to do this? Their emaciated bodies had nothing to rest on but the hard ground; very little shelter was furnished, and the food was of such a description that it did more to aggravate and increase the diseases that afflicted them, than to strengthen and nourish. This, with the utter want of medicine and such care as sick people require, all combined to make death a certainty.

I do not consider it necessary, however, to give a long description of this spot; but to give the reader a proper conception of the place, I will give an extract from the testimony of Dr. Bates, a physician from the state of Georgia, and employed by the Rebel Government at the hospital. He said: "I saw a number of men, and was shocked: many of them were lying partially naked, dirty, and lousy, in the sand; others were crowded together in small tents, the latter unserviceable at the best. I felt disposed to do my duty, and aid the sufferers all I could; but knowing it was against the orders to take anything to the men, I was obliged to slip whatever I took to them very slyly into my pockets. They frequently asked me for a teaspoonful of salt, or for orders of siftings of meal, that they might make a little bread. Again, they have gathered around me and asked for a *bone!* I found persons," he continues, "lying dead among the living sometimes, and thinking they merely slept, I have tried to wake them up, and found they were taking their everlasting sleep. This was in the hospital, but I judge it was about the same in the stockade."

These poor, wretched creatures, who, with trembling limbs and pain-racked bodies, that had been reduced by the terrible agony they had endured until they were almost beyond the semblance of human beings, covered with filth and vermin, were the ones that begged of their destroyers for a bone, a drop of water, or something to relieve their terrible sufferings. These men were no exiles for crime; they had left home moved by a sublime inspiration to help save the life and honor of the Nation. Many of them had been tenderly reared, and had fond, doting mothers in Northern homes, who had given them up to the service of the country with a patriotic devotion equal to the ancient Spartan mothers, and who were at this time hoping and praying for their safe return. Others had fond wives and affectionate children, in pleasant and peaceful homes, and oh! who can tell the utter misery and despair of these dying men, when they remembered their awful condition, and how they must have wished and prayed to be at home again? It was a frequent occurrence to hear them exclaim, "Oh, if I could only die at home, and after seeing my friends again!" It is hard to part in death with loved ones at home, when surrounded with all that love and kindness can do to smooth the way over the dark river; but to die like an outcast, yea, like a dog, was bitter and terrible indeed. But who can doubt that the great and merciful God, who has declared that without His notice "no sparrow shall fall to the ground," in his all-merciful Providence prepared the way for these poor, dying ones, soothed their sorrow, quieted their fears, and at last received them to himself in heaven?

On the 4th of the month, eighty-three prisoners came in, and they had a lot of good news; among it that we were now positively to be sent to our lines in the course of a few days. On the following day the air was full of all kinds of rumors in regard to an exchange, and a report also reached us that Atlanta had fallen. The prison was in a great bustle of excitement, and presented a more cheerful appearance than it had for some time, and all were anxiously discussing the probable truth of the good news. On the 6th, the rumors commenced to take a more definite shape, as an order came into prison that a number of detachments were to be ready to leave the prison: and on the following day six detachments, or about 2,000 men, left, as we believed, for our lines. Everything was now in a terrible state of excitement, and all but the poor unfortunates who were too far gone to hope to get away, were talking over the good news and of the prospect of getting into "God's land," as the boys expressed it, again.

It was pitiful to see the poor sick, who could not expect to go along. We tried to cheer them by telling them that they would no doubt all be taken as soon as the rebels could get transportation, but we felt that the hope for them was indeed small. On the following day, a large number more left; and, although we were not of the number, we felt confident that our time would soon come, so we tried to keep up our patience and as calmly as possible wait for our turn. On the 9th, 10th, 11th and 12th, the transfer of prisoners continued, and our prison was thinning out rapidly, the opposite side of the pen being quite deserted. On the 13th, our detachment was ordered to fall into line. We soon had our little property gathered together, and bidding our comrades an affectionate farewell, fell into line and marched to the south gate, where we halted for further orders. We waited anxiously during the night for the gate to open, but in the morning we were informed that the last train that had left before us had run off the track, and that a large number of men had been killed and wounded.

On the following day we received the unwelcome news that we could not leave for a few days, as the prisoners who belonged to Sherman's army were to be sent away first.

All kinds of rumors were now afloat, one being that a portion of Sherman's army was within a a short distance of our prison, and that we would in all probability fall into their hands. This somewhat broke our disappointment in not getting away, as we wished that if the prison would fall into the Union army's hands, we might be kept back to witness it, as then there would have been a certainty of our being released. We could not feel quite a certainty of it being the case if we were sent away; and then again, we felt a little as if we would like to have a chance to revenge ourselves on our jailers. Had our prison been captured, and Wirz fallen into our hands, it is not likely that the Government would have had any expense in trying and hanging him.

On the 17th, thirty men belonging to Sherman's army left, as we were told, for that army, and on the following day eleven hundred more were ordered to be ready to move on the next morning. I came to the conclusion to write a letter home, and gave it to one of these men with the request that he would have it forwarded as soon as he should get into our lines. The shipping of prisoners now stopped again for a few days, and we commenced to fear that we might after all be doomed to a longer stay in our miserable prison; but the guards assured us that we would all be sent away just as soon as they could get transportation.

A very disagreeable rumor now reached us that the rebels had built a large prison-pen for us at some other place, and that we would all be gathered together and put into it—in short, that it was to contain all the Union prisoners in the hands of the enemy, and was situated in such a place that there would be no prospect of our troops ever capturing it. We did not pay much attention to the last part of the story, as we did not believe that with the successes attending the Union forces, the enemy could have any part of the Confederacy long; but we did dread the prospect of again being disappointed in our hopes of being exchanged, and looked forward with dismay to again entering another prison, even if it was to be but for a short time.

On the 27th, three more detachments left, and on the following day we were again ordered to fall into line to leave. This time our expectations were realized, as far at least as leaving the prison was concerned, and the gates were at last thrown open, and we marched out with the earnest prayer that we might never get to see it again. As we marched to the station, we could not help shuddering at the remembrance of the terrible misery we had endured and the horrible sights we had witnessed since we had entered that miserable place. With all our joy at the prospects of getting away, we remembered with sorrow the many dear comrades who had so miserably perished, and we shuddered at the thought of our narrow escape. And even now, when assured over and over that we were going home, our minds were filled with fear and distrust that it might not be true, and that after all we would have to enter some horrible prison again.

We reached the station at about the time the shades of night had closed over us, and were drawn up in line along the side of the train that was to take us away. In this position we stood a few minutes before entering the cars, and Gilbert, who was one of the prisoners who did not have much faith in the truth of the report of our being sent to our lines, proposed to me that we make an attempt to escape. His plan was to wait until the order was given to get on board, when in the excitement and confusion of the moment we would slip under the car, lie down, and stay in that position until the train had moved off. The idea at first appeared to me to be a good one, and I agreed to make the effort; but after considering the matter for a moment, I remembered seeing the trains back for a short distance before leaving the station, and I reminded Gilbert of it. "Sure enough," he exclaimed, "it will never do; if they back the engine over us we will be crushed." So we gave up the plan, and entered the cars with the rest. The train, however, moved off without backing, and we were sorry a great many times after that we did not make the attempt. We would probably have succeeded in getting away from the train, but it would have been a hard matter to get away from the station, as some prowling rebels no doubt would have discovered us.

We arrived at Macon at about 10 o'clock, at which place we stayed until three in the morning, when we left for Savannah, Georgia. We arrived at that place at about 6 o'clock on the following evening. During the night we were placed under a strong guard, and marched through the city to a prison-pen a short distance from it. When we saw the "bull-pen," as some of the boys called it, we fully understood that the exchange was all a humbug; and the indignation of the men who believed that we would be sent to our lines knew no bounds. The most of us had, however, about come to the conclusion that such was to be our fate, so we were to some extent prepared for it; but as we marched through the gates and they were closed upon us, our feelings were not of the most amiable kind.

On the following day we had frequent showers of rain, and as I had a terrible headache, no doubt the result of the nervous excitement I had passed through for the last few days, I had a most miserable day of it. In the evening I, however, made an examination of our new prison, and found it at least a little better than the one we had left. We had also succeeded before leaving Andersonville in gathering up quite a number of pieces of old blankets and rags, which we had tied together in a bundle, and for fear something of this kind might happen, had brought them along with us. They became quite a comfort to us, and dirty and filthy as they were, they proved a most valuable addition to our stock, and helped much to enable us to endure the remaining part of our imprisonment.

Some of the prisoners in leaving Andersonville felt so confident of going home that they left their rags behind, and I have often thought that it was more than probable that our forethought in gathering them up saved our lives. We could cover the ground for a bed with part of them, and with the best, and Gilbert's old blanket, form a pretty good cover.

Our rations on the first day after our arrival at this place were quite slim, but on the second we received the best ration we had received since our capture. It consisted of one-half pint of good corn-meal, one-half pint of boiled rice, one-fourth pound beef, salt, molasses, and what was quite as welcome as any, a small piece of soap. The food was, of course, only what a hungry man would eat at one meal, but then it was clean and wholesome, and I felt quite refreshed after devouring it. I had intended dividing it into two meals, but it tasted so good I could not stop until I had finished it all. I had a good wash with the soap, and made the following entry in my diary: "Washed with soap for the first time in four months."

This prison-pen compared to some of the others in the South was small, and contained only a few thousand men. The most of the prisoners who had left Andersonville before us had been sent to Millen, Charleston and Florence prisons. It was fortunate for us indeed that we succeeded in getting a little shelter, for in the early part of the month we had a long rainy spell and several severe thunder-storms. On the 2d, 3d, 4th, 5th and 6th, it rained almost all the time. Our food, however, continued to be good; and, although only in such quantities as to make one meal per day, we could get along with it right well, and it was heartily enjoyed.

On the 3d, some Union citizens smuggled into our prison copies of the Savannah *Republican* and Augusta *Sentinel*, which gave a description of the defeat of the rebel army under Gen. Early by Gen. Phil Sheridan, at Winchester. These papers acknowledged that it was a great disaster to the rebel party, and spoke in the bitterest terms of Gen. Early, whom they declared to be incompetent, and as having been drunk during the battle. It was most glorious news to us, and gave us a renewed hope that the war would soon be over, and we would be enabled to go to our homes.

We soon found out that the city contained quite a strong Union element, and also that the people appeared to have more regard for us than in any place we had yet been in the South; and I have no doubt but that if the rebel officers who had charge of us would have let the inhabitants of the city do so, we would have met with treatment such as prisoners of war are entitled to.

On the 7th the weather again changed, and commenced to get cool; and on Saturday and Sunday it was quite cold and disagreeable. All day during Sunday we were compelled to move around to keep from getting too cold, and by evening we fully realized the fact that we would be sure to have a most miserable night of it. We now found how fortunate it was for us that we had gathered up the rags before leaving Andersonville; for I really believe we would have perished before morning if we had not had them to protect us during the night. In the early part of the evening we tried to keep warm by walking around in a ring and stamping our feet on the ground, but we soon found that we did not have strength enough to keep that up very long; so we came to the conclusion to lie down and sleep, and take our chances of living until morning. Making the best disposition of our bedding, we nestled together as close as we could, and tried to sleep. After shaking and shivering for several hours, we at last fell asleep, and slept part of the night; but it was one of the most miserable nights I have ever lived through, and I sincerely wished I might never see the like again. In the morning we were quite stiff, and could hardly get up; but fortunately the wind had fallen, and the sun came up bright and warm, and under the influence of its welcome rays we soon commenced to feel more comfortable. We were shocked to see, however, the large number that had died during the night, more than a dozen dead bodies lying close around us, and the mortality all over the prison was very great. The yellow fever was raging in the city, and had also made its appearance in the prison; and it was said that this cold spell was a blessing, as it helped check the disease.

The appearance of this dreaded disease had greatly alarmed us, and we received with joy the news that we were to be taken away for exchange. We did not place any confidence in the part of the story relating to an exchange; but the dread of taking yellow fever was so great that we felt glad to leave. Had it not been for this, we would have left this place for another pen with considerable reluctance, as we could not hope to better our condition, and feared another Andersonville was in store for us. Almost every day we had experienced some acts of good-will from the citizens of the town, and food, clothing, and even money, were smuggled into prison.

We left Savannah directly after noon on the 12th of October, and marched to the depot, where we were again loaded on the cars, but did not leave until evening. During the march from the pen to the railroad I witnessed one of the most brutal sights I had ever seen, and one that filled us all with the greatest indignation. Some of the sick could not keep up with the column, and a rebel officer, who I think was Lieutenant Davis, came on behind, and with a large stick or club of wood, commenced to beat the lingering men in a most brutal manner over the head and shoulders, in several cases knocking them down with such violence that they could not get up. A number of citizens who witnessed the brutal act, and even a few of his own men, commenced to cry "Shame!" and the cowardly scoundrel, intimidated I suppose by them, stopped his beating, but kept cursing us until we were loaded in the cars.

A large crowd had gathered around the train, and we soon found that the blacks, and also a considerable number of the whites, sympathized with us; and had the brutal officer who had charge of the train let the people help us, we would have received substantial aid before we left the city. Just before our departure a beautiful lady, accompanied by a black woman, who was carrying a large bundle of clothing, came to the car for the purpose of giving it to the prisoners. The brutal, pompous officer mentioned before, came riding up to put a stop to it. The lady seeing the officer approaching, and knowing she would not have time to distribute the clothing, ordered her servant to throw them into one of the cars. The colored woman trembled with fear, and appeared to be in doubt as to what to do—no doubt wishing to obey her mistress, and yet too much afraid of the rebel officer to do so—when the lady seized the bundle and threw it into the cars. The enraged officer called on one of his men to fire on the determined woman; but the guard made no effort to obey the brutal order, and the noble woman, who was as cool and collected as if in her reception-room at home, gave the officer a look of contempt and defiance, which said as plain as words, "Fire if you dare!" and walked away, followed by more than one earnest prayer that God would bless and reward her for her noble generosity.

We left Savannah, going westward, late in the evening, and the fact that we were going away from the sea-coast gave us satisfactory proof that we were destined for another prison-pen, and that our day of deliverance had not yet arrived. The rebels had as usual loaded us in common box cars, with a guard stationed at each door, and also four or five of them on the top of each car. Some time during the night the one at the door shut it, and then crept up on top to his comrades. He had hardly more than done so when some of the boys conceived the plan of making an attempt to escape. They carefully commenced to open the door, shoving it a few inches at a time, until finally, when they had pushed it open wide enough, they began to jump out. The night was pitch dark, and as the train was running probably at the rate of twenty-five or thirty miles an hour, it was, of course, extremely dangerous to jump, as the one doing so did not know whether he would alight in water, or tumble over some steep embankment; but we were so anxious to obtain our freedom that we did not stop to consider the chances of being killed in the attempt to get it. Unfortunately the boys were all too anxious and impatient for the first chance, and made too much noise, which disclosed what was going on to the rebel guards. Only the third man had jumped from the train when the rebels discovered the movement, and the sharp reports of several rifles and the quick shutting of the door put an end to the business.

Two days after our arrival at Millen, two of the three men were brought into prison: the other one was never heard of. One of them gave me quite an amusing account of his adventure. He was the first one to jump from the train, and it so happened that at the place he jumped there was a high railroad embankment, and down this he tumbled head over heels and heels over head, until he reached the bottom with a thump which nearly knocked the breath out of him. Finding, however, that he was not much hurt, he made off. He had proceeded but a short distance when he came to a large sweet-potato patch, and, after digging out as many as he could eat, he moved on until daylight, when he hid himself in a wood. Sometime in the afternoon he discovered that he was being pursued by bloodhounds; and now, thoroughly alarmed, he made off. He had proceeded but a short distance, when he discovered that it was useless for him to try to get away, so he climbed on a tree and waited for the appearance of his pursuers. The dogs soon reached his hiding-place, and directly after their owners, who were mounted. They commanded him to come down, and he obeyed, not knowing what was in store for him.

He had, however, fallen into better hands than he had expected, and they treated him kindly. On the way going to the railroad station, from where he was sent to prison, they let him dig up as many sweet-potatoes as he could carry; and when he came into prison he had a string tied around his pantaloons and his shirt filled with them, giving him the look of a "stuffed Paddy."

CHAPTER XIII.

MILLEN PRISON.

WE arrived at Millen, a station on the Georgia Central Railroad, early in the morning of the 13th of October, and in a few hours after our arrival we were taken from the cars and marched to a large prison-pen a short distance from the railroad. We had so little faith in the truth of the statement made by the rebels when we had left Savannah, that we were going to be exchanged, that it did not surprise us much to see this prison, it being only what we had expected all along. We had commenced to think that the rebels were such liars that we could not believe anything they said. I am sorry to be compelled to state that before I get to the end of the narrative I will have to confess that the scamps fooled us once more.

This prison-pen was sometimes known as Camp Lawton, and was quite pleasantly situated about 90 or 100 miles northwest of Savannah. After our entrance into prison I spent most of the day in examining our new quarters, and I found that they compared very favorably with Andersonville. It was in many respects the best-arranged prison we had yet been in. It was very large and roomy, and was, as we were informed, to contain all of the prisoners in the hands of the rebels; and, could the rebels have prevented Sherman's march to the sea, it would no doubt have been used for that purpose. Like Andersonville, it was situated in a country almost covered with large pine trees, and about as far away from civilization as the enemy could get us. About forty acres of land had been cleared away, and with the large logs an inclosure built on the same plan as at Andersonville.

A splendid stream of water ran through the prison almost in the central part; and this was a great comfort to us, as it gave us plenty of good water, and also the privilege of bathing. A very good arrangement had also been completed to carry off the excrement and filth of the prison; and had shelter been erected for the prisoners, and proper food been given them, it would certainly have been an arrangement that would have been a credit to the South, and a proper receptacle for the confinement of prisoners of war, and such as the laws of humanity required. No shelter was furnished; and this can certainly not be apologized for on the plea of inability to furnish it, as the abundance of timber all around us would soon have supplied all the necessary material.

A considerable amount of limbs and brush had been left in the prison, and the first arrivals secured this, and with it constructed a pretty good shelter; but a large number who came later had no shelter at all, and as they were almost naked, and the cold weather came on, they suffered terribly, and a very large number of them died. Scurvy and diarrhœa, the diseases so fearfully prevalent in the other prisons, were also raging terribly here, and rheumatism was much worse in this place than in any of the prisons we had been before. This was no doubt owing to the colder weather, and the fact that a large number of the prisoners who came to this place had the seeds of disease sown in their system before they came here.

When I first went to Millen the food was better than in Andersonville, and consisted of one pint of corn-meal, six ounces of uncooked beef, six spoonfuls of cooked rice, and a little salt. This was the ration for twenty-four hours, and with it those who were well enough to be up and about could get along; but the rations were soon after cut down, and were about as bad as at Andersonville. No food of any different character was issued to the sick, and no medicine given to those inside of the stockade.

As mentioned before, I spent a good part of my first day in prison in walking around and examining it. We had, however, located our ground and gathered a lot of wood and sticks, and with the aid of our rags and blankets, succeeded in making a pretty good shelter. Gilbert, who ever had an eye to business, suggested that we on the following day gather all the small sticks of wood we could find, as we knew that in a few days it would be hard to get, and also as much as possible improve our shelter; so on the following day we worked as hard as our feeble condition would allow, and by evening had a supply of fuel that would at least enable us to cook our rations; and our shelter would have at least passed for a pretty good dog-house—that is, for those who are not inclined to be very particular with their dogs, and where the climate is not too cold. It was certainly not a model of architectural skill, and was just large enough, in the event of our receiving one visitor, to compel at least one of the hosts or the guest to sit on the outside. After it was completed we looked on it with much satisfaction, and it was certainly a real blessing to us. We looked forward, however, to the approach of winter with horror, knowing that our little stock of wood would be gone, and, although there was plenty on the outside of our prison, we knew that if our jailers had the same spirit that they had at Andersonville, it would not do us much good.

Since our arrival in this prison the weather had been quite pleasant, and continued so until the 2d of November, when it became stormy and cold. A large number of prisoners had arrived from Andersonville and other prisons, and as many of them were almost naked and without shelter, their sufferings were terrible in the extreme. The mortality became very great, and a gloom and despondency fell over the prison which was fearful to behold. It was a common occurrence to find two, and sometimes three, who had laid down side by side to sleep, to have taken the sleep that knows no waking, their spirits having passed away during the night.

The night following the 22d of the month was cold, wet and stormy, and the medium of human language can not describe the utter wretchedness and misery of our prison during the night. Notwithstanding the terrible anguish and misery of our past prison life, that night overshadowed them all in the intensity of suffering. Surely the angel of death reaped a rich harvest that night, not only in those he carried away before morning, but in the many who eventually died from the effects of that night's sufferings. Huddled together in our little hut, our bed of rags and clothing wet from the water constantly dripping through our roof, shivering and cold, we suffered terribly during the night; and yet we were fortunate, compared to many others who were without any shelter, and exposed to all the storm. As already mentioned, some of these had been just brought from other prisons, and already sick and in a most helpless condition, were thrown in among us to die like dogs. Oh, who can sum up the villainy and crimes of the authors of the rebel brutality in these Southern hell-holes? Surely, if God metes out punishment to man for his inhumanity to his fellows, these demons will have a fearful catalogue to answer for!

In the morning the storm had ceased, and the sun came out bright and warm, but I was quite sick from the terrible freezing I had received during the night. Among the number that perished during the night, was one of our comrades by the name of John W. Mathias, a native of Carlisle, and a member of company C of our regiment. Poor boy! he was without shelter; and sick as he was, he could not endure the agony of that terrible night, and with many others miserably perished. Sometime during the night he crept up to where several members of his company stayed, and on his knees begged for the help it was impossible for them to give him. In the early part of the night we heard him praying that God would relieve him of his sufferings, and daylight revealed the fact that his prayers had been answered, for he was at rest. His poor emaciated body was lying almost imbedded in the mud, but his pure young spirit had fled to its Maker. Sadly we carried his body to the gate, and laid it down for burial with the large number of dead who had passed away during the night.

I thought then if I should ever get home I

would not tell of all the horrible scenes I had witnessed, and I would rather my book could be void of them; but to describe our prisons as they really were, I will have to write of some things that I would fain wish had never existed. I can, however, assure the reader that, horrible as some of the scenes described in these pages may appear to them, they are yet only a faint description of the reality, and much will remain forever with the unwritten history of the war.

It is strange that with all the known facts in the case, any doubt should exist in the North in regard to the terribleness of those Southern prisons, and of the brutality of the men who had charge of them. When men who enjoyed the comforts of home, and really know nothing about the Southern hell-holes, try to mitigate, or endeavor to raise a doubt as to the truth of the published atrocities in these places, it is time for the survivors, who are the best judges in the matter, to testify to what they have seen. "We speak what we do know, and testify that we have seen;" and it is only through the personal experience of those who endured the horrors of these places that the history of them can be given.

Sometimes when prisoners arrived from other prisons, we went among them to look for old friends, and occasionally found some in such a wretched condition that we could not help but wish they had closed their eyes in death before they came to this terrible place. It was so with our old friend William Rinear, a neighbor in our Northern home. We had left him in Savannah prison, then apparently in good health, and did not again see him until one morning I was walking through the prison, when I noticed a sick man who I thought resembled some one I knew. I went close to him, and found it to be Rinear. He was in a dying condition, and could only make out to talk to me a little. I asked him what I could do for him, and he said that some one had given him a brier root to make tea with, for the purpose of stopping his diarrhœa, and that if I wished to I might make him some tea; but that he did not think it worth while, as he knew that he was dying. He also said that he had made his peace with God, and was anxious to go. After staying with him for a short time, I went for Gilbert, and soon returned with him to see what we could do for our dying comrade. We looked for the brier root, but it was gone—some one had, no doubt, in my absence, picked it up. But it could not have helped poor Rinear anyhow; he was fast sinking away, and soon after passed to his eternal home. Sadly and with aching hearts we returned to our hut, feeling that it could not be long before we too would have to share the same fate, if we did not have a speedy deliverance.

On the following morning Fralich and I went to the spot where we had left Rinear, and found that his dead body had been carried to the gate. Instead of carrying the dead to a dead-house outside of the stockade, as was the custom in Andersonville, at this place they were carried to the gate, where they were laid inside of the prison until the arrival of the mule-team, when they were taken away to the burial-ground. We went to the gate, and, among a large number of others, we with some difficulty recognized the dead body of our friend. He, with the rest of the dead, had been stripped of all clothing, and presented a sight so sickening that we soon turned away with horror. We had walked away a short distance, when in looking back we discovered that the teams were coming in to load up the dead, so we stopped to watch the proceeding. With as little feeling or respect for the poor victims of their brutality as if they were logs of wood, the rebels threw them on the wagon until it was full—their arms and legs in some cases dangling out over the wagon—and then drove off. As we left the spot Fralich exclaimed, "John, I wish to God that every man in the North could witness this!"

During the latter part of our imprisonment in this prison, the rebels had again commenced to give us molasses instead of beef. The rebels appeared to have this article in abundance, and as some of the sick could not use it, it was, compared to other diet, quite plenty in our prison.

It was at this time that we struck upon an idea which was the means of helping us considerably. It was to take our ration of molasses, make candy, and sell it to the new prisoners who were coming in almost every day, and almost always had a little money. Gilbert was quite a good hand at making candy, and after he had transferred our rations into it, I went out to try my luck. I was fortunate enough to get among a squad of new prisoners who had just come from Sherman's army, and soon made a sale of it all. Elated with our good success, we determined to carry on the business on a more extensive scale. We took the money we had thus obtained, and with it purchased molasses from some of the prisoners who could not use it, and then with our next day's rations we made quite a lot of candy, and I soon had sold all of it, realizing quite a profit. By trading and purchasing we soon found that we could get all the molasses we wanted, and Gilbert and Fralich made the candy, while I did the purchasing and selling.

A large number of prisoners from Sherman's army were coming in about this time, and as my goods were quite a novelty in our prison, and also tasted good, I for some time had ready sale for it. With the proceeds we purchased sweet-potatoes and beans from the rebel sutlers, and what we did not use for ourselves we would trade off for molasses with the other prisoners.

We soon bettered our condition considerably. It enabled us for a few weeks to have more food, and we also added to our stock of bedding by purchasing an old blanket, for which we paid four dollars and seventy-five cents. We also purchased a little tobacco for Fralich, who was the only one of us three who used it—and now that he had more to eat, he became dreadfully hungry for some of the weed. We also became so extravagant as to spend fifteen cents for a newspaper, so the reader can easily understand that our condition was very much improved. It was also a great benefit to us from the fact that it kept our minds employed, and to some extent made us more satisfied with our lot. As is the case in all matters of business, the success of some will soon bring others into the field, and competition became so sharp that "candy business" was (to us a common phrase) soon "driven into the ground."

Fortunately for us, I, however, about this time discovered a plan which would again give us a monopoly of the trade; and I was not slow to avail myself of it. On one occasion I was among a number of prisoners who had just arrived, and calling out, "Here is your nice candy, five cents a stick!" Close to me, and also engaged in the same business, was a prisoner who presented even a more dirty and desolate appearance than myself. He was also loudly proclaiming the worth of his goods, and had just made a sale, when his customer came close to me and commenced to talk to one of his comrades about it. The one spoken to, pointing to me, said, "I would rather buy from that young man; he keeps his hands cleaner." Looking at my hands, I quickly came to the conclusion that if they were not as dirty as the other fellow's, yet there was much room for improvement, and that I might add to my capital in trade by giving them a good washing. I immediately went to the sutler, and, purchasing a small piece of soap, I went to the brook and gave my hands, arms, face and neck a good washing, until they were as clean as soap and water could make them; then fixing my hair as nice as possible, I again commenced business.

When I informed the boys of my plan they laughed heartily, and one declared that I would get rich some day, which, by the way, so far at least has proved to be quite a mistake. Assured now (if I may be allowed to use a slang expression), that I had the other candy merchants by the nape of the neck, I again sallied forth, and was soon loudly calling out, "This way, boys, for your nice clean candy!" at the same time assuring the crowd that it had been made with clean hands, and the most perfect care taken to keep it perfectly clean. As to how clean it was made I am willing to let Gilbert and Fralich tell—they know all about it. The dodge was successful, and I kept the monopoly of the business. I cannot say, however, that on the next day, when I saw that my principal competitor's hands showed a decided improvement, I felt very highly elated. I am afraid I had a good bit of the spirit that characterizes business men everywhere. The candy business soon after this came to an abrupt close, as the rebels again changed our rations from molasses to meat; and what was our loss was certainly a great gain to the rest of the prisoners. As it had greatly helped us, we had no reason to complain.

On the 3d of November about 1,000 prisoners arrived from Andersonville, who had been left at that place until this time. They reported that prison as being about empty, and that Sherman's army was surely marching in the direction of our prison. On the following day we were again informed that an immediate exchange would take place, but we did not pay much attention to it. On the 8th, the day that the loyal states re-elected Abraham Lincoln to the chief magistracy of the Nation, we concluded also to have an election. It would at least be good pastime, and we felt anxious to know how the majority of the inmates of the prison would vote.

The rebels, who had worked hard to convince us that it was the fault of Lincoln's administration that we were not exchanged, had greatly encouraged the idea, and were really the prime movers in it, thinking that McClellan would have by far the largest number of votes. Black and white beans were furnished to vote with—the black ones representing the Republican party, and the white ones the Democratic party. A ballot-box was placed inside of the prison, and men stationed there to see that all voted fairly. All then that wished to vote fell into line, and marching up, quietly deposited their votes. It did not, however, turn out quite as the rebels expected; and I do not think that if they could have foreseen the result, they would have been so anxious to help it along.

In the evening the votes were counted, when it was found that 3,014 had voted for Lincoln, and 1,050 for McClellan, giving Lincoln 2,964 majority. This proved pretty conclusively that although they might starve and kill us, they could not compel us to sue for peace by favoring a disgraceful compromise.

On the 13th a physician came into prison for the purpose of examining us and selecting seventy-five out of each thousand prisoners for exchange; and on the 15th this lot of men left, as it was said, for the Union lines, but on the following day they again returned to prison. It now became evident to us that the rebels must be somewhat confused by the situation, and we waited with great anxiety to see what would turn up next. On the 18th the sick were again taken out; and finally, on the 19th of November, 1864, we were informed by the rebels that the following day we would be sent to Savannah, Georgia, for the purpose of being exchanged. The news at first created some excitement, but the most of us did not put much faith in the report. The rebels had deceived us so often that we had lost all confidence in what they said. A few of the prisoners, however, who grasped at every rumor as a drowning man does at a straw, were at first almost wild with joy, and were constantly talking of the good times they expected to have when they could get home to loved ones again.

But in a few hours, after discussing the matter among ourselves, almost all came to the conclusion that the rebels were deceiving us; and if they did remove us, it was for some other object. They had deceived us so often that we could not help believing they tried to torture us, by holding out hopes they knew would never be realized. We were also aware of the fact that Atlanta had fallen into possession of Sherman's victorious army, and that he was making preparations to commence his great march to the sea. Prisoners from that army had informed us of its movements, and we soon came to the conclusion that it was Sherman who had given the rebels marching orders. Some of the boys could not help but taunt the rebels at every opportunity, by reminding them of it. "How do you like Sherman's marching orders?" became a common saying that could be heard all over camp, much to the disgust and annoyance of our enemies. That we were right in our opinion about the cause that compelled the rebels to remove us from Millen, is fully borne out from the fact that Sherman commenced his march from Atlanta on the 14th of November—six days before our removal—and that the situation of our prison was directly in the line of his march toward Savannah, which was the place where he reached the coast. On the 2d of December the advance of Sherman's army had possession of Millen. On Sunday, November 20th, a large number of prisoners were taken from the prison, put on cars, and sent in the direction of Savannah. The haste and fear displayed by the rebels convinced us that our troops were coming, and that our enemies were hurrying to get us out of the way. We were all in a tremor of joy and excitement, and could hardly keep our feelings within the bounds of propriety, as it would not do to get to be too demonstrative within the hearing of our guards. We began to entertain the hope that our troops would overtake us before the rebels could get us to another prison; but in that we were disappointed. We had, however, the utmost confidence that the Government would soon crush out rebellion in the South; and that if we could hold out a short time longer, our deliverance would come.

But we were also daily reminded of the fact that Death was reaping a rich harvest among us, and almost every hour of the day some poor fellows were being exchanged (as the boys expressed it), by that grim monster. Only those who 'have been in like situations can form any idea with what intense anxiety we watched every movement of our enemies, and every act and word that would give us any hope of being released from our terrible sufferings. New prisoners coming into prison were eagerly seized upon, and compelled to relate again and again to eager crowds all the news they possessed of the movements of our armies, and the prospect of an exchange of prisoners. Sometimes one of the new arrivals would succeed in getting a newspaper into the prison; it would soon be going the rounds, and be read and handled until very little of it was left.

The nights were beginning to be quite cold, and as the old prisoners were almost naked, they were suffering from the effects of it. Scurvy, diarrhœa and rheumatism were also telling fearfully on us, and day after day we saw our comrades carried away dead, after suffering all the agony and misery the human system can be afflicted with. In their eagerness to clothe themselves, some of the prisoners would strip the rags from the dead and carry their nude bodies to the gate, where the rebels would load them on mule-teams, and haul them away for burial. It was a terrible sight to see their poor emaciated bodies thrown into the wagon, with as little respect as if they had been logs of wood. Some might think that it was a hard thing to rob the dead of the little covering on them; but it is truly said that "self-preservation is the first law of nature," and the prisoners tried to justify themselves by the thought that their poor comrades had passed through their sufferings, and as they were unconscious of any indignity heaped on their bodies, it could be no harm to take what they had to better their own condition.

The prisoners were taken away as fast as possible, but our detachment did not leave until the morning of the 21st, when we were marched to the station, and put on the cars. At twelve m. we left for Savannah, where we arrived at nine p. m. We stayed in Savannah over night, and in the morning were again put on the cars and taken South. Where we were going, no one appeared to know; but one thing appeared certain —we were not to see the end of our bondage yet. Before starting we were furnished with ten crackers, which was quite an improvement on our former rations. The weather was extremely cold for the time of the year; so much so that our guards, who were natives of Georgia, told us they had never experienced weather of that kind so early in the winter. Most of the prisoners were on platform cars, and suffered terribly, and a few of the weaker ones froze to death. We were on the cars till the next morning, when we stopped at a station a short distance from Blackshear, Georgia. It was a wild, desolate-looking place, only one house being in sight. We were then told to get off of the cars, as the train would stop for an hour or two, and we would have the privilege of warming ourselves. I had been fortunate enough to get into a closed box-car, so did not suffer much from the cold; but the men on the open platforms were in a sorry condition. I was in the act of getting out of the car, when a prisoner, who had been on one of the platform cars, came to inform me that a member of our regiment was dying in the cars he had left. I hastened forward, and found the poor fellow to be William Dutton, a member of Company C, and a native of Chester, Pa. He was in a dying condition. I went and told Gilbert and Fralich of his situation, and they helped me lift him from the cars. Some of the men had built fires, and we were going to carry him to one of them, when a rebel officer told us not to do so, as that would kill him. We tried to bring him to, but poor Dutton was past recovery. After his death Gilbert went to one of the rebel officers and requested permission to bury our dead comrade. The rebel officer procured a spade for us, and a few steps from the railroad track we dug a grave and buried him. Poor Dutton! a few days before he was rejoicing in the hope that he would soon be released and get home to his family. Little did he think that his body would so soon be buried in the wilds of Georgia, where no loved ones could come to shed tears over his grave. His case was a peculiarly sad one—he had enlisted for three years, and was captured the day before his term of service expired. In his pocket we found a letter that he had received from his wife, a few days before his capture. It was such a letter as a fond, loving wife would write under the circumstances, rejoicing in the belief that her husband would soon be united to her after so long an absence. I kept the letter, and after my release wrote to his widow, informing her of her husband's death. William Dutton was a true, quiet, peaceable man, and was respected by all who knew him. He was an earnest Christian, and spent most of his time in reading the Bible, and quietly waiting his Master's call. And who can doubt that death came to him as an angel of mercy? How applicable the following words of the poet:

> "It is not death to die—
> To leave this weary road,
> And, 'mid the brotherhood on high,
> To be at home with God.

> "It is not death to close
> The eyes long dimmed with tears,

> And wake in glorious repose,
> To spend eternal years.

> "It is not death to bear
> The wrench that sets us free
> From dungeon chains, to breathe the air
> Of boundless liberty."

We stopped at the station for several hours, when we were again put on the cars, and left for Blackshear. After we left the station I was informed that McCoy, a member of Company G of our regiment, had also frozen to death on one of the hind cars, and his body was left lying on the ground near the railroad track. We arrived at Blackshear at three p. m., when we were marched into the woods, and put under a strong guard. The rebels informed us that in the morning we would be paroled and sent to Savannah or Charleston, and at one of the two named places we would be delivered to the United States authorities. We placed very little reliance on the first report, but in the morning everything had the semblance of reality. The rebels made preparations for paroling us, and we commenced to think that at last our long-delayed hopes were going to be realized. In a short time a thousand of us were paroled, and put in the cars. We did not leave Blackshear, however, until six in the evening, when we started for Savannah, at which place we arrived at three o'clock in the morning. We left Savannah at eight a. m. for Charleston, where we confidently expected to be put on the United States fleet. The rebels had at last succeeded in fooling us, for subsequent events proved the parole to be all a sham.

The rebels were evidently perplexed about the situation, and did not know what to do with us. Sherman's army had reached and captured Milledgeville, Georgia, and his cavalry had destroyed the railroad between Augusta and Millen; if they should get possession of the railroad between Savannah and Charleston, and compel Johnston's army to move northward, we would have to fall into the hands of the Union troops. The rebels, no doubt being badly pressed for men, and needing the heavy guard that guarded us at some other point, came to the conclusion to give us a sham parole, so as to be able to get us into some other prison without guards. No guards accompanied us, and if we had had the least idea they were not acting in good faith, we would have fled from the train and made an effort to get to Jacksonville, Florida, which place we knew to be in the possession of our troops. But we were completely fooled. We had, however, for a short time at least, the satisfaction of enjoying the prospect of soon being at liberty again.

The weather had again become very pleasant, and we were in high spirits at the prospect of so soon being in "God's land." Some of the men were noisy and demonstrative in their joy; others were sitting quietly enjoying the prospect of so soon being with loved ones again; and all waiting with terrible suspense to get to the end of the journey: but what a bitter disappointment was in store for all of us! We had hoped to get to Charleston before night, so as to get a sight of the dear old flag, as it floated from the ships in the harbor. But we did not reach there till after dark, and then all our joy and pleasure was changed to bitter sorrow and disappointment. Immediately after our arrival a strong guard of rebel soldiers surrounded us, and we realized the terrible fact that we were destined for another Southern hell-hole. No language can express the bitter disappointment and despair that at first took possession of us. Some of the sick ones gave up entirely, and died in utter despair. The most of the prisoners, however, soon rallied, and tried to take the most philosophical view of the matter the situation allowed. We came to the conclusion that our enemies must be hard pressed to resort to such dirty means to accomplish their objects, and the hope that they would soon be compelled to give us up revived in our hearts.

Soon after our arrival we were taken from the cars and formed into line for the purpose of marching to the depot, in the northern part of the city. As we formed into line a large crowd of citizens gathered together, and in the vilest language commenced to abuse us. The women appeared to be the most vicious, and almost exhausted the English language to find words mean enough to fling at the d——d Yankees, as they were pleased to call us. "What do you uns want down 'ere, anyhow?" was an expression we were compelled to hear quite frequently. One of our boys ventured to reply to one in the crowd who had made that expression that he did not think our wishes had been much consulted in regard to our coming so far South, and if they would just give us a chance to get away, we would bid them a long farewell. "Yes," replied this dilapidated specimen of Southern chivalry, "if I had the power you would never get from here, for I would hang every one of you," to which the Yankee replied, "How fortunate for us that you are not one in authority; you have the appearance of being a most blood-thirsty fellow, and the only wonder is to us that you are not in the front, fighting. Your friends are wanting reinforcements pretty badly up about Columbus, and if you will just shoulder your musket and march in that direction, you will find plenty of Yankees to catch and kill."

The prisoner's remarks were greeted with hearty laughter by some of our guards, who evidently did not feel very kindly toward the fellows who were willing to help to do the blowing, but not the fighting. Our boys, although in the hands of their enemies, could not be stopped from talking, and almost always came off victorious in the many tongue-encounters they would get into. Some of the women who had been thus worsted commenced to throw water at us, and it happened to be anything but clean. I had always been an ardent admirer of the fair sex, but on that occasion I came to the conclusion that when it comes down to pure "cussed" meanness, a woman can just be a little meaner than any one else. There was, however, one class in that throng that was in sympathy with us, and who would have gladly helped us if they would have had the privilege. Their sympathetic looks, as we were marched away amid the howls and imprecations of our race and color, told plainly enough what they would do if they had the power. The reader of this, who may have been unfortunate enough to enjoy Southern hospitality when a prisoner of war in the South, will have no trouble in coming to a conclusion as to who the class were that I refer to. It was the poor, despised black race, who were always and under all circumstances the prisoner's friend. On the way going to the depot, where we got on the cars for Florence, South Carolina, we marched through a part of the city, and we were to have at least one enjoyment before leaving Charleston. About the time we left the lower depot, the Union guns on Morris Island and the Federal fleet in the harbor opened fire on the city, and the fiery missiles commenced dropping into it. The flash of the guns in the distance, the long streaks of fire coming through the air, the crash of the large shells as they struck the buildings, and the terror of the people, made a scene no pen can describe; as the night was dark, it added to the brilliancy of the bombardment. It was amusing to us to see the terror and fear displayed by our guards. Judging by the way they conducted themselves, we supposed they had never been under fire before, and so great was their fear that we began to hope they would flee and leave us.

I have often wondered why it was that none of us appeared to have any fear, as we were marching along under the fire of the Union guns; and I can only account for it from the fact that the conviction was fast settling upon us that we would have to perish in some Southern prison anyhow, and that we might just as well die from the fire from our fleet as to starve to death. As we were marching along, one of the prisoners remarked that he wished the Union forces would open fire with ten thousand guns and sink the city. When reminded by a comrade that in that case he would also perish, he remarked, "I would not care, if it destroyed the rebels."

At midnight we left Charleston for Florence, South Carolina, where we arrived at about five p. m. We were camped in a large field over night.

When we left Savannah on the 26th, we received a piece of beef and one pint of corn meal for that day's rations. Somehow we always did get more to eat when in that place than anywhere in the South; but on the two following days, the 27th and 28th, we did not get anything; so that when we got to our new prison, we were suffering terribly of hunger. We expected that perhaps we would get a pretty good allowance; but we were to suffer another disappointment. When the ration came it consisted of one pint of wheat flour—only that, and nothing more. Unprepared as we were to properly prepare it for eating, it was the most miserable food we had been furnished with yet. The most of us could not do anything but mix it with cold water, and eat the paste. The reader can form an opinion as to how palatable such a dish, without salt, would be.

At eight o'clock we were commanded to fall into line, and march to the prison-pen. As we came near the gate a prisoner who had become weak-minded, and evidently clung to the hope that we were going home, commenced to weep bitterly, and exclaimed, "Another bull-pen! I thought we were paroled, and going home." Poor fellow! he was rapidly nearing his eternal home, for in a few days after his body was carried back through the gates for burial.

CHAPTER XIV.

Florence Prison—Terrible Condition of the Prison—Sad Death of the Drummer Boy—Paroled, and leave for Charleston—Delivered to the United States Fleet—Departure for Annapolis—Admitted into the Hospital—Receive Furlough, and Start for Home.

AFTER our entrance into this prison we as usual first located our ground, and then made a survey of our new quarters. I cannot use the word *home* in connection with these hell-holes; it seems to me entirely too sweet a word. The prison was constructed on the same principle that Andersonville was, and resembled it in a great many respects. A stockade built of logs closed us in from the outer world, and a small stream of impure water, with a swamp on either side, ran through the prison.

The ground inclosed contained about twelve or fifteen acres, of which four or five bordering on the stream were so swampy that they could not be occupied. The dead-line at this place was marked by a small, narrow ditch, and the same deadly significance attached to it as in the other prison-pens, it being certain death to cross. Unlike the other prison-pens, no sentry-boxes were erected on the top of the stockade, the guard standing on a lot of ground which had been thrown against the stockade from the outside. No shelter was furnished the inmates, but as at Millen, a considerable lot of offal from the trees that had been cut to build the stockade was left on the inside; and this furnished the first inmates with material to build shelter, but did not help the later arrivals much.

On our arrival we found the prison densely packed, and all of the wood had been gathered up by the earlier prisoners. We were, however, fortunate in securing shelter directly after our entrance into prison, in this manner: Two of the first inmates of the prison had erected a shelter by digging about twelve or fifteen inches into the ground, and over this they formed a roof with limbs, brush, and earth. A fire corner and mud chimney were at the one end, and the entrance at the other. It was a warm nest during dry weather, but when it rained the water soaked through, and made it of course a very unhealthy place. Both of the occupants had taken sick and died. We succeeded in getting possession of this place, and were thankful indeed for the shelter it afforded

It would be utterly impossible for me to try to describe our feelings as we marched into this prison. We were broken down in body, and almost in spirit; and the thought would be continually coming into our minds, How can we ever expect to live over the winter in this terrible place? Quite a number of men, to escape the horrors of the prison, were enlisting in the rebel army; not, of course, in the expectation of doing the enemy any real service, but for the purpose of saving themselves by getting shelter and enough to eat, and in the hope that some chance might present itself by which they might escape to the Union lines.

The food we received was of the worst description, and hardly enough to keep any one alive. It generally consisted of one pint of corn-meal, or wheat flour, and sometimes a few raw beans. Sometimes we received salt, but as often none; and when we did get this article there was so little of it that we could hardly taste it when mixed with the food. Fralich and I discovered that by putting our salt together and dissolving it in water, we could get a better taste of it by dipping our mush into the water. In this way we dined together until we were separated. It was certainly more social than elegant-looking to see us with little wooden spoons dip each mouthful as we ate it into the same cup, which contained the precious salt.

I did not see any meat of any kind while in this prison, and, as already stated, we sometimes got wheat flour instead of corn-meal. This was the worst diet of any we received in prison, as we had no way to prepare it. No medicine was issued to the sick inside of the prison. A hospital department was connected with the prison, but comparatively few of the sick could be admitted, and consequently the mortality inside was very great. As at Millen, the dead were carried to the gate, and then hauled away to the burial-ground, which was located on a wealthy Union man's farm, a short distance from the prison.

The officer in charge of this prison was one Lieutenant Barrett, one of the most cowardly and brutal wretches that ever lived, and a fit companion for the brutal Dutch Captain Wirz and cowardly Davis. This Lieutenant Barrett frequently came into prison and fired a pistol over the heads of the prisoners, to see them dodge around to get away, and their fright appeared to give him intense delight. It was about this time that I witnessed one of the saddest and most brutal acts I had yet witnessed in my prison life. It was a rule of the prison that all the inmates, in obeying the calls of nature, would go to the part of the prison set apart for that purpose. This was of course right and proper, so far as it applied to men who could go there; but in the following case the attempt to enforce the rule was as senseless as it was brutal.

Among the inmates of our prison-pen was a small, tender-looking drummer boy, about thirteen years of age. He had been a prisoner but a short time, but his health soon gave way, and he commenced to suffer with the diarrhœa. Weak and faint, he got up and proceeded to go to the water-closet arrangement of the prison; but had proceeded but a short distance, when he found that he could not go any farther. A brutal guard, with a malignant spirit that would have disgraced an imp from the infernal regions, and who it is hard to believe was human, deliberately raised his rifle and fired at the child. The bullet sped on its deadly mission, passed through the body of the demon's innocent little victim, and he fell dead on the ground. A cry of horror rang out from those who had witnessed it, and the poor little corpse was tenderly lifted from the ground and borne to a tent.

It would be impossible to describe the scene that followed. Strong men wept like children, others raved and swore vengeance, and all expressed it as the most dastardly, cowardly outrage they had yet witnessed. Had it been one of the men it would have created some excitement, though we had witnessed that quite frequently before; but to see this innocent child shot down like a dog, and for an act he could in no way avoid, aroused the men to the most dangerous pitch of excitement. Plans commenced to be quietly discussed about making an attempt to break out, and it would have been a sad day for the rebels in Florence had we succeeded in doing so.

The companions of the dead boy washed his

body, and after fixing him for burial, all who wished had the privilege of seeing him. As I looked on the dead body of the child, I thought I had never looked on one more beautiful and innocent-looking. His beautiful curly hair hung in ringlets around his brow, and his pure white face looked as peaceful as if he were sleeping. Yes, he was sleeping the sleep that knows no waking. Murdered by a rebel monster, his little body lay a monument of rebel brutality before us; but, thank God, man's brutality stopped here: "They can kill the body, but that is all they can do." His pure spirit had left the tortured body, and winged its way to where devils and fiends could not disturb him again.

During the early part of the month the weather had been quite pleasant; but on the 7th it became quite cold and unpleasant, and continued so until the day before I left prison. On the 11th we had a severe rain-storm; and as we could not keep the water from getting through our roof, we became wet and very cold, and I found to my dismay that I was getting sick. I began to suffer intensely from rheumatism, and it was most fortunate for me that at this time arrangements were being made to parole the sick. On the following day our detachment was ordered to fall into line and be examined. A large number of sick were to be paroled and sent away, and the doctors made an examination to get the required number. The object was to get the men who were in the worst condition; but men whose term of enlistment had expired had the preference, the rebel authorities no doubt thinking that they would be of no further service to the Government. On that ground they might have rested easy in regard to the sick, for it is safe to say that of all that class who were now sent to the Union lines, not one would again be able to perform military duty. A few bribed themselves out by giving the rebel doctors rings and other trinkets. I had suffered fearfully with rheumatism the night before, but in the morning I felt somewhat better. I was, however, so weak that I could hardly stand in line until the examination was over. The first time the doctor passed down the line I was not taken, and I had just about made up my mind that I was to be doomed for a longer imprisonment, when he again returned and said I was to be taken out to the hospital. The hope of being sent to our lines made me anxious to go, as we were informed that all in the hospital would certainly be sent away. Had it not been for that, I would have preferred to remain with my comrades, and die with them, before taking my chances in that place. As I bade them a sad farewell, fearing that I should never see them again, Gilbert and Fralich, although less fortunate, spoke words of cheer. Gilbert exclaimed, "John, it's a lucky thing for you, for you cannot expect to make it much longer here; and I think we shall all soon get out, for the rebels are on their last pins!" We did not, however, have much time to talk, for I was soon taken away and put into the hospital.

This place was in the northwestern part of the prison, but was divided off from the other part of it. It was under shelter, but it was in the most horrible condition. The men were lying on the cold ground, with only a slight covering, and so filthy and lousy that the sight they presented was horrible in the extreme. The United States Sanitary Commission had sent a considerable amount of clothing and hospital supplies to this place, and it was said that the rebel doctors distributed them fairly among the inmates at one time after the other, as they would be most needed, with the exception of a large number of white sheets, which had been intended for the beds of the sick. The rebel doctors said that as the men slept on the ground, these fine sheets would do them little good, and so made arrangements to trade them off to the citizens of the vicinity for sweet-potatoes, which were to be given to the sick, and which the rebels said would do them more good than the bedding.

A notice having been put up that sweet-potatoes and other food would be received in exchange for the hospital goods, a large number of citizens, mostly ladies, gathered, anxious to get a good bargain. Somewhat similar to the farmer in Vermont, who when his house burnt away, and after applying to his neighborhood for relief, found that every man for five miles around was bringing relief in the shape of turnips, and to stop the further arrivals of that kind of relief, he was obliged to post one of his sons at the gate and inform his friends that no more turnips would be received—so in this case all came with sweet-potatoes, only it differed from the turnip donation in the fact that they expected to get about ten times the worth of their yams in the despised "Yankees" bedding.

A large amount of sweet-potatoes were gathered together in this way, and it was said that the sick had for some time all of that kind of diet they wanted. I have yet, however, to learn that sweet-potatoes are very beneficial to sick people; but the doctors had no doubt an eye to business, as it would save so much food to the Southern Confederacy. The prisoners inside of the prison also for a short time received rations of these potatoes, and among them they were gladly received.

On the following morning after my entrance into the hospital, the doctors again came around and examined us. This was to fill up a detachment, which was to be immediately sent away, and this time I was one of the fortunate ones selected to go. I was immediately taken outside, and signed a parole, that I would not take up arms, perform any field service, or any military duty, until I should be duly declared exchanged. In company with a large number of others who had been paroled, we were kept in a large field a short distance from the prison. As I had once before been paroled by the rebels for the purpose of deceiving us, I could not feel altogether at rest, and a terrible fear possessed me all day. I knew now that with me it was a matter of life or death, as my health had given way so badly that if I would be sent into the prison again, a few short days would be as long as I could survive.

We were not guarded, but I was now too sick and weak to make an attempt to escape, and impatiently I waited to see what would turn up next. The day was a most beautiful one, and could I have felt positively certain that we were soon to go home, I could have lain down in peace and calmly awaited the order to start; but the fear that perhaps after all it would not be so, kept me nervous and restless. Finally, at about three o'clock p. m. we received orders to fall into line and proceed to the station, a short distance from us. The most of us were really hardly fit to walk at all, but the hope of deliverance kept us up; and slowly, painfully, but gladly, we proceeded on the way, and by four o'clock we were loaded on the cars. In a few moments after, the shrill shriek of the engine announced to us the glad tidings that we were going to start. The cars commenced to move, and we were on the way to Charleston, at which place we were to be delivered to the Union authorities.

As we could not all get inside of tne cars, some of us had to get on top, and during the night I made quite a narrow escape from being thrown off. The night was quite cold, and being so exposed to the air, we suffered considerably.

When I was taken from the hospital I had taken the privilege of throwing the old blanket I had for covering over my shoulders, and taking this, I wrapped it around me, and lying down on the car, fell asleep. The motion of the car kept moving me gradually around, and I was in a most dangerous position, as a sudden jerk of the car might easily have thrown me off. One of the men, seeing my danger, pulled me back and wakened me. When I discovered the narrow escape I had made, I was too much frightened to sleep again; and as we were getting most miserably cold, we were heartily glad when daylight appeared. It was after sunrise when we came in sight of Charleston, and as the sun came up clear and warm, we soon felt comfortable, and we enjoyed the sight very much. In the distance we saw the Union fleet, and we watched anxiously to get a glimpse of the dear old flag, and it filled our hearts with joy to think we would so soon be under its protection again.

After our arrival in the city we were immediately taken from the cars and marched to the wharf, where we were loaded on a Confederate steamer, and soon after steamed out of the harbor for the Union fleet. Some of the rebels on board tried to frighten us by telling of the danger we would have to encounter in passing the torpedoes they had planted to blow up the Union fleet, should they attempt to land and take possession of the city; but we soon came to the conclusion that our enemies would be pretty sure to take care of their own precious selves, so we did not bother much about it.

On the way going out we had a very good view of Fort Sumter, and it looked as if it had passed through a terrible siege. The one side looked more like an immense battered-down pile of bricks than a fort. We had also a good view of the Union iron-clad fleet which was doing duty in the harbor. The new Ironsides especially looked formidable, and it filled our hearts with joy and pride as we looked at her frowning guns and starry flag.

The rebel steamer steamed directly for the steamship New York, which was to receive us. As we came near the Union steamer, the prisoners, impatient to get on board of her, commenced to crowd to one side of the rebel ship, and the rebel officers had considerable trouble to manage her, the weight being almost all on one side, making the ship unruly. It was only when the impatient boys discovered that their conduct was retarding their exit from the rebels, that they could be prevailed upon to obey orders. One of the rebel officers, who no doubt felt disgusted with the impatience the prisoners displayed to get out of their hands, and their devotion to the old flag, exclaimed, "Well, you men do certainly feel anxious to get out of our hands!" Quick as a flash an Irishman replied, "Yes, and begorra we hopes niver to see the likes of you again." This created a hearty laugh, in which the rebels themselves joined. They also acknowledged that, judging from our appearance, we must have had a pretty tough time of it during our sojourn in the Southern Confederacy.

As soon as the two steamers were lashed together, the prisoners made a rush to get on board the Union ship, and in a very short time the rebel steamer was relieved of her load. It must have been a strange sight to the rebels to see the boys gather around the old flag, and witness their devotion to this precious emblem of their country. Some cried like children, others sang and shouted for joy, while others sat down and quietly watched the demonstrations of their more noisy comrades—their faces, however, indicating a peace and joy they could find no words to express.

During these demonstrations of joy, I closely

watched the countenances of several of the rebel officers, and I could not but think they were touched by the scene, and that their hearts warmed for the dear old flag. It looked so grand and noble compared to their rag, that I thought perhaps they would not care much to see it wave over all the land again.

Directly after getting on the Union vessel, we were told to take off all our clothing, and with what blankets we had, drop them into the sea. Taking my diary and a few things from my pockets, I soon went through that performance, and I saw with no regret my clothing, baggage, lice and all, float away. We were then washed and furnished with a clean new suit of "Uncle Sam's" blue, and also a good, warm, wholesome dinner. The coffee was especially appreciated by us, and after having partaken of our dinner we felt so much better, that with the same kind of diet we felt that we would soon be well and strong again. In the afternoon we were transferred to the steamship "Star of the South," and soon after the good ship was bearing us away from the terrible scenes that had so long surrounded us. I could hardly realize the fact that I was at last going home; and even now, when I knew that I was out of the hands of the enemy, I felt so nervous and my mind so disturbed, that during the first night after my release I found it impossible to sleep. Weak and sick as I was, and having hardly any sleep the night before, I felt the importance of a good night's rest; and I closed my eyes and tried to compel my mind to rest, but all in vain.

During all my long imprisonment I had heard nothing from home, and my mind constantly wandered away to the scenes of my boyhood, and wondered how I would find things there. I had no doubt but that some of my friends had given me up for dead, and I feared that some of them had passed away in my absence; so I felt as if I could not wait until I could write to them and hear from home. My mind also frequently wandered back to the horrible pen I had left, and to the comrades who were still there. We had suffered so long together that our mutual afflictions and sorrows had bound us together like brothers; and it seemed almost selfish to rejoice at my own escape, and they still in "durance vile." I felt rejoiced at my own release, but the thought of those who were still in the hell-hole I had left troubled me considerably. I am happy to say that they both returned safely to their homes some time after my release, but with broken-down health.

On the following day the weather was windy, but cool and pleasant, and I longed to go on deck; but I was taken quite sick in the latter part of the night, and suffered fearfully during the day; so much so that I was commencing to fear that perhaps after all I would never see home. On the following night, however, I succeeded in getting some sleep, and felt somewhat better in the morning.

At about 9 a. m. we reached Fortress Monroe. I expected that perhaps we would be put into one of the United States hospitals at this place, and judging from my former experience there, I felt that we could not be put in a better one; yet I wished we would proceed farther North, and get as near home as possible. I soon found that my wish would be gratified, for we soon after left, and sailed up the Chesapeake bay. We arrived at Annapolis, Maryland, at ten o'clock on the following day, Monday, December 19th. As we steamed up to the dock we felt that we were indeed in "God's land" again.

The wharves and shores were crowded with people, some of them being from the North, who were looking for friends; and the sight of the loyal throng, who with beating hearts and trembling voices were inquiring for friends, and who had a kind look and word for us all, made us feel that we were indeed among friends. The magnificent band belonging to the St. John's College hospital, which was stationed on the dock, first played "Home, Sweet Home," and then "Hail Columbia." The scene that followed it would be impossible to describe. It was useless for any of us to try to keep our eyes dry,

IN "GOD'S COUNTRY" AGAIN.

and on the shore some of the men and women wept like children.

As we were taken to the hospital, I heard frequent expressions of indignation, one old gentleman exclaiming, "My God, can it be that in an age and country like this a man must look on such a scene!" I wondered what the old gentleman would have said if he could have seen us before we were washed and put into clean clothing.

The hospital we were admitted to was called the St. John's College hospital, and after being again washed, and our clothing taken from us, we were furnished with hospital clothing and put into nice clean beds. The contrast from our wretched condition in prison was so great that it almost seemed like a pleasant dream, and my mind could not sometimes fully realize that it was all true. Kind, attentive physicians worked to bring us back to health and strength again; nurses, both ladies and gentlemen, gathered around us, willing to attend to our every want. The food was all that the most exacting ones could wish for—although, as we were in too weak a condition to have all we might have wished for, some of the men at first complained a little in regard to the quantity of it; but the doctors and nurses explained the matter so nicely to them that they soon became satisfied.

We were informed that as soon as we should

be strong enough, we might go to the table set apart for the convalescents, where we would get all the food we wanted. In the meantime only such diet was given us as the doctors would prescribe in the morning when examining us. This was, however, of the very best kind, and so complete was the arrangement that the patient could hardly ask for any delicacy that could not be immediately procured, and it always was, if the attending physician did not think it would injure the sick applicant. Long suffering and the horrible scenes they had witnessed had made some of the men very weak-minded, and they needed constant attention and waiting on; but in every instance that came under my observation, the duty was discharged with the greatest fidelity.

The night after our entrance into the hospital was cold and stormy, and O! how grateful I felt that a kind Providence had safely guided me into this haven of rest. As I have already stated, I could sometimes hardly think it could be true that I was safe away from the enemy; and in the morning the nurse informed me that I had frequently jumped up and felt and examined the bed and my surroundings, when, being assured that I was safe, I would lie down and go to sleep again.

On the following day I felt much better, and in a few days could be up again. I now wrote a letter home, and then spent the remainder of the day in reading and examining the papers. On the following day a large ship-load of released prisoners arrived, and as the authorities at the hospital were short of room, it was announced to us that all who were able to go home might have a sixty-days' furlough. We were soon all in a tremor of excitement, and every one trying to be as well as possible. Comfortably as we were situated, yet we felt so anxious to get home that we forgot the dictates of prudence, and I at least would better have stayed where I was for some time time to come. The doctor in charge of the ward I was in did not not want to hear of my going; but I begged so hard that I was at last permitted to go, and with a number of others I was put on a steamer bound for Baltimore.

We had hardly more than left when I felt that I had made a mistake in leaving the hospital; but it was now too late, and I was compelled to make the best of it. At Baltimore I took the cars for home, and arrived there on the following day, but in a sad condition. The great desire to get home had kept me up; but once there the reaction came quick, and I was soon taken very sick. I was pleased to find, however, that death had not broken our family circle during my absence. Father had, a few hours before my arrival, started for Annapolis, but was overtaken by a messenger, who informed him of my arrival, when he returned home.

The sickness that followed was long and terrible, and for almost three months I could not lift an arm, and for several weeks was unconscious of my own existence. Finally, however, through the skill of our good old family physician, Dr. P. S. Clinger, and the care and attention of loving friends, I so far recovered as to be able to return to the hospital. The movement was, however, made too soon, and I was again taken very sick.

Finally, on the 7th day of July, 1865, after being almost seven months under medical treatment, and fourteen months after my capture, I was discharged from the hospital and sent home; not to again enjoy good health, however. The strain on my system had been too much to hope for that; and a broken constitution and wrecked physical frame will ever be to me a horrible reminder of prison-life in the South.

CHAPTER XV.

ST. JOHN'S COLLEGE HOSPITAL.

THIS hospital was especially intended for the treatment of released prisoners of war, and I can not close this volume without these words of praise in its behalf. It was beautifully located in the suburbs of the antique city of Annapolis, Maryland, and at first only embraced the building of the St. John's College. It was, however, soon found to be too small, and the Naval Academy buildings and others were used for hospital purposes. A large number of hospital tents were also erected and filled with sick.

To this place were sent the wrecked and broken-down creatures who had survived the horrors of Southern prisons, for medical treatment before being sent to their homes. A large corps of able surgeons and nurses attended to the wants of the inmates, and all that human skill and attention could do, was done to save the poor emaciated victims of rebel brutality, and win them back to health and strength again.

A considerable number were, however, too far gone for human skill to save; and the soldiers' cemetery near the town contains the graves of hundreds of these men, who had reached the Union lines only to die.

Beside the regular supplies issued by the Government, the United States Sanitary Commission and other aid societies sent immense amounts of hospital supplies, and the arrangements for feeding the sick were as perfect as could be made.

The spiritual wants of the inmates were also well attended to, religious meetings being held regularly, and well attended. A Sabbath-school was also organized for the convalescents, and all those who were able to attend. Mrs. Palmer, the wife of the chief surgeon in charge of the hospital, and a number of other Christian ladies, took a very active part in this school, and undoubtedly accomplished much good.

A good band, which daily discoursed sweet music on the grounds, was one of the most pleasing features of this grand institution. A small volume might be written on the management of this hospital, and the scenes connected with it; and it would indeed be in strange contrast to the horrors of the prison-pens these inmates had come from. In those prisons the destruction of life had been a studied method; but in this hospital the prevention of it was the object striven for.

THE END.

www.ingramcontent.com/pod-product-compliance
Lightning Source LLC
Chambersburg PA
CBHW022142300426
44115CB00006B/312